Resisting Extractivism

Resisting Extractivism

Peruvian Gold, Everyday Violence, and the Politics of Attention

MICHAEL WILSON BECERRIL

VANDERBILT UNIVERSITY PRESS
Nashville

First printing 2021

Library of Congress Cataloging-in-Publication Data

Names: Wilson Becerril, Michael, 1988– author.
Title: Resisting extractivism : Peruvian gold, everyday violence, and the politics of attention / Michael Wilson Becerril.
Description: Nashville : Vanderbilt University Press, [2021] | Includes bibliographical references and index.
Identifiers: LCCN 2020039778 (print) | LCCN 2020039779 (ebook) | ISBN 9780826501578 (paperback) | ISBN 9780826501585 (hardcover) | ISBN 9780826501714 (epub) | ISBN 9780826501721 (pdf)
Subjects: LCSH: Gold mines and mining—Environmental aspects—Peru. | Gold mines and mining—Moral and ethical aspects—Peru. | Violence—Environmental aspects—Peru. | Environmentalism—Political aspects—Peru. | Environmental justice—Peru. | Social responsibility of business—Peru.
Classification: LCC HD9536.P42 B43 2021 (print) | LCC HD9536.P42 (ebook) | DDC 338.2/7410985—dc23

LC record available at https://lccn.loc.gov/2020039778
LC ebook record available at https://lccn.loc.gov/2020039779

"*¡No jueguen con el agua!*" (Don't play with the water!) seemed to be my grandmother's favorite phrase. As children, my cousins and I would collect water in buckets and chase each other around her backyard, aiming for each other but splashing most of the water on the grass and concrete. As a kid, I never fully understood her problem with our games. I used to think she did not want us to catch a cold and get sick, given that her second favorite admonition was "Put on a sweater!" As I have grown, I have come to understand her message differently: water is not to be wasted.

My grandfather worked up to become head mechanic in a cement mine and factory, which had been established originally as a British company in the 1880s but taken over by its workers (including my great-grandfather) and turned into a cooperative in 1931. Above all, however, my grandparents were farmers—tied to their small plot of land by economics, culture, and no doubt, politics. Dark-skinned, rural, and humble, their place in the country's postcolonial social hierarchy meant they lacked access to formal education (Mexico did not institute public instruction until they were married adults), but they were infinitely wise, colossally funny, and deeply in touch with their land. My mother, their only daughter out of five children, and my father, a half-Mexican immigrant from the US, were hard-working artists and entrepreneurs who spent much of their time in downtown Mexico City, so raising my sister and me fell largely to my grandparents.

This book is dedicated to their memory. For José Jesús Becerril Benítez, a diligent, quiet, and pensive farmer who taught me to whistle with birds, care for plants, watch the rain, and appreciate the little things that are tragically taken for granted. And for Josefina García Cuellar, a matriarch, soccer aficionada, and tireless raconteur who sat on a wheelchair from as early as I can remember until she passed away in 2006 but was never anything remotely close to meek, and who showed me the power of laughter.

Contents

Figures and Tables

TABLES

FIGURES

Acknowledgments

If you are a poet, you will see clearly that there is a cloud floating in this sheet of paper. Without a cloud, there will be no rain; without rain, the trees cannot grow; and without trees, we cannot make paper. . . . You cannot point out one thing that is not here—time, space, the earth, the rain, the minerals in the soil, the sunshine, the cloud, the river, the heat. Everything co-exists with this sheet of paper.

THÍCH NHẤT HANH, *The Heart of Understanding*, 1988

In any study that relies on extensive fieldwork, the list of people who deserve credit far exceeds the space allotted to dedicatory sections. As the epigraph to this section illustrates, I have everything for which to be thankful. Preparing for, conducting, and writing this research is to the credit of many people who have my eternal gratitude.

This work would not be possible were it not for all the people in Peru who—in parks and restaurants, in their offices and homes, at events and in our various expeditions, and far more—shared a moment with me to discuss their views and experiences. Many people, including those who did not officially participate in this research, generously invited me into their lives and to their proceedings; cared for me when I was sick; ran back to my hostel, after meeting me, to gift me books or show me fascinating media; stayed up late talking with me about politics and society; facilitated my conversations with others; offered me mementos, kind words, and useful advice or materials before we parted ways; and otherwise transformed difficult logistics into unforgettable memories, enduring relationships, and, I hope, useful research. I thank Alicia

Abanto, Stéphanie Rousseau, Liliana Alzamora, Mirtha Vásquez, Teresa Santillán, Liz Puma, Gerardo Damonte, Nelson Peñaherrera, Luis Riofrío, Lenin Bazán, César Medina Tafur, Luis Villafranca, Nilton Deza, Maritza Paredes, Charito Reyes, Eduardo Dargent, Paula Muñoz, José Carlos Orihuela, Ximena Waarnars, Vladimir Gil, Silvana Baldovino, Nadia Gamboa, Guillermo Salas, José de Echave, Ronald Ordóñez, Raúl Benavides, Javier Torres, Shreema Mehta, Andrew Miller, Martín Estévez, and my good friend Jefree Roldán, among many others. In addition to the people who participated in this study in any small or major way, this book is inspired by and dedicated to all who have struggled for justice and a better future. The world and I owe them incalculably.

Secondly, I was lucky to know and have the support of many mentors. Kent Eaton was, from our earliest conversations, a constant source of light able to guide me out of intellectual uncertainty. Kent unswervingly found potential in my work and opened many doors for me to think about and carry out this research. I also owe infinite thanks to Mark Fathi Massoud, an exemplary instructor and writer without whose encouragement, support, and friendship I would not have survived graduate school; to Eleonora Pasotti, who consistently provided the perfect balance of razor-sharp criticism and enlivening reassurance that every apprentice craves; and to Jeffrey Bury, whose field expertise, contacts, and advice were essential to this research. These four people were kinder, more caring, sharper, and wiser mentors and role models than I could have imagined. They always surpassed my hopes and needs as their student. I am immeasurably grateful for their generosity, grace, inspiration, and empowerment. Despite being always busy, they read and improved countless poorly written drafts, wrote letters on my behalf even when I requested an excessive number, and vastly improved who I am personally and professionally.

Likewise, I am grateful for the mentorship of Nancy Ries, Megan Thomas, Sylvanna Falcón, Hiroshi Fukurai, Ben Read, Ronnie Lipschutz, Cecilia Rivas, Ana María Seara, Xan Karn, Andrew Rotter, and many other faculty and staff at UCSC and Colgate University, and for the support from colleagues and friends, especially Mario Avalos, Earl Hidayetoğlu, Andrei Tcacenco, Stephanie Montgomery,

Sam Cook, Cassie Ambutter, Alfredo Reyes, Edher Zamudio, Karina Hurtado, Ingy Higazy, Délio Vázquez, John Wang, Sophie Rollins, Randy Villegas, Aaron Augsburger, Estelí Jiménez-Soto, Rafael Delgadillo, Logan Puck, Augusta Alexander, and Anna Ríos Rojas. And I want to inscribe here a very special thanks to all of my students at UCSC, its Pathways to Research mentorship program, and Colgate University—hundreds of people who unflinchingly brightened my day, sharpened my thinking, and inspired my commitments.

Many others are similarly responsible for shaping my thinking, interests, and personality. I am grateful to all the activists with whom I have organized for more than fifteen years, as my conversations with them largely provoked my research questions, and their efforts have kept me aware of the stakes in this work. I am indebted to Jennifer Collins, Sally Kent, Beverley David, Nerissa Nelson, Elizabeth Wabindato, Ismaila Odogba, David Lay Williams, Stephanie Alemán, Eric Yonke, and other friends at the University of Wisconsin–Stevens Point. Participants in various international academic and activist fora where I have presented my work have made it more accurate and legible. I deeply appreciate Adilia Caravaca and Mihir Kanade, my instructors at the UN University for Peace; Noemy Blanco and my other hosts in Indigenous communities in Costa Rica and Guyana; my colleagues, mentors, and friends from various projects, including the Institute on Qualitative and Multi-Methods Research; and Maiah Jaskoski and Maria Rasmussen, my leaders in a US Minerva Research Initiative study on violence.

This research received crucial financial and intellectual support from the United States Institute of Peace, the International Center on Nonviolent Conflict, the University of California, the UCSC Politics Department, and the UCSC Research Center for the Americas. Not least of all, I am immensely lucky to have met Zachary Gresham. I thank Zack, my project editor Joell Smith-Borne, the anonymous academics who peer reviewed this research, and the whole team at Vanderbilt University Press for their skilled, encouraging, and thoughtful partnership.

I am thankful for the support of all my friends and my family around the world—especially my mother Laura Becerril García, whose compassion and social skills made me an organizer; my father

Michael Wilson Aguayo, a bedrock of my political and intellectual disobedience; and my aunt and uncle, Carlos and María González, my first mentors, careful critics, and loving guardians. Finally, I want to reserve special recognition and gratitude for my sister, Melissa Wilson Becerril, and my partner, Rachel Anderson. Through good times and hardships, Melissa has been a lifelong role model and source of support. Looking up to her has shaped me profoundly. Rachel too has been my moral compass, my greatest editor, the antidote to my afflictions, and my leading inspiration. As the first sounding board for my ideas, she is critically responsible for making this research worth reading. Her clarity and consistency are truly unparalleled. I thank both of them for making the world brighter, leading the way, challenging me to improve, and teaching me to see criticism as a gift made from love.

When I started graduate school and my research, I was locked in a mortal battle of cellular proportions, a battle with cancer that decimated me physically and psychologically. Through the following years, my mentors, colleagues, students, friends, and family helped me heal and grow anew—into someone who is more self-critical, a keener listener, and better equipped to maximize the impact of my short time on Earth. I thank them all from the bottom of my heart. Anything worthwhile in the pages that follow is owed to these many people. Any errors are, of course, entirely mine.

Introduction
Enacting Violence

Awakened by an unfamiliar racket and agitated by the presence of unauthorized intruders, about one dozen Tambogrande residents approached a team of mining company geologists drilling exploratory holes into the ground near their coastal town. "Get the hell out of here," the locals demanded, "you have no permission to be drilling here." The geologists panicked—they were from out of town, untrained in community relations, and generally unequipped to de-escalate conflict—and they quickly called the company's regional manager, who was stationed at the region's capital city about a half-hour away. Their regional manager arrived in town shortly thereafter, his truck spreading dust onto the scene. His white-collar shirt, lizard-skin boots, gold watch, and gold belt buckle over crisp blue jeans imposed a remarkable contrast against the worn shoes and dust-covered clothes on the farmers, some of whom had brought tools like pitchforks.[1]

The manager could have reminded the locals about the state's permission for the company to explore the area. He could have apologized for the misunderstanding. Instead, his response was to deny the locals and seemingly to pick a fight. Speaking with a cosmopolitan, urban, coastal accent, he said, "You are nobodies. You are all shit," and began rolling the sleeves on his shirt. "It was as if he was ready to fight all of them," said Martín, the geologist who first told me this story, chuckling as his memory returned to that once-tense experience. The confrontation eventually quieted, but the damage was done. That evening, local activists went to the drill site and set fire to the company's perforation machinery.[2] According to Liliana Alzamora, a teacher and leader of the movement against the mine, moments such as this sealed the fate of the Manhattan Minerals Corporation's gold mining project in Tambogrande—and indeed, of the firm.[3] However, interactions like it remain unexplored aspects of conflict escalation.

It is perhaps understandable that discursive, symbolic, micro-foundations of conflict, such as the ones my interviewees described and I witnessed during my fieldwork, are difficult to study and to grasp, let alone to intuit how they relate to physical, explosive, "spectacular violence."[4] When analysts, state agencies, civil society organizations, and donors seek information about conflict, many tend to unconsciously crave broad conclusions and easy slogans almost impulsively, such as *research shows Latin America is the world's most dangerous region for environmental defenders*.[5] The public generally tends to want stories that represent a general phenomenon, so it is also drawn to large numbers. Depending on one's priorities, these may be statistics of bodies counted (*at least 270 people were killed and 4,614 people were injured in Peru's social conflicts between 2006 and 2016*[6]), currently active conflicts (*since peaking at 306 cases attended in 2009, the number of conflicts registered in Peru has remained stably above 200, and consistently, a large majority are about mining projects*[7]), or jeopardized investment (*according to one rightwing observer, the toll of "obstructing" mining investment could be higher than US$70 billion*[8]).

Many people likewise draw on official statements and media reports, which react to public outbursts of conflict but rarely cover the tensions that boil under the surface in daily life. However, if we share the objective of people working to transform conflicts in Peru—to develop participatory institutions that address conflict democratically, foster mutual resolutions, and prevent violence—then we must pay closer attention to how violence is experienced, discussed, and given meaning. We must critically inspect how structural inequalities are reinforced, normalized, and transformed through ordinary, minute interactions. There is no singular grammar of violence, which means the concept itself must be analyzed in context, rather than taken for granted. As Stephanie Montesanti, Wilfreda Thurston, and others have argued, the production of violence is profoundly intertwined with the social fabric, which is historically constructed alongside ethnic, gender, and class lines, and manifested in everyday life and personal spaces.[9]

Book Objectives

Motivated by the scale and deadliness of conflicts over contemporary resource extraction, this book builds a ground-up theory of violence by centering and analyzing the voices of people closest to it. It interrogates violence beyond the spectacle, studying it as a contested category, political discourse, and dynamic social process, particularly within the context of organized resistance to extractive "development" projects.

This work should first interest people who seek grounded analyses of resistance. It will be particularly relevant and useful to people organizing for social change, especially regarding extractive projects. My research compiles and delivers fresh insights about the analytical and practical efforts of activists working on the ground to improve their communities over many years. The ethnographic stories and their theoretical analysis contained here will be useful to people interested in environmental justice and social change, both inside and well beyond Peru. My intention is for this study to be adapted where useful, criticized, and improved by generations of organizers and activists.

This research is also meant for readers more broadly interested in the meanings of violence and conflict. Building upon a rich tradition, my work problematizes standard conceptualizations and offers an original approach to understanding what violence is, where it comes from, what it does in people's lived experiences, and how best to confront it. Students of Latin America will also appreciate the contextualized analysis of how Peru's political culture influences the dynamics of gold mining conflicts—because of its postcolonial legal framework, history of internal conflict, concentrated media monopolies, and the discourses that dominate public discussions of mining in the country.

Finally, this book aims to assist other stakeholders involved in resource conflicts: policymakers, corporate decision-makers, actors in nonprofit and international organizations, and others who may be searching for ways to direct resources, offer support, stop contributing to violence, and help build durable alternatives.

Violent Frames and Representations

What leads people to take up violence against one another, and why do actors entangled in it choose to eschew or forego violent means of waging and resolving conflict? In my search for answers to these questions—through experiences in activism, reading, and conversations during my fieldwork in Peruvian mining communities—I came to understand violence as much more than an event of physical damage. Again and again, interviewees spoke to me about facing "ideological violence by the state,"[10] discussed pollution as "environmental terrorism,"[11] and decried the stinging yet "subtle violence" of everyday encounters.[12] They presented conceptualizations of violence as material damage and as a discourse—as living conditions and as a framework to interpret reality. Because of this, it became clearly necessary, and most productive, to critically interrogate the very practices, physical and discursive, by which actors—including myself—articulated, perceived, assigned meaning to, and thereby recreated violence.

As a concept, violence defies definition. Any perspective of it is inherently politicized, filtered by worldviews, and shaped by conscious choices as well as subconscious biases or assumptions. Meanings are imparted onto it, transmitted, and misinterpreted through everyday practices and attitudes, some of which may be considered violent in some instances but are not framed as violent at other times. Violence therefore is difficult to operationalize and understand unless one can maintain a critical lens to the very ways that it is given meaning. Studies of violence tend to ignore these questions, cloaking unchecked biases or assumptions under a pretense of objectivity. A reflexive and critical analysis of violence, accounting for how it operates more broadly, requires conceptualizing it as an everyday phenomenon and social process.

Contrary to the popular perception that violence is an anomaly or an aberration from the norm, violence is quotidian and "hidden in plain sight."[13] It is in interactions as well as in structures—environmental, economic, racialized, gendered, and distributed unequally.[14] Violence is relational, constructed, lived, co-created, and experienced materially as well as symbolically. It exists in memory, emotion, pain, and physical trauma, as well as in economics, the configuration of institutions, and the ideologies that drive state control. And most importantly, it cannot be disentangled from its structural and historical contexts, which are—in the case of Peruvian mining conflicts—marked by the exclusion and exploitation of Native and Black people, their territories, and their ecological surroundings. These processes, while associated with long histories, are ongoing presently as living legacies of the colonial period, during which strict hierarchies based on race and gender were violently enforced. Dominant state, corporate, and media discourses offer new brandings and a flavor of legitimacy to these legacies, but their effects continue to manifest in the dispossession of impoverished people of color.

For people living in precarious or vulnerable conditions, such as subsistence farmers whose land is coveted by powerful corporations, or women in places where femicide is common, everyday life is anything but nonviolent.[15] What constitutes violence includes not only images of flames engulfing company equipment in the front pages of newspapers, but also the results of blood samples in mining areas, proving that a majority of locals carries heavy metals in their blood at levels surpassing the standard levels of medically accepted risk—as well as authorities' efforts to cover up the results.[16]

Although less attended than a brawl between protesters and police, violence is the suffering of a low-income family whose child was born with unexplained spots on her skin, likely because of their exposure to pollution through the sources of water used on their skin, teeth, crops, animals, and so on. Water pollution and depletion are certainly physical forms of violence, especially when hundreds of thousands of people and ecosystems downstream are affected. Insecurity is a condition lived in everyday experience, but most of its forms rarely receive public attention—they go unnoticed by sensationalist and inflammatory definitions of violence, and by otherwise well-meaning actors uncritical of their internalized bias and unwilling to check their complicity with violent structures. To be sure, violence is not absent from society until the moment a crowd sets company property on fire; rather, the status quo is constructed upon, and relies for its existence on, a wide range of structural violence and historical injustice, characterized by authoritarianism, systemic exclusion and exploitation of othered populations, and accumulation by dispossession.[17]

Consequently, concealing these forms of violence and inconvenient realities is also a necessary aspect of the modernization project. This is what Henri Lefebvre referred to as a dual production of space and reality, where social norms are built to systematically highlight the wanted and conceal the undesired.[18] A strict control over narratives is required to keep workers producing, consumers shopping, markets expanding, and profits flowing (for a few). It is partly because these practices go largely overlooked that actors with little access to institutional power seek to draw attention by engaging in spectacular violence, such as property destruction, looting, and arson. Although these explosive moments get noticed by the broader public, physical confrontations encompass neither the full manifestations and understandings of violence that study participants articulated, nor the tremendous local organizing and political efforts of rural communities contesting mining projects—the vast majority of which are not only nonviolent but also explicitly anti-violent. In other words, the dominant, event-driven logic of violence tends to reinforce what I problematize in this study as "the politics of attention," in its selectivity about what is noticed and concealed.

More than a mere conceptual clarification, this understanding is of major methodological and practical import. That most types of violence go overwhelmingly ignored reflects not only media bias, but also a core debility of academic studies about violence—and of efforts to confront it. If violence exists in many diverse forms, then the study of violence is fraught with superficiality and unchecked bias. These problems hinder the potential to analyze, let alone to transform and prevent, violent conflict. In fact, they may exacerbate it, by providing the logical and structural mechanisms by which people see violence as justifiable: by the state against its people, by non-state private actors against their opponents, and by people disaffected by political institutions.

Violence can be found in experiences lived but not reported. It is in systemic discrimination, unnecessary aggressions, one-upping, masculinisms, classist arrogance, and structural exclusion. It is palpable, as one interviewee said, when mining company employees rev their truck engines to make noise or dust at "anti-miners" walking by, simply to annoy and intimidate them. Late at night and in the early morning, those employees bring the same trucks to harass protesters at home, shining their bright lights through the windows, pressing hard on their vehicle pedals, and honking loudly as families inside try to sleep. I have witnessed this same toxicity escalate to physical harm at road blockades, when angry drivers menace protesters with their cars. And it is similarly felt in moments such as when someone refuses to concede on something that would cost little other than pride, as it happened during one "dialogue table" the state set up to mediate negotiations after a violent conflict between Barrick Gold and farmers in La Libertad. There, company operators prevented negotiators from offering substantial concessions; this combined with pressure by activists on their own spokespeople and ultimately thwarted the chances of reaching a temporary settlement.

As this book will demonstrate, violence is more than physical and more than an event; it is structural and embodied, symbolic and material, institutionalized and epistemic, deeply personal but also inextricably social, and rational as well as emotional. For these reasons, it must be treated as contingent and contextualized. It is the gasoline in the atmosphere, and it can be sparked by spontaneous decision making, long-term planning, unclear or incohesive commitment to nonviolent discipline, impulsive reactions to provocation, and feelings of anger and hopelessness. Indeed, the exchange of blows between police and protesters is sometimes triggered by someone hurling racist and classist insults, as it happened, for example, on the most violent day of the Conga protests in Cajamarca city in July 2012. As captured in videos of the confrontation in downtown Cajamarca, a woman protesting pleads to police, "Why are you like this? Why do you speak to us like this? Why do you mistreat us?" To this, one riot police officer audibly replies, "Because you are dogs, *concha de su madre*!"[19] Police killed four protesters that day. These examples crystalize the interaction between structural inequalities, desperation or a sense of one's dignity being violated, the rhetorics that frame our understandings, and the outbreak of physical confrontations; they suggest attention to feelings like disrespect and to language more generally. Within contexts of asymmetric conflict and inequality, everyday factors such as insulting words can make the difference between a peaceful protest and violent confrontation.

Violence is a discourse that gives meaning to experiences, a concept that can confer and wrest legitimacy. It can be found in the attitudes, rhetoric, and behavior of people on various sides of conflict—in their various animosities, resentments, distrust, and conspiratorial thinking. For example, mining supporters and company actors often repeated their notion that a web of environmental NGOs was responsible for Peru's violent resource conflicts. Similarly, some mining opponents gratuitously blamed mining companies for most of their social problems. Clearly, the various forms of violence that occur within and surrounding Peru's resource conflicts are mediated by discourses. These help people to interpret experience, to justify actions such as state-sanctioned corporate land grabbing, and to organize societies. And most importantly, language, discourses, and interpretations help people shape their material and symbolic realities.

Perhaps one of the clearest examples of this dynamic is how, before president Alan García ordered military police to shoot Indigenous protesters in the northern Amazonas region of Peru in 2009, he used his pulpit to refer to the protesters as "not first-class citizens" whose backward views would not be allowed to dictate the fate, and stall the progress of, millions of Peruvians. Among other venues, García articulated these notions in an open letter to *El comercio*, in which he framed Peruvian Natives as unproductive obstacles to their country. In his words, they were like "manger dogs" who not only refused to become productive but also refused to allow others to exploit natural resources that belonged to the nation.

In such statements, García—like many others whose similar views are diffused through media and dominate public debates—drew an offensive line between Peru's citizenry and the "anti-development" protesters, demarcating the latter as enemies outside that border. In the aftermath of the confrontations, during which ten Indigenous people and twenty-three police were killed, and many more were injured and hospitalized, the police funerals became a national spectacle, attended by high-level politicians and covered widely in the media to honor the "fallen heroes," victims of a "genocide of police," in president García's words.[20] This contrasted with the criminalizing and racist language with which protesters and their cause were condemned as they buried their dead quietly.

Framing people as violent serves to justify state violence.[21] Mainstream media and politicians perform this practice cynically, but beyond their openly biased and sensationalized representations, it is even more important to notice that scholarly literature on violence has also tended to pathologize non-state actors, which effectively forecloses the possibility to better understand and prevent violent conflict. By failing to critically reflect on how their own representations can obstruct social justice and legitimize specific forms of violence, such as violent policing and repression, observers reify the power imbalances that will lead to future violence, and they end up reproducing the very thing they purportedly oppose.

Experience, Interpretation, and Reflexivity in Ethnographic Research

As Keisha-Khan Perry and others have written—especially from within the fields of feminist and critical race and ethnic studies—social science is never a politically neutral practice.[22] Research, including the positions of the researcher vis-à-vis the researched, embodies and reifies structural power relations, which are constructed over centuries through phenomena like colonialism and state formation. These ongoing processes are economic, political, military, and intellectual projects.[23]

When studying something so intensely political as human violence, the pretense of objectivity can be not only naïve, but also problematic. To name something *violent* is to condemn it, and the act of classification depends on, or at least activates, a moral boundary.[24] Violence is a process, not an event, and as such its beginning and end depend on the observer, who may occupy a position of relative social privilege above the people characterized as violent. Moreover, because there are many overlapping types of violence—structural, gendered, racist, economic, ecological, physical, indirect, and symbolic—the very choice to focus on one narrow definition of violence, and ignore the other forms of violence that may be at play in a given context, has a concealing effect. For example, representations of violent protest, insofar as they ignore the structural conditions in which it exists, serve to legitimize various forms of state and private repression, which is understood as attempts to punish political opposition through both overt and obscure means.

In their shallow obsession with objectivism, positivist researchers tend to ignore the institutional, practical, epistemological, and historical constraints that have shaped both the researcher's position vis-à-vis "the others" and, more broadly, how power constitutes "valid" and "unreliable" knowledge. This lack of positional awareness between the researcher and the researched is not merely an oversight, but actually considered valuable.[25] Attachments and commitments to those studied are treated as obstacles, for observers must remain impartial outsiders for their knowledge to be reliable. The result is an approach to violence that privileges official sources of information despite their clear bias, and when it does consider multiple viewpoints, it tends to treat issues as if there were only two sides, reducing multifaceted problems and our capacity to understand them. Most commonly, it also fails to take into account unequal power between the actors involved (especially between the writer and the people under observation, a divide reified by this approach). In sum, this approach produces reductive, criminalizing, and therefore ultimately, "violent" representations. And it consists of more than a majority—positivism is a hegemonic force within the social sciences, capable of influencing what works and types of knowledge merit funding or publication.

To understand violence as a physical and figurative construct within Peru's mining sector, I had to resist the pressures posed by the academic mainstream and instead notice in-depth the relationships of power that violence generates, whether or not they grabbed the attention of those who set the record. To put it one way, it was necessary to take note of what is left unnoticed, what is left out of conflict accounts. I would have to examine what is concealed or highlighted, brought to light or shoved under the rug—and what effects these practices may have. Such matters could not fully be understood from a distance nor by probabilistic studies of large numeric data. Any potential to generate a more productive and transformative understanding of violence required immersion: I had to privilege the partial perspective rather than dismiss it, witness the experiences of people "living with violence," and listen to as many people with a stake in these conflicts as possible.[26] I had to avoid the trap of false binaries such as objective/subjective, insider/outsider, researcher/researched, or supporters/opponents, and instead engage in a kind of work that was reflexive about positionality, power, and the co-creation of knowledge.[27] Accordingly, these commitments led me to adopt an ethnographic approach, in which who I am, and what authority I had to speak, would be suspect rather than assumed or unacknowledged.[28]

My positionality as a fieldworker was that of an activist, University of California researcher, a white-skinned Latin American living in diaspora, and, significantly, a non-Peruvian. This foreign position presented crucial limitations, as well as surprising and useful opportunities.[29] My outsider status was betrayed whenever I was slow to translate words from English to Spanish during my conversations, or when I misspelled in my correspondence, especially in the first weeks of my fieldwork. My first language is Spanish, but I have lived most of the second half of my life in English-speaking countries, and my theoretical reading and training has been dominated by this second language. I therefore admit that sometimes, after a while, returning to Spanish feels as if it were my first *and third* language. But beyond this clumsy reacquaintance with Spanish, being a non-Peruvian researcher entailed more important obstacles. A crucial one, constantly in the forefront of my mind, was that I could enter a place and ask people about violence, with the option of leaving—of returning, most likely unscathed, to a more fortunate and comfortable life in California. I could spend several months using water that descended from the nearby mines for drinking, showering, and brushing my teeth, as well as eating plants and, occasionally, animals that were raised on that polluted water; and while at first this was an uncomfortable realization, it was never lost on me that, unlike the people in the communities that hosted me, I could eventually leave this temporary risk behind.

More broadly, conducting this study as a non-Peruvian committed me to become familiar with the people who generate mainstream discourses of mining in Peru, the venues through which their frames travel, and the people who are contesting these.[30] My fifteen months of fieldwork coincided with an election year, so my research was also inevitably steeped in contemporary local, regional, and national politics. Given the prominence of Alberto Fujimori's party in the country's political establishment, this required my study of events such as his coup d'état of 1992 and its corrosive effects on political institutions and public trust.[31]

One of the most salient legacies of his decade in power is distrust in media, given Fujimori's practice of bribing and censoring reporters, editors, and entire newspapers and broadcast outlets during his decade in power.[32] I would slowly learn, for instance, about the presidential death squad, Grupo Colina, and its acts in places like Santa, Áncash, where they left Sendero Luminoso graffiti to frame the guerrillas for a massacre; or about how the Movimiento Revolucionario Tupac Amarú took the Japanese ambassadorial residence and held its residents hostage between December 1996 and April 1997, leading Fujimori's government and international media to orchestrate a spectacle around the militarized repression that ended it. What could be the broader, complicated effects of the administration's media manipulation, or of its death squads? How did its use of emotions like fear influence political culture and actors' strategies?

Similarly, this work required learning about the collusion and support Fujimori received from other governments and economic elites, and about the favors received by massive domestic and transnational corporations (including the gold mining company, Yanacocha[33]) during his corrupt administration. To understand violence called for knowing the numbers of people disappeared by state forces, and of people killed by the state and guerrillas during the internal armed conflict—facts which strongly shape contemporary discourses of violence and terrorism, often conflating these with leftwing politics altogether.[34] I would have to know about the anguish of two hundred thousand Indigenous women forcibly sterilized, a product of the Fujimori regime's racist and classist policies of population control.[35] (Where did this state-sponsored ethnic cleansing program come from? How deep are its roots? How was it excused? And to what extent does it help understand contemporary resource conflicts?) Further, I needed to grasp the enduring power of Fujimorismo today, when it remains a dominant party in Peru's legislature. Of course, it is no longer the 1990s, and the experiences of everyone living in Peru could not be reduced to accounts of fear, authoritarianism, and media manipulation even during those turbulent times. These are merely some examples of the background and commitments I lacked.

On the other hand, I do not interpret my outsider position as a reason to ignore what happens in places to which I am a supposedly distant stranger, both because identities are not fixed nor singular, and because this may serve as an excuse for people to not care about conflicts and violence in which they (we) are complicit, even indirectly, as members of global societies, as affluent consumers within a transnational political economy, and as co-inhabitants in the global ecology.

In actuality, instead of factoring in as a reason to ignore what happens in Peru, my position presented me with privileged access to a population that is consciously secretive and traditionally difficult to access: mining company actors. Whereas actors in the mining industry might be reluctant to grant an interview to someone with an Indigenous last name and dark skin, my University of California credentials, white skin, male body, Scottish patronym, and Mexico City accent opened doors to me—in many cases, in unprecedented ways. I could gain invitation to interviews in mining company headquarters and the presidential palace in Lima, and these interviews would further open doors to me in the mining provinces I visited. And because of their superficial ascriptions about who I was, people in positions of power provided candid and revealing interviews, including confessions of nefarious tactics to repress their local opponents. My intersecting privileges and outsider position could be used to access, uncover, subvert, and alter power inequalities. I therefore used my activist-scholar training and my privileged identity to access understudied populations, and to study power from above.

This access is methodologically as well as theoretically significant: too many scholars spend their time uncovering social movement strategies, networks, and forms of mobilization. Copious studies of social movements may help activists find effective strategies, but they may also be helping those who want to understand social movements simply to outmaneuver and silence them. Following the Baconian theme that knowledge is power, focusing on the organizing strategies of social movements and subaltern peoples is a service to the state and to companies that wish to better *know* them in order to *control* them. Activists and the oppressed may have less need for studies about their shortcomings to be published in the global North, and more for how economic and political elites operate. Thanks to my positionality, this study can help to fill that void.

To make the most out of my privileged positions, maximize the potential of this study, and address the distances constructed between researcher and researched, it would be necessary to conduct this study with self-criticism and concern for the politics of research. If this exercise was to be useful to those who shared their time and thoughts with me, I would need to abandon and critically reverse the dominant model of detached and hierarchical research. I would have to adopt an immersive, participatory, and collaborative approach, as opposed to assuming the authority to commodify people's stories for self-serving purposes.[36] Likewise, it was of utmost importance for me to question and recognize the limits of my experience, and to not overstate the potential of my immersion to "fully" understand Peruvian culture and politics.

Immersion would force me to be more accountable.[37] Through relational fieldwork, first-hand experience, and participant observation, I would not only develop a more complex and finer understanding of violence as a social process, but more importantly, I would also forge bonds that would make me more engaged, more conscious about whose voices were centered in my analysis, more aware of the effects (and limits) of my work, and more critical about my choices and representations.

To summarize, being an outsider could allow me to contemplate cultural particularities that Peruvians might take for granted, such as everyday customs or dominant discourses that are not prevalent elsewhere, and it provided me with unprecedented access to the halls of power. At the same time, it also required me to recognize my privileged position as a researcher, my limited knowledge as an outsider, and my responsibility to "catch up" and do background work. Ethnographic fieldwork meant not only doing interviews, participant observation, and archival research, but also developing a nuanced view of political economy and state developmentalism under military regimes, learning about the country's media panorama, and appreciating the details and intricacies of recent political developments—for example, what "the Montesinos method" of blackmail entailed. Moreover, I would study and become acquainted with Peruvian and sub-regional slang (such as *chapar*, which can mean to "catch" something, like a thief, or to "score" something, like a new set of kitchenware) as well as with the uniquely Peruvian and sometimes racialized connotations of words and phrases that cannot be directly translatable into, in my case, Mexican Spanish.

I opted to acknowledge and remain constantly critical of these limits, instead of ignoring them or assuming my fieldwork would overcome them. By critically reflecting the role of research as a political process, I forced myself to attend to the different tensions and power relations at play at each stage, from design and fieldwork to writing, revision, and publication.[38]

Position and Distance in Violence Research

Mask no difficulties, mistakes, failures. Claim no easy victories.

AMÍLCAR CABRAL[39]

A central argument of this study is that violence must be studied in depth, in context, and discursively, as opposed to through superficial glances typically offered by probabilistic models. My critique of violence necessarily contains a critique of the study of violence, and it calls for a relational approach to its conceptualization, which in turn requires locating it in people's experiences and studying them in context via immersion. This reconceptualization centers research as an affective and relational process that intervenes in these experiences. Ethnography examines how practices of meaning production generate political phenomena, which is especially important when studying a concept as complicated as violence. Political ethnography—insofar as it is guided by positional awareness, intentionality, and participatory approaches—can generate denser, more complex, and more accurate understandings than the statistical methods that dominate social sciences, especially political science. More importantly, it is also more likely to build reciprocal relationships and research accountability. These strengths raise the potential of research to help confront violence in its various senseless, brutal, subtle, and oppressive forms.

Mining in Peru has generated an alarming rate of conflict. Given the number and diversity of these conflicts, they present a prime context in which to study actors' strategies in subnational politics. To build theory about why some conflicts over mining become more violent than others, this work relies on extensive ethnographic fieldwork, including unprecedented access to activist, industry, state, and media actors. Additionally, cross-case comparison can generate patterns and theories that can be broadly applicable. This study therefore merges ethnography with a qualitative comparison of case studies to analyze, and theorize, the critical agency of different actors, including those attempting to show an alternative, more sustainable path to development.

Book Roadmap

This book unfolds as follows. After this introduction, the first chapter summarizes my central argument about the escalation of violence in Peruvian gold mining conflicts, based on a within-case and comparative analysis of actors' strategies across four cases, including their different processes, trajectories, and outcomes. Furthermore, it outlines the methodology and contributions of this study, including how I selected the four different cases and how I gathered and analyzed all sources of evidence. Next, Chapter 2 situates my research questions in a theoretical, legal, cultural, and political context that helps to answer why some of Peru's resource conflicts become more violent, and likewise, how violent conflicts are managed, transformed, and resolved.

That chapter concludes by suggesting a framework that responds to the most important shortcomings of extant studies. The book then enacts that framework in its detailed description of four gold mining projects, each a separate chapter. Chapter 3, the first empirical chapter, is a case study of the Tambo Grande mine project. The analysis focuses on the mechanisms by which locals organizing against mining were able to turn a violent confrontation and arson into a successful nonviolent struggle. Because of this transformation, and with help from activist media and outside supporters from Lima and beyond Peru, including Oxfam International, the movements there stopped the Manhattan Minerals Corporation's proposed project.

In Chapter 4, regarding the La Zanja case, I explore the interaction between different kinds of strategies adopted by the company, including investment projects termed "corporate social responsibility" and different types of repressive actions against local opponents, both in the exploration phase and since the construction of the mine. Next, the Lagunas Norte case study in Chapter 5 elaborates these themes, although through slightly different dynamics. Barrick Gold, the company there, used mainly investment strategies and some repression, and yet this combination reached similar results as in La Zanja: it locked the contenders into routinized conflict.

The fourth and final case study, in Chapter 6, demonstrates how companies such as Gold Fields are becoming increasingly sophisticated in their community relations strategies, namely by refusing to use repression and by intentionally countering the condescension that often marks interactions between locals and company officials. These practices have effects on the level and tone of conflicts faced by these companies, but the Cerro Corona mine also demonstrates the limited potential of such superficial changes to eradicate the many forms and meanings of violence that manifest in the relationships between wealthy transnational companies and rural, typically low-income actors in postcolonial contexts. While minor changes have depoliticized interactions between locals and company officials (who boasted in interviews about their need to conceal their privilege from locals and "blend in"), such changes ultimately do little to alter everyday forms of violence. That case builds on the previous chapters by analyzing what "dialogue" means to the different parties; specifically, it inspects the intentions, processes, and effects through which different spaces for dialogue are crafted or demanded by the state, companies, and civil society.

Finally, the conclusion summarizes the study's key implications within and beyond Peru, discusses its limitations, and offers some proposals for action to help confront the different forms of violence—selectively noticed and unnoticed—that are increasingly enveloping conflicts over natural resources.

Incendiary Ethics: Resistance in a Vulnerable Planet

The kind of strategy people adopt to resist the onslaught of global capital is quite often not an ideological choice, but a tactical choice dependent on the landscape in which those battles are being fought.

ARUNDATHI ROY[40]

That many people have died over resource extraction and in resource conflicts, inside and well outside Peru, is not particularly news, but it is now urgent. Extractive conflict has been integral to what we understand as Western modernity, a period marked by the colonial imposition, and slow globalization, of two European constructs, capitalism and the nation-state. Resource plundering motivated colonial exploration, the enslavement of Black Africans and their descendants, Indigenous genocide and displacement, and the construction of legal systems that would legitimize these economic relationships. Incentivized by private and corporate profits, the state sustains capitalism through the control of populations and territories. State control is not only exercised through physical violence—including beatings, killings, imprisonment, and displacement—but also by shaping the public's subjectivities through discourses of "development," "nation," and "security." In a global context of a growing climate crisis occurring alongside growing global demand for subsoil resources like gold, copper, steel, oil, and natural gas, the stakes and tensions at the heart of such conflicts are immense.

In Peru as in similar contexts elsewhere, biased mainstream commentators frequently accuse environmental activists of being backward, anti-development, and even terrorists. In framing protesters as threats to national progress, these dominant narratives effectively serve to dehumanize people, portray them as unredeemable, and justify their deaths as an inevitable part of a broader project of modernity.[41] While the people who benefit from the institutionalization and consolidation of this model tend to be affluent, white, male, and from the global North, those who bear the most violent collateral damage inherent to this system are overwhelmingly Black, Indigenous, dark-skinned, and especially women. Therefore, one cannot abstract these fluid discourses from the white supremacist and patriarchal legacies of colonialism that have marked what modernization meant, and for whom, in these landscapes for longer than five centuries. Such discourses and the commentators who mainstream them are not only uncritical of, but also partly responsible for, how extractive capitalism intersects with various forms of state and corporate violence—components of modern "development" as a neocolonial, unevenly beneficial and burdensome, and whitening project.

Companies' social and environmental responsibility is endlessly touted in official speech, everyday conversations, online social networks, broadcast media, propagandist journalism, and research papers. Meanwhile, the formation of political movements in response to resource extraction in Peru has been typically *ignored* (when confrontations are treated as merely spontaneous events), *pathologized* (or treated as culturally backward, criminal, or violent), and *repressed* (where the former two responses help to justify state and corporate violence, land theft, and systemic exclusion) by mainstream representations found in media, state, and academic discourses.

This work demonstrates how, contrary to these gendered tropes, classist assumptions, and racist representations, many local movements in Peru's rural contexts are explicitly working to promote "sustainable development" and stop various types of violence. In actuality, sustainability is a concept they are theorizing, expanding, and responding to with much greater nuance and sophistication than is typically acknowledged in dominant accounts. Highlighting and analyzing the ideas, theorizing, and actions of people in these movements can help mitigate the climate crisis, advance environmental justice, and build more enduring forms of peace.

Resource conflicts interweave inequities and galvanize neighbors against the combined forces of global capitalism and the state. Precisely for these reasons, they are central to understanding and transforming the multiplying crises our planet faces. Only resistance that consciously cuts across these interrelated problems can strike at the heart of the problem and build alternative futures. Those on the receiving end of the extractive global order ought to learn from, and support, the leadership of marginalized communities that—in complicated ways and despite the increasingly sophisticated forms of repression wielded against them—are bravely organizing to contest and reverse the dynamics that are literally destroying the planet.

CHAPTER 1

Between Violence and Not-Violence in Resource Extraction

Because of the scale, intensity, and compounding effects of climate change, protecting the environment has never been more important, but in many places, doing so can be a deadly task. In 2012, the organization Global Witness began systematizing world data regarding violence against environmental activists—people organizing to contest, for example, projects over land grabbing, water, dams, logging, gas, agro-industry, oil rigs and pipelines, infrastructure, and mineral extraction. Ever since then, the organization has consistently identified Latin America as the world's most dangerous region for environmental defenders, and specifically Brazil, Honduras, and Peru as places where this issue concentrates. This book investigates why conflicts related to resource extraction have taken a violent turn in the past decades, particularly in Peru.[1]

One-third of the world's mining investment concentrates in Latin America. Peru is a remarkable example: minerals represent about 65 percent of its export income and have guaranteed its standing as one of the world's fastest growing economies. Gold alone accounted for 18 percent, decidedly the largest share, of Peru's total income for the period between 1995 and 2015.[2] Perhaps this is why the most common and deadliest conflicts in Peru today, by far, are related to mining. At least 270 people were killed and 4,614 people were injured in Peru's social conflicts between 2006 and 2016.[3] The Peruvian ombudsperson's office, an independent state agency in charge of auditing and protecting human rights, registered well above two hundred conflicts within the country each year consistently between 2008 and 2017. The vast majority of these, about two thirds on average, have been linked to resource extraction, and most of all to mining specifically.[4]

The death rate in these conflicts is truly staggering. Between 2005 and 2009, the Río Blanco (formerly Majaz) mining project in Piura caused seven deaths. In June of 2009, thirty-three people were killed when the state armed forces opened fire on Indigenous protesters who were occupying roads and an oil duct in the Amazonian province of Bagua. Six of the twenty-four total victims produced by Peru's conflicts in 2012 were killed by police while protesting the Conga open-pit mining project, backed by the World Bank and suspended for years. Between 2011 and 2015, at least five people were killed over the Tía María project, owned by Grupo México. Nearby in Cusco, during the same period, four people were killed over the Espinar mine. And between 2015 and 2019, the largest conflict story in Peru was the Las Bambas copper mine, a Chinese investment that would surpass Conga as the country's largest mining project; five people died over this conflict alone between September 2015 and October 2016.

These examples are only a handful of the many mining conflicts that continue to plague politics in Peru, not to mention in other places beyond, as the global demand for minerals grows. Each year, dozens of mining projects—old and new, big and small—burst into conflict. However, mining conflicts vary immensely, even among similar cases. Only a few escalate into open violence; some remain mainly nonviolent or show few signs of tension, and even violent conflicts are sometimes resolved. What explains this? Why do some conflicts burst into violence, and when do they not? Why do some stagnate and become routinized, and how can they be resolved sustainably?

These questions are at the heart of human rights and development issues in Latin America today. Literature on resource conflicts tends to focus on violence as a possible outcome of weak institutions, but violent coercion is only one way that different actors participate in complex processes of negotiation over natural resource management that involve institutions, collective actions, digital media, under-the-table acts, and distant allies. The extent to which conflict will unfold, including when it will be violent or nonviolent, and in what ways, remains largely under-theorized. Therein lies a puzzle that may help to understand how to resolve conflict pluralistically, democratically, and durably. To do that, this research builds onto existing scholarship on resource management; violent conflict and everyday violence, including gendered violence and resistance; regional histories and their accompanying cultural, political, and economic formations; and corporate strategies and accountability.[5]

Significance of the Study: Contributions to Policy, Practice, and Scholarship

Gold is treasure, and with it, those who possess it do as they wish in this world and succeed in helping souls into paradise.

CRISTÓFORO COLOMBO

Humanely if possible, but at all costs, get gold.

KING FERDINAND OF SPAIN

Enough is enough. These people [Indigenous protesters] do not wear crowns. They are not first-class citizens. That 400,000 natives could say to 28 million Peruvians, "You don't have a right to come around here"? No way. That is a very grave error, and whoever thinks that way wants to take us to irrationality and to a primitive retrocession.

ALAN GARCÍA[6]

It is difficult to overstate how much Latin American societies, politics, economics, cultures, and landscapes have been deeply shaped by a long history of resource extraction,[7] but beyond merely representing a protracted process, this phenomenon is an urgent and intrinsically planetary concern. As people across the world have fueled demand for energy and minerals, natural resources have become the engine behind many countries' economic growth, expanding the strategic importance of extractive industries and the frontiers of extractive capitalism. In Peru, this situation has led to a massive rise in social conflicts, galvanizing communities to contest their rights—on the streets and in courtrooms, in occupied buildings and internet blogs, and through local elections as well as arsons and kidnappings.

To defend their own paths to "development," locals-turned-activists have barricaded themselves in buildings, sought mediation from domestic courts and international agencies, defended themselves from police and private guards, blockaded roads, detained unauthorized resource prospectors, confiscated property, set fire to company equipment and vehicles, and more; likewise, they have faced arrests, police violence, defamation, intimidation, and other forms of repression. Their efforts have placed issues of water pollution and scarcity, dignified livelihoods, benefit redistribution, and equal representation at the center of the country's debates. At the same time, irresponsive institutions, state-corporate repression, and racist discourses (such as those president Alan García used to justify repressing the Indigenous people protesting against extractivism in their territories in 2009) have contributed to anger, desperation, provocation, and a general sense among different stakeholders that taking matters into their own hands, even through illegal tactics such as property destruction, is necessary.

Why should anyone care about Peru's gold mining conflicts, and what broader insights can be gained from a semiotic and comparative understanding of violence? Rural conflicts over extractive projects affect more than local politics and governance, companies and states' revenues, and national politics—they can also disrupt macroeconomic forces and international relations. Furthermore, because local territorial dynamics are increasingly tied to international commodity chains, conflicts over natural resources transcend traditional ways of conceiving of locality and space.[8] They involve and link people on various ends of commodity chains, from sites of extraction to retail, consumption, and waste. And ultimately, unsustainable resource governance threatens ecological stability, which is already an immeasurable problem. Thus, even before they escalate to overt violence, resource conflicts are critical obstacles to justice and peace.

Contentious politics take place on physical, legal, and discursive levels. In Peru, resource conflicts are infamously at the center of the country's political agenda. Moreover, in addition to their salient character in public debates, Peru's resource conflicts have become a "conceptual epicenter"—they invoke and transverse political, economic, and cultural issues such as violence, corruption, justice, gender, race, class, development, sustainability, and democracy. Therefore, as Peruvian friends seriously committed to transforming conflicts often reminded me during my fieldwork, the field severely lacks in-depth and empirical studies, especially those that balance dense case understandings with comparative analysis to draw patterns. In places such as Peru, where resource conflicts are notorious (to such an extent that news media frequently address them as "our daily bread"[9]), studies such as this can make a significant contribution to policy, practice, and scholarship.

By examining patterns in the trajectories and outcomes of conflicts, this book has the potential to make a lasting impact, not only in academic literature but also for practitioners seeking pathways to dialogue and peace. It is especially intended to assist company agents, civil society, activists, state actors, and international supporters. First, the work will help company actors improve their local engagement. This study emphasizes and will provide useful insights about the agency of company employees across the corporate structure. This applies to both their long-term strategies to engage local opponents, and the everyday relationships that they establish with people in the areas near their project. Second, the cases and theory presented here elucidate mechanisms about when activism is effective, at what, and when it is not. These will have practical value for civil society organizations and local activists seeking ways to effectively attain justice and promote their communities' wellbeing, especially when contesting extractive projects. Third, the research contributes recommendations for policymakers seeking to develop robust institutional mechanisms to channel conflict nonviolently and prevent violence—particularly in the context of Peruvian political culture, but relevant beyond those boundaries. And fourth, the theoretical conclusions here will speak to outsider actors, such as the thoughtful people I interviewed in intergovernmental organizations and transnational solidarity groups searching for ways to direct resources and provide their support, even across long distances.

In sum, this research reflects a serious underlying intention: to assist policymakers and state officials in fomenting democratic governance and preventing violent conflict, to assist companies in protecting their investment through understanding the adverse effects of short-term conflict avoidance strategies, and to assist communities in stimulating their human and economic development in ways that are democratic, equitable, and sustainable. By focusing on cases beyond the headlines and understudied dynamics of conflict management, this investigation will help in promoting forms of development that are commensurate with local needs, aspirations, and capacity.

Mining and the Spaces of Violence in Peru

The recent, tremendous expansion of extractive industries in the global South has fed and enriched theoretical debates about the causes of extraction-related conflicts.[10] As broad as the bodies of literature on subnational conflicts and resource conflicts have become, each field and the spaces between them remain incomplete in important ways. Specifically, at least one of the following issues applies to extant works.

First, selection bias predominates. Studies of large and explosive conflicts abound, but they tell us little about more common cases, where conflict has been managed and even mutually transformed. In addition to the tendency to only study large-scale, widely publicized, and unrepresentative cases (such as the Conga mining project in Peru), research on resource conflicts typically focuses on protestors and the state. Insofar as they ignore the agency and repertoires of mining companies in dealing with local populations, their conceptual and theoretical frameworks are too narrow.[11] This study attends to both of these types of selection bias by focusing on more "ordinary" cases as well as by analyzing the behavior of all stakeholders in parallel, including company actors. I gained extensive access to contacts in two of the mining companies I studied (and limited access in the other two), ranging from executive officers in Lima to provincial managers and employees in the mining districts. Interviews and participant observation conducted with these contacts help to illuminate the complex perspectives and practices of actors in different corners of the industry. As one might say, they help to "see like a mining company."[12] Far from uniform, the behavior and views of industry actors vary widely; systematically understanding their agency is crucial to this research.

Second, strategic choice is largely unexplained. Existing studies tend to take conflict for granted, without unpacking the choices of tactics available to stakeholders as forms of negotiation. Protesters' choices have been studied extensively in other contexts, such as struggles against authoritarian regimes, but scantly within resource conflicts.[13] Theories linking violence to "resource rents" have focused on groups that seek to loot resources in order to fund civil wars, which does not account for social movements contesting extractive projects.[14] Similarly, studies of resource conflicts have tended to focus on the state as a rent-seeking actor willing to loot resources and repress the local population if necessary.[15] States' interest in generating tax revenues from extractive projects, and their will to use violence to do so, may induce grievances. However, this line of arguments runs into a few major problems. For one, if repression is understood as a strategy to contain opposition, then it cannot be the singular explanation for that opposition also. Repression emerges during conflicts as one of their possible effects, but not as their original cause—even if it may be a factor that exacerbates conflict. Furthermore, these types of grievances are noticeable in many places where conflict does not manifest, so they are inefficient explanations for conflicts, and they are even worse at explaining the shapes and dynamics of those conflicts, whenever they do occur.

Additionally, studies of mining firms' community engagement strategies center, critically or optimistically, on the growing phenomenon of corporate social responsibility (CSR) practices, but they have largely fallen short in understanding the shape and character of conflict (e.g., estimating why conflict may develop violently versus in other ways), how CSR interacts with other forms of corporate-community relations (such as the reliance on state repression and private coercion), or the roles of discourse, specifically how it reproduces constructs of race and other structural forms of oppression.[16] Therefore, we lack an account of actors' full range of strategic repertoires. This book intends to unpack these overlooked explanatory factors.

Conversations on negotiation tactics and strategies are common—formally and informally—among mining company actors, both within a given company and between different firms in the industry. Likewise, questions of tactical efficiency and ethics, framing, the costs of escalation, and the balance between short-term and long-term goals are at the center of activists' deliberation and planning. However, we know little about these strategic and ethical choices within resource conflicts. More crucially, we lack a contextualized understanding of how the legacies of armed conflicts—such as Peru's civil war between the state and insurgent groups (formally between 1980–2000)—give currency to terms like *violence* and play into these choices and deliberations. A rich and growing body of research has become increasingly rigorous in arguing for the strategic and moral value of nonviolent means of waging conflict—not only on moral grounds, but also because of its strategic efficacy.[17] This underscores a central puzzle: if nonviolent negotiation is not only morally, but also strategically, a superior method, then why do some actors continue to use violence? And when do they not?

Third, outsiders' roles are portrayed too simplistically. While the importance of outside attention to resistance was already prominent in early twentieth century anticolonial thought, it remains a nascent area in the study of resource conflicts.[18] This is the case even as the levels of interaction, connectivity, diffusion of ideas, and coordination with transnational actors are higher than ever—in fact, activists in the global South are increasingly "marketing" their plight to supporters in the global North.[19] Literature on transnational activism provides analytical leverage in examining the strategic choices of actors involved. However, the interests of locals often do not align with those of their "allies," such as nongovernmental organizations (NGOs).[20] Furthermore, whereas the literature focuses on NGO-community alliances, I found that companies also work with many NGOs in a number of capacities previously unaddressed in studies such as this.

Finally, discursive contention is overlooked as a site of violence.[21] Peru's established media and public debates, corporate public relations, and official ideology (manifested in policies, official pronouncements, and politicians' speeches) have constructed over time a hegemonic—although highly contested—pro-mining and extractivist discourse. Their highly circulated rhetoric consists primarily of two general propositions: first, that mining is central to Peru's identity, and that the country's natural endowments must be utilized to foster investment and grow its economy; and second, that Peru's resource conflicts are caused by protestors who are anti-mining, violent, anti-development, and even environmental terrorists—criminals who, motivated by greed and ignorance, are responsible for denying their country the development it deserves.

Media pundits such as Jaime de Althaus, Mariella Balbi, Phillip Butters, and Aldo Mariátegui, for example, frequently and famously portray mining-related activists as violent ideologues, corrupt manipulators, or backward, ignorant, and manipulated—and then these pundits' allies in academia and government repeat their rhetoric.[22] Their discourses may drive conflict escalation and erode resolution efforts, given their dismissive and polarizing tones. This study finds that such reductive narratives not only miss the nuances of conflict (e.g., how violence is often started by people in favor of rather than opposing mining), but also exacerbate distrust and alienation.[23]

Creating peaceful and sustainable development requires building understandings, relationships, and institutions that can mitigate and channel conflict nonviolently, credibly, democratically, and inclusively.[24] Toward this end, research participants stated

FIGURE 1. Photograph of contested graffiti on the walls of Cajamarca City, 2016. Activists spray-painted many walls around Cajamarca city with "agua sí, mina no" (yes to water, no to the mine) messages, but I noticed many of the tags had been altered to say "yes to the mine," crystalizing how narratives, and their venues, are sites of political contestation.

their need for systematic analyses of the discursive, symbolic, and everyday aspects of these conflicts. This research presents an ethnography of subtle forms of violence, and it explores how meaning-making practices render certain types of pain or damage noticeable and other types invisible.[25] By excavating how everyday interactions that underlie conflicts are strategically concealed in the short-term, this research may assist in the prevention and transformation of violence over resource extraction.

To grasp the dynamics at play in these conflicts, it is of critical importance to conduct research that analyzes empirically beyond the polarizing discourses that dominate questions of mining in Peru. At the same time, to dismiss the role of discourses would be to omit a large part of the story. It is crucial to understand, in context, the processes through which aggression escalates, is given

TABLE 1. Issues and Gaps in the Literature about Peruvian Mining Conflicts

Selection Bias	Strategic Choice	Outsider Roles	Discursive Contention
Studies tend to concentrate on large, spectacular, and unrepresentative cases of conflicts, as well as on protesters and the state—not industry actors	Actors' full range of strategic and tactical choices remains under-theorized and unexplained in the context of resource conflicts	External allies are treated simplistically (e.g., as uniformly beneficial to activists) and in ways that ignore the effects of outsiders on actors' tactical choices	Racialized, class-based, and gendered discourses of development and modernization in Peru are largely absent from studies of extractive conflicts

meanings, and de-escalates. Narratives and concepts therefore must be examined as sites of conflicts.

Previous explanations for political violence have attended to factors (such as grievances or scarcity) that over-predict violent behavior at best, and at worst are problematic and racist pseudo-science, given their Eurocentric evaluations, "cultural" assumptions, and generalizations disguised as explanations. The clearest examples are scarcity-based analyses, which are not only over-deterministic,[26] but also tend to congeal with the increasingly widespread rhetoric that reduces ecological collapse to "overpopulation." In effect, this victim-blames the poor and the global South and in turn exculpates overconsumption by the more affluent and whiter global North, thereby creating a cozy overlap between these analyses and fascist biopolitics of population control, forced sterilization of the other, militarized xenophobia, and violent ethno-nationalism. Instead, this book traces conflicts' different forms to previously understudied practices that frame and give meaning to minute interactions and daily relations. Moreover, its original comparative analysis demonstrates how the sequencing and combination of stakeholders' strategies matter in conflict trajectories and outcomes.

This research provides an original analysis of how discursive forms of power are interwoven with company strategies and everyday life. Combined, these factors have the strongest explanatory potential in understanding violent escalation by different sides.

Far beyond just a lack of understanding, it is important to theorize the processes that actively sow distrust, discontent, and resentment leading to violent escalation. This study therefore builds on previous insights to deepen understandings of how insincerity (of promises, agreements, land-sale valuation, and false dialogue as pacification), lack of transparency, arrogance and impunity, and everyday coercive tactics can lead to violence—and more importantly, how they can be addressed in order to prevent it.

In these ways, this research grows from and contributes to rich bodies of work studying violence and resource extraction, both separately and, more rarely, together. It helps to reconceptualize everyday, compartmentalized dimensions and meanings of conflict in subnational contexts. Moreover, it provides analysts and practitioners the tools to understand how, when, and why conflict erupts into overt violence, and secondly, the types of frames and outside attention that may entrench this cycle or dislodge it. Thus, the project builds onto debates about violence, its causes, and its alternatives. Studying the conditions that lead to actors' choices helps to understand the propensity of conflict escalation, the results of campaigns, and the prospect of finding durable solutions that resolve differences through deliberation.

Argument: Company Strategies, Attention, and Everyday Violence

Whether they are mining company employees or supporters, opposition activists, or ambivalent bystanders, the stakeholders variously involved in mining projects deploy fascinating and rivaling explanations for the rise of violence over mining in Peru. When asked to comment on why they thought Peru's mining conflicts often become so violent, interviewees in this study offered diverse answers, ranging from the role of local histories and politics to the importance of structural and macroeconomic changes. Some of the most commonly repeated explanations that interviewees offered included the role of outsider NGOs. According to many of those I interviewed, particularly among people generally sympathetic to mining, NGOs were vested in conflict in order to exist and fundraise, and thus had a material incentive to exacerbate rural conflicts. Another recurrent theme expressed by several people was that protesters understood violence as a way to force companies into offering material concessions, so that the latter could avoid any public embarrassment. Whether accurate or not, such answers represent discourses that influence choices, as analyzed in the chapters that follow.

To understand how worldviews are shaped and translated into practices, laws, and lived experience, this study centers and critically analyzes the narratives that people in various sides of Peru's resource conflicts used to explain violence. Contrasting these claims against as much additional evidence as possible, it then independently theorizes causal explanations for the varying levels of violence across cases of Peruvian gold mining. These findings form a common thread, but they can be clustered among three themes: the importance of company strategies, the politics of attention, and the role of everyday violence.

First, based on ethnographic analysis of the process of conflict in four cases (the Tambo Grande, La Zanja, Lagunas Norte, and Cerro Corona gold mining projects) and a comparison of these mechanisms across the cases, this investigation's central finding is that the most accurate explanation for violent protests are the community-engagement strategies of corporate actors—whether these are persuasive and meant to pacify, such as corporate social responsibility programs, or more coercive means of silencing opposition, such as intimidation and judicial repression. Company strategies are a surprisingly overlooked factor in extant studies. However, above all competing explanations (including the role of outside attention and support, the average framing through which media covered protest, and others), variation in corporate strategies across the cases best explains both (a) the levels of violence adopted by social movements and local opponents, and, in combination with the strategic choices of local opponents, (b) the final results of each conflict. Table 2 depicts this theoretical argument, expanded below, about the causal mechanisms in each case.

TABLE 2. Theorizing Explanations for Violent Actions and Case Outcomes

	Company Strategies	Violent Collective Action	Media Attention and Framing (of Activists)	NGO Support	Case Outcomes
Tambo Grande	Coercion	Arson, then a transition to nonviolence	Favorable overall	High	One-sided victory for the movement
La Zanja	Coercion (with persuasion)	Arson and property damage; no transition to nonviolence	Mixed (criminalizing and favorable)	Low	Routinized conflict but partly demobilized movement
Lagunas Norte	Persuasion (with coercion)	Arson, property damage, and dead police; no transition to nonviolence	Criminalizing overall (except for minor activist media)	None	Routinized conflict with active social movements
Cerro Corona	Persuasion	None; entirely nonviolent, low-level organizing	Hardly any, but favorable when it has been present	None	One-sided victory for the company

HOW COMPANY STRATEGIES EXPLAIN VIOLENT PROTEST

When the mining companies used coercion against their local opponents, this directly correlated with activists' use of tactics that are widely framed as violent, such as property damage. When companies used both repression and investment in combination, this was met with mixed violent and nonviolent opposition strategies. And when they used persuasion only, activists who expressed their willingness to use property destruction nonetheless did not engage in it, partly because it would have been perceived as unjustifiable against a company (Gold Fields, at its Cerro Corona mine) that explicitly refused to engage in coercion from the start.[27]

Table 3 goes beyond the simplified "persuasion-versus-coercion" typology in Table 2, expanding the company strategies in each case into six categories, ranging from development-oriented investment (such as channeling funds for sustainable farming), to coercive practices like intimidation. As it shows, thanks to its insignificant

TABLE 3. Expanded Typology of Company Strategies

	Persuasive Strategies			Coercive Strategies			
	Corporate Social Responsibility		Media Strategies		Repression		
Case	Development Investment	Philanthropic Compensation	Public Relations	Opponent Defamation	Legal Persecution	Private Intimidation	Result for Company
Tambo Grande	No	Yes	Yes	Yes	Yes	Yes	Defeat
La Zanja	Yes	Yes	Yes	Yes	Yes	Yes	Mixed
Lagunas Norte	Alleged	Yes	Yes	Yes	Yes	Alleged	Mixed
Cerro Corona	Yes	Yes	Yes	Alleged	No	No	Success

persuasive strategies, the Tambo Grande project fared worst of all, with a one-sided victory for the social movement against it; and on the other hand, the company that used no forms of coercion, Gold Fields, has reached the most successful outcomes.

Companies that combined persuasion and coercion as their responses to conflict created a perverse incentive that encouraged violent escalation, both because people resented being treated with repression and because escalation was a proven means to gain concessions from powerful companies and also from the state. Beyond only shaping protest, the combination of repression and investment also impacted the overall outcome of each case: namely, it locked actors into prolonged, frequently reactivating tensions—as I detail next, it dangerously routinized conflict.

HOW COMPANY AND LOCAL AGENCY EXPLAIN CASE OUTCOMES

The cases, selected for their contextual similarities, exhibited variation in their respective level of violent collective action and, ultimately, in their different conflict outcomes. During my fieldwork, I noticed four possible, mutually exclusive "ideal types" of project outcomes. One possibility is that the mining project is cancelled and its opponents gain a unilateral victory in the long-term (as opposed to a temporary postponement for only a handful of years), as was evident in the Tambo Grande case. A second possibility is the inverse: a unilateral victory for the company and a neutralization of its opposition, through persuasion and/or coercion. The Cerro Corona case might get closest to this type. Although rare, a third possible outcome is that stakeholders reach something akin to a mutual resolution that satisfies company agents as well as their opponents. The Cerro Corona case could also be argued as having reached this outcome, although I witnessed there a sense of enduring resentment and opposition, demobilized but perhaps not satisfied. Finally, there is a fourth, unstudied outcome of extractive projects which entails a more ambiguous *routinization* of conflict. In these cases, including the La Zanja and Lagunas Norte mine, confrontations become recurrent or cyclical—normalized and even institutionalized into the relationships, rules of engagement, and daily interactions between company actors and their local opponents.

This study argues that these outcomes are mostly influenced by how companies address communities, in the short and long term, and on how local opponents choose to respond. When companies responded to community opposition mainly with *coercion*, they exposed themselves to backfire effects, galvanizing resistance as opposed to quelling it. In one case, Tambo Grande, this ultimately led to activists' unilateral victory. When they responded to local opposition mainly with *persuasion*—via investments in local development, industry, agriculture, or philanthropy—companies pacified enough opponents to effectively quell resistance. As the Cerro Corona case shows, company operators did not merely demobilize opponents; using a strategy of heavy investment, they actually went further, generating seemingly amicable everyday relationships with locals, including some of their loudest opponents. Finally, when companies responded to opposition with *coercion alongside persuasion*, they routinized conflict, rendering it a part of the fabric of company-community relations—a dynamic fully neglected in the literature.

Routinization might be due to the combined effects of repression, which builds resentment and perhaps prolongs conflict, and of investment, which pacifies that tension at least temporarily but typically without addressing the underlying problems at the roots of those tensions, such as entrenched inequalities, racist discrimination, or ecological concerns.[28] Two of the four cases I studied, the La Zanja and Lagunas Norte projects, resulted in an ongoing pattern wherein social movement escalation is eventually followed by public confrontation and repression, which then triggers conflict mediation mechanisms, leading to company investment promises that, if unmet, foster resentment and restart the cycle of escalation. This may be because such promises are not kept, leading to a renewal of resentment and mobilization, and because local actors see conflict as an opportunity to "extract from the extractors."[29] At any rate, conflict has returned in deadly waves every couple of years in both the cases where companies used a mixed strategy. However, a key difference in the outcomes of those two cases, La Zanja and Lagunas Norte, is that the company that used more overt forms of repression was slightly more successful at demobilizing its opponents.

Company strategies set conflicts on particular paths, but how protesters organize after confrontations can make the difference in the results of each case. Two additional insights are therefore necessary to solve this study's research puzzle and, ultimately, to contribute theory that will improve approaches to environmental conflicts, violence, and resistance. First, this research finds an important, even if not altogether straightforward, role played by outside attention—from media, solidarity groups, supporter NGOs, the state in Lima, and the broader public—in shaping how violence "works." Second, by problematizing the politics of how attention is drawn to violent events, this work also underscores the importance of the everyday, rarely noticed relationships built among and between local, company, and state actors. These two findings are summarized below by the concepts of "everyday violence" and "the politics of attention."

THE POLITICS OF ATTENTION: ORDINARY LIFE AND THE SPECTACLE OF VIOLENCE

Peru's resource conflicts showcase how violence is directly tied to attention, and how these dynamics impact conflict stakeholders differently depending on their structural power. The key manifestation of this link between violence and attention is how, whether or not they are directly involved in perpetrating it, stakeholders on all sides of conflict use violence in one way or another, at least discursively. This is because violent events, and the heightened attention these bring to remote localities, present people with an opportunity to try and draw some kind of benefits, material and symbolic. Nevertheless, the relationship between violence and attention is strategically important to conflict actors for completely different reasons if they support or contest mining projects. I will parse out these two central points in the following paragraphs.

While only some actors directly perpetrate physical damage, this study finds that almost all actors involved in conflicts *use* violence, to some extent. Most people I interviewed, across various corners of mining issues in Peru, are "nonviolent" personally—they identified as people who rejected and would not use violence. However, most actors do not think that all or any violence is unjustified. On the contrary, almost all of them could justify its use in specific circumstances such as self-defense, wars for independence, punitive justice, the violence of incarcerating a human being, which some see as a necessary evil, and other settings. In other words, people who explicitly stated that they opposed violence could also identify qualified instances in which they could perceive it as necessary or legitimate, even if they would not engage in it personally. This demonstrated the challenge of categorizing actors as violent or nonviolent, which is reductive, othering, and potentially criminalizing. Instead, their narratives led me to realize that people on multiple sides of conflict—even those opposed to and unwilling to engage in violence—were using the phenomenon of violence, at least rhetorically, thereby endowing it with symbolic and material life. To articulate it is to enact it; to give it meaning is to give it a form.

Because explosive moments of physical violence garner attention from media, the state, and the broader public, they give people variously involved in conflict a chance to reframe debates. People use violent events to create narratives and be recognized; they may be trying to frame themselves as helpless, powerless victims, or inversely, as more than just victims but actually courageous agents of change; and similarly, they may be trying to frame their opponents as evil, backward, or corrupt. They hope to alter discourses that can translate into attitudes, practices, and policies favorable to them. They thereby shape what violence is and does, imbuing it with meanings and affecting future interactions, as well as broader worldviews, norms, habits, relationships, policies, laws, cultural and economic structures, and more. And in most cases, people do not engage in these practices naively or pre-politically, as is commonly argued in scholarly literature; rather, they do it with strategic intention and political consciousness.

This critique of the politics of attention shows how violence can be used to discredit, but it can also be used to gain favorable attention. People tend to assume that violence will result in negative backlash; however, contrary to this conventional expectation, the cases here reveal how violence can be instrumentalized to delegitimize enemies as well as to gain legitimacy and outside support, moving ambivalent bystanders into the realm of passive and then active allies. After a violent confrontation, people attempt to, and sometimes can, credibly convince the public that they are morally justified victims, that opponents are criminally responsible and deserve punishment, and that violence is sometimes necessary. Understanding this is crucial to identifying the causes and effects of violence—in Peru's subnational conflicts and beyond.

Whether they generally sympathize with protest or are in favor of its repression, most people understand that publicly violent events attract attention, so these events become part of actors' calculations. However, the opportunity to reshape public debates holds more potential for people contesting mining than for its advocates. Structurally, Peru's legal institutions, political speech, and established media are aggressively in favor of resource extraction as the country's main pathway toward economic development, and they discredit and silence those who disagree. When the status quo is tipped so heavily in their favor, mining supporters have less to gain from upsetting this normalcy.

The institutional and legal frameworks that structure the possibilities of interaction between companies and their opponents are so favorable to mining, and so repressive to its opponents, that the absence of outside attention to local conflicts benefits mining companies. Company supporters willing to use violence or coercion against outspoken opponents do so counting on the belief that state, NGO, and media actors will pay very little attention to what happens in what are understood as remote, isolated, rural, and presumably underdeveloped spaces. This lack of attention presents a cover and feeds the perception that companies can act with impunity. Whenever they need, mining companies also have greater power to shape public narratives through their access to established media outlets (especially concentrated media conglomerates such as Grupo El Comercio, whose owners have been invested in mining since its founding[30]), where they portray themselves as environmentally and socially responsible, and as victims of corrupt local and external agitators who manipulate ignorant, needy peasants for self-gain. They therefore invest in publicity strategies that inoculate them from scandals, backlash, and declines in their stock value. At a fundamental level, company supporters almost never feel the need to act illegally, for the law works in their favor.

On the opposite end of the spectrum, people who protest a mining project (for diverse environmental, economic, or cultural reasons) believe they have more to gain from unsettling that order and that status quo, which is why some have engaged in spectacles of violence, such as the burning of company property. Activists perceive the lack of attention to their cause as an obstacle to attaining tangible victories such as concessions from the mining companies, interventions from state mediators, or resources and support from outside groups. As several interviewees revealed separately, they therefore believe that spectacles of violence can be used successfully to draw attention, reshape the public debate, gain allies, and pressure their opponents to offer concessions. Of course, this is not always the case, and I was skeptical of such claims—until I heard them repeated by interviewees across the board: activists, mining company agents, scholars, journalists, police officers, and more. Given their respective interest in the dynamic, and how common the claim was, I set upon investigating it empirically.

Companies and their supporters have strong public relations strategies, more resources, and far greater access to national politicians and media, thus greater control over public debates. However, protesters in at least one of the cases, Tambo Grande, used a moment of violent confrontation and property damage to actually gain attention and support. What explains this surprising outcome? Based on the comparative analysis of the case studies, this research proposes that the success or failure of these attempts—whether or not mining opponents can use favorably the heightened attention brought about by violence—depends on two particular, equally necessary factors: (a) their access to diffuse media in which they can shift the conversation, and (b) how convincing they are in reframing themselves as legitimate and, most importantly, nonviolent.

VIOLENCE, FRAMING, AND OUTSIDE SUPPORT

Here is how the process developed in the cases. If and when it happens, an incident framed as violence raises attention beyond the local level, inviting responses from regional and central governments, media, and nongovernmental organizations. If, in these contexts, protesters arrive at a credible and decisive transformation of tactics, marked primarily by committing publicly to nonviolence and framing their opposition as responsible for any violence, they may shift the debate. Escalation reframed as nonviolent can help to exploit the attention originally brought about by a violent confrontation. At the same time, committing to nonviolent tactics is insufficient; the groups protesting also need access to diffuse media through which they can share their reframing. If the coverage of the confrontation is mainly criminalizing, or it is not diffuse enough to reach broad audiences, even a credible and decisive shift to a nonviolent framing will not draw much support for the protesters.

Contrasting the cases shows how, to draw support and use the politics of attention in their favor, protesters needed both a credible tactical adherence to nonviolence and access to media. Protesters against the Cerro Corona project remained entirely nonviolent but had no real media coverage. Protesters in La Zanja and Lagunas Norte gained some access to media, but they were unable to present themselves as committed to nonviolence. Especially in the latter, media narratives heavily criminalized the movement, except in the coverage from a regional university's news broadcast and a local radio station. Only the movement against the Tambo Grande mine counted on both a credible transformation to nonviolence *and* access to various media through which they could diffuse their frames; this combination allowed them to use attention to draw more supporters to their cause, eventually tipping the conflict in their favor.

To put it simply, coercion takes place slowly and subtly over time, as well as directly and openly. When it provokes escalated tactics, confrontations may reach a level that can be framed as violent. This then draws attention, which mostly—but surprisingly, not always—portrays protesters in condemning or criminalizing ways. Heightened outside attention offers people engaged in conflict, including ambivalent residents of the surrounding area, an opportunity to use the violence to draw material and symbolic benefits. Indeed, activists can channel outside attention favorably despite the violent event that brought it, depending on their media framing and access. If they decisively and credibly take on a nonviolent frame, and have access to media to diffuse this framing, they can use violent events to their favor.

These dynamics help to explain why various sides of a conflict might adopt tactics that escalate into explosive forms of violence. From this follows a third central finding of this study: understanding the politics of selective attention requires accounting for violence as a multifaceted phenomenon that transcends spectacular events.

FEELING AND MEANING EVERYDAY VIOLENCE

Problematizing the role of attention in conflict escalation presents fundamental conceptual and methodological implications for the study of violence. These coalesce around two main points. First, the event-driven conceptualization of violence reinforces the dynamics I referred to above as the politics of attention that exacerbate conflict. Violence must be treated as a process and everyday phenomenon, which is symbolic as well as material, structural as well as embodied, and it must be studied in context. Attending to its origins, microdynamics, and operations beneath the surface is crucial to transforming and preventing it. Everyday effects (such as the feeling of one's dignity being violated through subtle racialized insults and microaggressions) can provoke a nonviolent protester into a physical confrontation.

Language has understated but major consequences on Peru's resource conflicts, often in surprising ways. Specifically, I will show how people on various sides of conflicts use culturally resonant frames, for example to portray themselves as powerless victims, their opponents as "ungrievable" or beyond rescue, and violent actions as justified.[31] This reframing opportunity may incentivize escalation to violence, but maneuvering the discursive terrain of conflict may also have an opposite, disciplining effect on actors' strategies: as people learn how their opponents use frames to delegitimize them, they adjust their tactics and manicure their public image strategically.

Second, while violence can be found in the tone of voice, rhetoric, and attitudes with which company operators address locals—for example, in condescending or deceptive ways—reforming these practices is not enough to prevent violence. This research demonstrates the limits of discourse in understanding the lived experience and material conditions of people involved in these conflicts. For example, as companies learn from previous confrontations and mistakes (their own and those of others), they are increasingly dedicating time and resources to training their staff in human-relations strategies. Junior, medium, and large companies alike hire highly skilled sociologists and psychologists as "social relations managers," and they send staff to programs and conferences where they can learn about conflict avoidance from others in the industry. However, as I suggest in the final chapter, a focus on conflict avoidance is a poor substitute for engraining a genuine concern for human rights within company culture.

Companies are intelligently changing the way they address and relate to people in the places they refer to as their impact areas, developing strategies to pacify opponents with increasing nuance. But changing the tone or amicability of everyday encounters with locals does not automatically make "not violent" the relationships between company operators and their local hosts. These overtures may also backfire if they are accompanied by repression, which provides both symbolic and material incentives for conflict to become routine and rational. More importantly, the everyday violence at play within, and exacerbated by, conflicts over resource extraction should not be mistaken for a discursive-only problem. While training for friendlier or less-condescending attitudes toward locals and opponents has helped companies depoliticize their community relations, these superficial efforts of conflict avoidance do little to resolve most of the forms of violence that result from extractive capitalism, such as underdevelopment, pollution, gendered violence like human and sex trafficking, or the racist histories and institutions that underlie land tenure. In actuality, at least one case study (Gold Fields' Cerro Corona) shows how these discourses legitimize and occlude other forms of violence and domination. Interrogating this depoliticization is therefore necessary to meaningfully build relationships, address violence, and construct durable peace.

In short, violence has a social life that outlives events and media snapshots, and its roles are better understood as processes than as instances. Corporate, media, and academic discourses are biased toward representing violence as an event. However, violent events are the results of social relations, which are built every day. The social fabric is historically shaped by forms of violence, some of which may be hardly noticeable sparks but over time accumulate into solar proportions. Because it is present in the small, nuanced interactions that accrue into anger, boiling resentment, and persistent distrust (long before and long after the attention-grabbing event observers categorize as violent), then reframing our shared understandings of violent conflict will assist in finding better forms of conflict transformation and violence prevention. Violence must be analyzed as semiotic and discursive, but with a critical perspective. Altering discourses alone, while leaving broader structural inequalities intact, does not help to eradicate violence—neither in its everyday embodied forms nor in how it explodes into spectacular moments. In fact, how discursive practices are used to conceal material violence is exactly what must be exposed in order to build more peaceful institutions and social relations.

Synthesis

The arguments above can be summarized as follows. The community engagement strategies of mining company actors explain why locals contesting mining projects (for whatever environmental and redistributive goals) resort to violent collective action, although not in determined or straightforward ways. Repression intends to provoke undisciplined reactions by protesters, but this research also finds that repression in combination with compensation may generate even higher levels of violence and ultimately routinize conflict as an integral aspect of company-community relationships.

Although their local opponents identify various everyday forms of violence related to mining projects, company actors work hard to keep scandals and negative attention at bay; they profit from inattention, which provides impunity. Corporations simultaneously use investment programs and media to frame themselves as beneficial, and rely on established media's selective gatekeeping about what types of violence are worth public attention—a selectivity shaped by racist and classist discourses, as well as by deeply ingrained cultural biases that otherize, pathologize, and delegitimize local opponents to mining projects. These dynamics call into question how observers--including journalists, academics, and the public--participate in these problematic framing tendencies, thereby helping the state and corporations enact different forms of repression. The public's selective attention ignores people's everyday experiences of harm and violence, but instantly criminalizes their protest.

Sometimes, activists feel that all the damage and trauma to which they are subjected daily does not matter to anyone. Their complaints go nowhere or are ignored, and their activism is shut down through increasingly subtle means of pacification and coercion. Their suffering is treated as normal; perhaps it is even legal, or at least culturally legitimized by a public that is either indifferent or actually invested in the things hurting them. In those contexts, it is more likely for people to arrive at the conclusion that their pain will not be resolved until they get the media and the government's attention, by any means necessary.

Two things result when outside attention is drawn to violent conflict: first, activists might gain an opportunity to frame their causes favorably and solicit support, including from NGOs, mediators, and the state; and second, companies enter into crisis-management and promise solutions. This has created a recurrent pattern where conflict escalation is followed by mediation, and later by unkept promises, feeding resentment. As this conflict cycle becomes normalized, it may entrench itself in the very fabric of company-community relations. Therefore, by pacifying and concealing tensions in the short term through investments or public relations strategies—all while simultaneously sowing conflict through arrogance toward local concerns and repression of their opposition—companies encourage and effectively routinize violent escalation.

Protesters use a range of nonviolent methods to voice grievances, organize communities, and make demands. However, theories of nonviolent resistance show that public attention is crucial for these dynamics to galvanize support and succeed. The paradox is that violent protest is generally more successful at drawing attention than most forms of nonviolence—despite the latter's moral appeal and the risk of delegitimization that comes with the former. The question becomes: what kinds of resistance can draw both attention *and* favorable framing? In part, the answer requires an interrogation of what is framed as violence or nonviolence, by whom, and to what effect. Disrupting this binary by understanding local agency and the microprocesses of conflicts can unlock this puzzle. With different results, activists publicly framed their actions as nonviolence, accessed friendly and diffuse media, narrated their own stories, and gained support. In one case, this worked to fully stop a major state-sponsored mining project.

This research is a critical interrogation of violence—as a concept, dynamic, discourse, and social process, particularly within the context of mining conflicts in Peru. It argues that everyday violence and the politics of attention explain why people, including those organized to contest mining projects as well as mining company actors and mining supporters, adopt coercion and different levels of violence. In turn, the strategies of these various and amorphous sides explain the shifting processes and the outcomes of each case.

Research as Witnessing

According to the United Nations Environment Programme, conflicts over land, water, and other natural resources represented at least 40 percent of all subnational conflicts between 1950 and 2009, and these types of conflict were twice as likely to relapse within five years.[32] As the planet warms, it is more critical now than ever to understand resource conflicts and the dynamics that lead them to escalate. A primary challenge in doing this is that violence is a difficult concept to study, especially from a distance. Explanations for political violence must account for its contexts, its construction, and the relationships, networks, and legacies it generates.[33] To excavate such contingent factors, it is necessary to conduct "thick," in-depth analysis that can trace these processes, dynamics, and causal mechanisms in a grounded way.[34] However, Peru's numerous resource conflicts demonstrate common patterns that deserve inspection. To draw theories that are useful more broadly, comparison across cases is needed. Therefore, this study merged ethnographic within-case analysis with a controlled comparison of cases to arrive at the findings outlined above.

I used a controlled comparison based on John Stuart Mill's method of difference.[35] First, by restricting the scope of the study to one particular industry (mining), one specific mining sector (gold), a subregion of a single country (the north of Peru), and a specific time frame (conflicts between 2000 and 2015), I could arrive as closely as possible to holding constant the variation among other factors that may drive case outcomes. Second, I chose cases that shared similar conditions but had different results along the factor to be explained: the levels of violence each project reached. This setup allows me to identify, trace, and analyze the dynamics that explain how similar cases can lead to contrasting outcomes—insights that may apply in other contexts.

I selected four "paradigmatic" cases that best reflected the range of escalation in Peru's gold mining conflicts: Tambo Grande, La Zanja, Lagunas Norte, and Cerro Corona. Despite their contextual similarities, a crucial factor that varies across the cases is how corporations responded to local pressures, learned about these relations, and adapted; ultimately, these differences shaped the cases' divergent outcomes.

Data for this study was collected during two fieldwork periods. First, I visited Lima to establish contacts and narrow my case selection in July to September 2014. I then lived in Peru for just over thirteen months between August 2015 and September 2016. I spent most of my time living in mining areas in the north of the country and made several trips to Lima. Through this immersion I conducted more than 250 formal interviews, collected and coded more than nine hundred archives (including stakeholders' internal reports and publications, media clippings, and official documents), and participated in or observed dozens of processes with actors involved variously in mining conflicts.

Interviewees include mining area residents in various occupations; movement leaders and participants; mining employees, managers, and executives; members of local, national, and international organizations; municipal, regional, and national government officials in various related offices; and journalists and academics based near the cases as well as in Lima. The study treats participants as partners whose concerns and questions are centered in my analysis, and with nuance rather than as monolithic or mystical, or determined by their many affiliations. Given my training and my objective of uncovering power relations, a key guiding principle in this study is to seek and highlight the voices of people who are seldom heard in studies and reports of this kind, particularly people whose identities crosscut multiple marginalized social categories given their position as women, people of color, Indigenous, Afro-Peruvian, gender nonconforming, disabled, economically impoverished, and/or houseless people. The challenge was to do this while simultaneously being critical of, rather than reifying, any such socially constructed and heterogeneous categories. Participants provided informed consent for this research, which was approved by a full IRB ethics protocol. (For more on my data collection and analysis methods, see this book's Appendix 2, "Notes on Methodology and Methods.")

Critical discourse analysis of all the sources outlined above, assisted by several layers of qualitative coding, provides a thick description of the cases.[36] This helps to weave a complex story and trace the processes by which people perceive events, make choices, frame their perspectives, and shape the outcomes of cases. Then, controlled comparison of cases helps to build theory about conflict mechanisms and the prospects of resolution efforts. Adopting a carefully reflexive, immersive, participatory, and systematic research design, this in-depth comparison of four gold mines in northern Peru contributes original insights about the processes through which conflicts become violent, as well as those that lead actors to eschew violent means of waging conflict.

Before turning to each ethnographic case, I will next set the stage for each by detailing the theoretical, cultural, and legal terrain of the study.

CHAPTER 2

Everyday Life, Mining, and Conflict in Peru

[Mining companies] leave us the pollution. Legally, they do it, but it is pollution. In fact, it is several types of contamination. The cost of everything increases: it is *economic pollution*. Second, there is *moral pollution*. . . . There is corruption of authorities, officials, and leaders. They have successfully distorted laws and elections. Barrick has funded four different candidates in Otuzco. For what? They do not want us to choose for ourselves. That is pollution as well: *political pollution*. When they come, alcoholism and violence increase. *Social pollution*. Then there's *environmental pollution*. They jeopardize the quality and quantity of water. They discredit us. . . . They try to divide the social organizations that oppose them. They bring parallel organizations like a "new" Ronda to discredit and replace local authorities. They distort how we organize, and they accuse us of being anti-mining terrorists. That's another damage: criminalization. Meanwhile, they do not comply with agreements that they sign. We are not anti-miners. What we want is justice.

ANONYMOUS ENVIRONMENTAL LEADER,
speaking to a workshop in La Libertad, on November 19, 2015[1]

Introduction: A Life of Gold

Gold is a site of struggle. On the one hand, the treasured metal is a valuable commodity; a cross-cultural symbol of fortune, luxury, and status; a metaphor for victory, success, and prosperity. The Quechua-speaking Natives of Tahuantinsuyo (known as the Incan Empire) thought of it as the lifeblood of the sun, their highest deity. The mineral element is malleable and enduring, and its utility ranges from that of a superconductor, present in electronic devices that are in growing global demand, to an edible food garnish for the affluent and extravagant. On the other hand, its aesthetics and glitter conceal an ugly truth.

Gold is a conflict mineral, a storied reason for bloodshed across much of the world for longer than, but especially during, the last five centuries. Pillaging precious commodities like gold has motivated and currently motivates colonial exploration, conquest, subjugation, exploitation, and ongoing dependency.[2] Lust for gold brought Francisco Pizarro and his conquistadores to Cajamarca in 1532, and it is what today maintains Cajamarca, now home to South America's largest gold mine, as Peru's main gold producing region. But perhaps that same lust for gold is why in recent years Cajamarca has been consistently ranked as Peru's poorest region, despite hosting such a promising, large-scale, international investment project for more than twenty years. Today, in mining areas within and beyond Cajamarca, authorities and residents report severe pollution, water scarcity, lead and arsenic in locals' blood, and other problems, such as mass die-offs of river fish.[3] Meanwhile, gold's scarcity and historically high market value continue to lure exploration and exploitation, causing displacement, pollution, corruption, human and economic underdevelopment, and violent conflict along its global paths—from the sites where it is extracted to where it is retailed, consumed, used, stored, wasted, and left to decay.[4]

The price of gold has grown drastically since its lowest recorded point at US$239 per ounce in December 1970 (adjusting for inflation at 2020 Consumer Price Index levels). The highest price on the record was nearly $2,300 in January of 1980, followed closely by a peak that surpassed $2,000 in late 2011. However, as this book went to press, 2020 was on track to shatter the all-time highest record—partly as a result of the COVID-19 pandemic, which not only shifted markets dramatically but also moved a significant part of human activity toward the internet and electronic devices.

According to the World Gold Council, just over half of all gold produced becomes jewelry, one quarter is kept by private investors, 12 percent ends up in central banks and state vaults, and about 10 percent of all gold demand is created by the electronics industry.[5] Even though people in the United States alone throw away an estimated $60 million worth of gold and silver from discarded phones every year, less than 30 percent of the world's total demand is satisfied by recycled gold, which means that over 70 percent of the gold produced each year is extracted from the subsoil, feeding a mining boom during the past two decades. Thanks to high demand for technological gadgets from countries in the global North and other rapidly growing markets—including India and China, which together account for 50 percent of global demand—mining exploration budgets more than doubled in just two years, between 2009 and 2011. One quarter of the industry's total exploration budget in 2011 went to Latin America.[6]

Latin America produces more than one-fifth of the world's gold, with Peru and Mexico as the region's largest gold producers (first and second, respectively).[7] Most medium-to-large gold mines there use open-pit, mountain-top removal to blast through rock and gather earth, creating large holes that appear as mostly concentric from a bird's-eye view. Massive fleets of diesel-powered industrial load vehicles then each carry about 180 tons of mined rocks and dirt, along with roughly 8.5 ounces of gold, to where it is processed. To separate the gold from rock and earth, the most common and cost-effective method is cyanide heap-leaching. Machines pulverize the soil and rocks, which are then spread onto watertight and artificial ponds; there, the materials are flattened and sprayed with a cyanide-and-water solution meant to dissolve and drain the soil. Engineers then mix the gold and cyanide with carbon, which bonds with the gold particles, and then another acidic solution (typically, hydrochloric acid) is used to separate the carbon. The liquid gold-and-acid solution is then poured onto electrified steel, which attracts the metal. Once gold-plated, the steel is exposed to temperatures high enough to melt the gold, which is then drained, isolated at last, and usually smelted into iron bars for transportation.

The cyanide pools leftover in tailings dams—the formal term for colossal, artificial structures used to store toxic waste—can be reused to a limited extent, but a small mine still consumes thousands to millions of gallons of fresh water each day. This water cannot be recovered, as it is mixed with the more than 1,900 tons of cyanide that an average medium-to-large gold mine uses yearly.[8] If they are not deliberately dumped into soil or water, tailings are dumped at the end of a mine's lifecycle—typically two to three decades.[9] In 2012, investigators revealed that nine of the world's largest mining companies dump their tailings into rivers, lakes, or the ocean, including companies that operate in Peru such as Barrick, Newmont, Vale, Rio Tinto, and Xstrata.[10]

Along the way, the process generates additional forms of pollution: the mountain-top removal process exposes sulfides in rocks to air and water, creating sulfuric acid and releasing it into the atmosphere. Similarly, other poisonous substances contained in rock, such as arsenic, cobalt, copper, cadmium, lead, silver, and zinc, get washed away with rainwater and artificially leached water, and are thus carried downstream, where even trace amounts are hugely dangerous to aquatic life, wildlife, broader ecosystems, human health, and local economies. Highly toxic chemical agents such as cyanide, stored at the mines, often spill or leak from containers that are usually uncovered and susceptible to heavy rain and flooding. There are thousands of tailings dams around the world, and two to five of them experience major failures each year, such as when the tailings dam collapsed at the Vale company's Córrego do Feijão mine in Brazil in 2019, spilling twelve million cubic meters of sludge, killing nearly three hundred people. Furthermore, mercury and other hazardous heavy metals are common bi-products of refinement. According to the US Department of Energy, nearly 80 percent of the materials used in the process become toxic and irrecoverable.[11]

Water usage depends on the ore grade (or concentration of minerals in the soil) at each site, which varies immensely, and on the type of processes the miners use. Also, each observers' methods of measurement may also vary, so it is useful to aggregate estimates from across various peer-reviewed studies; one such comparison of these estimates found that efficient mines require an average of 260 metric tons of water and 200 gigajoules of energy for every 32 ounces of gold they produce; in addition, each 32 ounces of gold produced generates 18 metric tons of greenhouse gases such as carbon dioxide and 1,270 metric tons of waste solids.[12] To put these figures in perspective, producing a single half-ounce, 18-carat gold ring requires, on average, mining more than five metric tons of earth, burning more than 833,333 watt hours of electricity, and permanently contaminating more than 1,000 gallons of fresh water—the planet's most important resource.

Although seemingly disconnected, wider structures, actors, and dynamics are linked across geographical boundaries by socio-environmental conflicts. The mass extraction and production of minerals for global consumption require water, land, electricity, petroleum, workers, policing, legal systems and cultural norms, infrastructure like roads and processing plants, transcontinental transport, increasingly globalized networks, and more. Furthermore, the environmental and human risks of mining are only part of its hidden costs. Tensions arise far before production begins, as mines tend to require the displacement of people living on the surface land and blocking access to concentrated metallic deposits. Those residents may also be self-sustaining or small-scale farmers and Indigenous peoples, they may hold religious or cultural attachments to their land, and they may be women with particular gendered roles and relationships to their land (as primary food providers and caretakers of their families). Thus, more than just resource-intensive operations, mines are further entangled in complex social contexts, histories, and politics.

This research argues that, despite cases' heterogeneity and contingencies, the most significant causal explanation for the escalation of Peru's gold mining conflicts rests on the agency of company actors, which includes instigating everyday violence. Their strategies (and lack thereof) for approaching and responding to communities and local opponents are, in contrast to alternative explanations, the factor that best helps to understand why locals undertake tactics beyond the realm of what is typically considered nonviolence, such as arson, temporary detainment, and physical violence. Most previous studies of resource conflicts have altogether ignored or downplayed this factor.

This chapter surveys theoretical frameworks—from within as well as from outside of Peru—and the political context that may help to answer why some of Peru's resource conflicts become more violent, and how violent conflicts transform away from violence. I argue that answers to this question must integrate critical, qualitative approaches to violence, nonviolent agency, and resource conflicts in their contexts, taking account of actors' relationships, choices, and the structures that may shape those.

Contested Ecologies: Natural Resources and the Promise of Development

> Those on the frontlines of these struggles are often not environmentalists—they are communities defending their livelihoods, the right to participate in decision-making and recognition of their life projects. Nor is this, as governments and companies try to paint it, about a balance between development and conservation. It is rather about the meaning of development itself, who is sacrificed in the name of development and who decides. Pollution is not democratic, nor is it colour blind.
>
> LEAH TEMPER[13]

The demands of international trade, an expanding global consumer class, and the adoption of neoliberal policies over the past two decades have caused the prices of primary commodities to boom. This has encouraged many countries, especially those with a history of export-led economies, to adopt aggressive forms of resource extraction (in the form of drilling, mining, fracking, processing, damming, logging, and industrial-scale harvesting) as their main engine for growth. Lucrative opportunities for multinational corporations, the spread of new technologies that increase the scale and reduce the costs of resource extraction, and financial speculation on commodities markets are sustaining a trend for export-led growth and a dramatic rise of extractive activities.[14] These are noticeable worldwide, but foreign direct investment and states dependent on it are expanding the frontier of resource exploration into more remote, resource-rich areas of the global South. For instance, while labor and environmental regulations in the European Union make extraction expensive, states like Peru and Brazil deliberately weaken their own regulations, speed up the approval of extraction projects, and deploy security forces to protect investments.

Natural resources are a frequent and increasing source of conflicts across the world. According to the United Nations Environment Programme, "there is significant potential for conflicts over natural resources to intensify in the coming decades."[15] Corroborating this, the Heidelberg Institute for International Conflict Research suggested that natural resources were the second-most frequent cause of conflict around the world in 2010, and the most frequent cause of conflicts in Latin America in 2013.[16] Given the frequency of such conflicts, and in order to channel and resolve them nonviolently, it is necessary to understand their recurring patterns.

Extractive industries are known to introduce a number of complex changes to rural areas. Locals and governments welcome many of these changes with open arms, as they represent the very promise of extractive industries: increased economic activity; an injection of cash into the local economy; jobs; higher revenues for local service providers, such as restaurants, hotels, transportation workers, and other businesses; and not least, more resources for governments at the local, regional, and national levels, which may translate into greater investment into human development goals like education and healthcare. For communities in many subnational regions, extraction may seem to be the only possible revenue-generating economic activity available. However, extractivism can lead to severe problems.

Environmental degradation, including resource depletion and contamination, is accompanied by negative social effects.[17] These commonly include dislocation of local economies; displacement and acculturation of Indigenous peoples, which threaten to cause the extinction of languages, traditions, and whole cultures; integration of people into urbanized lifestyles and the global cash economy, where they may not succeed, causing them to end on the streets (especially if they sold their land for what, as people often realize later, was too small a price); rupture of local social bonds, loyalties, and patronage schemes; decay of traditional norms and structures; rise of local corruption, alcoholism, crime, sex trafficking, and drug trafficking; negative health indicators, such as higher child mortality rates, malnutrition, and lower educational attainment; heavy burdens on local infrastructure; and more idiosyncratic effects—for example, how controlled explosions at mining sites sometimes damage homes and other buildings nearby.[18]

The intrusion of extractive industries may jeopardize locals' survival in a number of interrelated ways: *economically*, if they farm for trade and self-sustenance; *biologically*, because they need clean water; and in some cases, *culturally*, if their identities, symbolic systems, and languages are attached to specific aspects of their particular ecosystem—such as burial sites, bodies of water, or mountains considered to be sacred—that will be jeopardized or destroyed by extractive industries. Furthermore, locals frequently complain that companies reap massive gains from mining investment, but they ignore consultation with locals, offer few employment opportunities, and pay back minimal taxes. In so doing, companies inadvertently set the stage for discontent and conflict among populations that surround the resources in question.

At the heart of conflicts over resource management today are different ideas about what constitutes progress and development. The hegemonic, dominant perspectives on this matter—promoted and mostly taken for granted by public officials, international financial institutions, economists, and media spokespeople—are the Eurocentric ideas that nature is for individual use and that economic growth, as measured by GDP indicators, translates to progress for all. People who defend this economistic bias believe that material and intangible things must be *commodified*, as trade is the key operator in their formula. In this view, the worth of things (including humans and their labor, nonhuman animals, plant species, nonsentient material, and social phenomena such as education) depends on their price as regulated by market forces. Nature is valued only by its potential to render economic profits and material benefits.[19]

The undeniable negative impacts of extractive industry put in question the value and credibility of the dominant views of capitalist extractivism and its model of development. Critics of this ideology, emerging from various combinations of feminist, Indigenous, anticolonial, antiracist, and ecological perspectives, typically focus not only on how the benefits and burdens of extractive activity are unevenly distributed, but also among whom. The benefits of extractivism are concentrated among people who are white, affluent, male, urban, and based in the global North. Meanwhile, its negative impacts disproportionately affect women, people of color, Black and Indigenous peoples, global South peoples, those who are gender and sexuality nonconforming, self-sustenance farmers, low-income workers, and impoverished people—and especially people at the intersection of these.[20]

Furthermore, perspectives critical of extractivism tend to overlap in their preference for alternative views of development, where ecological and humanitarian concerns should take primacy over economic growth. In some iterations of these diffuse approaches, living things are explicitly acknowledged as mutually dependent and reliant on a delicate balance with nonliving things, including natural processes such as the water and nitrogen cycles. That is to say, they measure progress not by the scale of economic transactions but by the well-being and longevity of life in a fragile ecosystem.

Untroubled States

Postcolonial countries like Peru inherited a global political economy and infrastructure where their role is primarily to export raw material resources in exchange for manufactured value-added goods produced in the colonial metropoles, a subordinate role cemented by international trade agreements and institutions like the World Trade Organization. However, the governing factions that temporarily take the reins of the state have some agency over the model of development they adopt. In Peru, as in many Latin American countries, the state played a heavy hand in the economy until especially the 1990s, when it succumbed to the dominant development model known as neoliberalism (a fundamentalist ideology for economics, politics, and society based on the primacy of market forces over the state's traditional responsibilities to its populace, espousing principles of individualism, austerity, privatization, and the downsizing of public services).

Because of its erosion of the liberal notion of a social contract, wherein the state is responsible for the well-being of its inhabitants, neoliberalization in general has been associated with increasing social instability.[21] Furthermore, when it comes to socio-environmental conflicts specifically, the neoliberal push to reduce the state has mutually reinforcing consequences.[22] Starting in the 1980s, "governments all over the world were forced to provide more attractive conditions for capitalists," chipping away the state's credibility as an impartial mediator of tensions and leading communities to believe they have to make their claims extra-institutionally.[23] Finally, neoliberalism replaces the state's responsibility for provision of social services with individual responsibility and the will of the market; therefore, in underserved areas, communities are encouraged to look to mining and other extractive companies to provide basic services. Mining companies go as far as to pay for the vehicles, meals, and transportation of local police departments. In short, neoliberalism is known to heighten inequality and exacerbate social conflicts, and meanwhile it also restricts the state's capacity to resolve these. The absence of the state is therefore at the heart of institutional failures to resolve conflicts before they erupt into violence. Indeed, my findings on the politics of attention suggest that people undertake property destruction precisely to reverse the state's growing absence, forcing it to respond to their claims.

The vacuum generated when states exculpate themselves from subnational conflicts only increases the importance of private company actors' still-understudied discourses, strategies, and everyday agency. However, evidence makes clear that the state should reverse course and take a greater role in ensuring equitable and sustainable resource management. Social movement actors and environmentalists in the country are working toward that objective by taking positions of state power at the national, regional, and municipal level, but the electoral success of parties like Frente Amplio, Tierra y Libertad, and Movimiento Acción Social is regionally constrained and significantly impeded by post-war narratives of "left-wing terrorism."

Cursed by Wealth

Many areas or countries that are richly endowed with natural resources, especially minerals and hydrocarbons, paradoxically tend to exhibit negative outcomes in terms of persistent poverty, chronic underdevelopment, and growing inequality. Scholars argue this is because the abundance of profitable natural resources might contribute to a sequence of economic and political distortions, such as patronage or clientelism, that undermine the quality of both democracy and development, especially in the context of weak institutions and postcolonial states.[24] In other words, the abundance of resource wealth may create incentives for state actors to disregard the public and engage in corruption, thus eroding trust, democracy, and well-being.

The "resource curse," as this phenomenon is known, affects national governments as well as their subnational units. For example, in one of the most relevant and effective studies on this matter, Javier Arellano-Yanguas compiled and compared quantitative data from mining and nonmining districts in Peru. His robust study results demonstrated that, despite companies' considerable efforts to invest in voluntary philanthropic schemes and corporate social responsibility strategies, areas with mining activity performed worse than nonmining areas. Not only had mining areas failed to improve on indicators of social and economic development over time (such as the poverty rate and the percentage of people with access to education, sanitation, and water), but worse, they actually had experienced a downturn. The study also used qualitative evidence of links between company investment and conflict, local clientelism, and political corruption. And damningly, the contrast between mining and nonmining regions showed that mining as a percentage of regional GDP had no statistical effect on regions' economic well-being—contrary to the propaganda, promises, and rhetoric of its supporters, and to local expectations.[25]

In short, the benefits and burdens of extractive activity, especially one that is as resource-intensive and that creates as much toxic waste as gold mining does, are unevenly distributed between the many stakeholders involved: area residents, mine workers, state officials, company managers, owners and shareholders, retailers, consumers, etc.[26] Such inequities, in addition to the dispossession of locals from their territories and the risks of water and soil pollution, have unsurprisingly provoked various reactions from farmers, Indigenous peoples, and civil society more broadly. However, grievances do not always manifest into conflicts, nor do they determine the shape of conflicts. More fundamentally, a key problem of the resource conflicts literature is that privileged observers commonly depart from the assumption that violence originates out of protest, whereas everyday life in sites of resource extraction is characterized by different types of violence (ecological, economic, social, and political) operating under the surface, but typically unattended by media, the state, and even academic researchers. Violence is in the water and the air, in locals' polluted bloodstreams, and in the plants and animals in their gardens. It is in the food they eat. Violence is in how you are perceived and treated because of the historical construction of subjectivities, which for the last five hundred years have been colonial in nature and inegalitarian by design.

The reasons behind conflicts surrounding natural resources are heterogeneous and contingent.[27] Therefore, more details are needed to contextualize and explain the emergence of environmental conflict and its varied internal dynamics.

Neoliberal Extractivism in Peru's Post-Conflict Context

This section presents a framework to consider contentious politics over natural resources in Peru—including how different people perceive and then act upon them. I review key traits in Peru's cultural, legal, and political context that set a particular stage for these dynamics. This context may hold clues about why conflicts over natural resources become violent. It consists mainly of four relevant and interrelated factors: (1) Peru has one of the most extractive-industry-friendly legislative frameworks in Latin America; (2) its post-conflict scenario is marked by authoritarian legacies; (3) judicial authorities have license to inflict harsh punishment on protest activities; and (4) Peru's media, politics, and economics have generated an industry-friendly hegemonic discourse. Each of these factors and their possible effects deserve brief elaboration.

PERU'S EXTRACTIVE FRAMEWORK

The mining sector has been deeply important to Peru's economic development over the past several centuries, as well as to its rapid economic growth over the past three decades.[28] As is clear from its concentration of the world's mining investment, Peru has adopted one of Latin America's most neoliberal, no-holds-barred approaches to regulating resource extraction. Mining law existed and has been reformed several times since before Peru's independence from Spain in 1821, but the 1990s marked a profound shift in Peru's institutional design to accommodate mining investment.[29] Alberto Fujimori's authoritarian administration (1990–2000) enacted a series of liberalizing reforms meant to attract investment and reduce the regulations seen as a "barrier" to it.[30] In addition to changes in the tax and customs codes, such as "tax stability" contracts meant to protect miners from future tax changes (expanded by subsequent governments), legislative decrees 662, 664, and 818 created a framework for private, largely foreign investment in natural resource exports. His government privatized more than two hundred mining operations, and by 1995 also legalized the expropriation of communal land for mining purposes. Most forcefully, perhaps, Legislative Decree 708 in 1991 established mining as an activity of "national interest" and modified a wide range of labor, land, and environmental regulations to fast-track mining concessions, construction, and expansions.[31]

The world price of metals climbed steadily during this time, reaching record highs and creating a powerful incentive for the state and mining companies to pursue and expand operations. In turn, subsequent governments have maintained, expanded, and mildly modified these codes.[32] Alan García's government (2006–2011) altered forestry laws and Indigenous land rights in a series of reforms that became the central concern of the 2009 protests in the Amazonian province of Bagua, where Indigenous-led protesters occupied roads and an oil duct. That particular conflict resulted in thirty-three deaths in only one day.[33] Later on, a quintessential example of these kinds of legal changes under Ollanta Humala's presidency (2011–2016) is a series of reform "packages" criticized as anti-environmental, and approved in 2014.[34] Among other things, these allow Peru's president to dispose of protected reservoirs and communal lands.

Besides the broader macroeconomic and political forces driving these reforms, scholars such as Francisco Durand have demonstrated how Peru's extractivist and neoliberal legal framework has been influenced, to some extent, by mining firms as agents in pursuit of interests. A prime example is Reflexión Democrática, a powerful lobby in the country founded in 2004 by Alberto Benavides Ganoza, founder and then CEO at Buenaventura—one of Peru's oldest and largest mining firms—and a partial owner of Yanacocha, La Zanja, and Cerro Verde. On his retirement, Benavides Ganoza was replaced as Buenaventura executive by his eldest son, Roque Benavides, who was also the president of Peru's largest corporate lobby, Confiep, in 1999 and 2000.

Extractive interests have captured the state across Peru's fractured political party system. Lobby firms draft legislation and persuade lawmakers on behalf of clients, but Durand elucidates other means for private firms to influence the state and the public—including via image consultants, nonprofit organizations, and policy think tanks. For example, the Instituto Peruano de Economía (IPE) is "Peru's most influential think tank on economic and labor policy"; it was founded in 1994 with a World Bank donation, and since then has been funded by companies including Buenaventura, Las Bambas, Cerro Verde (owned by Buenaventura), and the Southern Perú Copper Corporation. The IPE's work was instrumental in the anti-environment structural reforms passed in 2014.[35]

AUTHORITARIAN LEGACIES OF CONFLICT

Peru has only recently emerged from a period of internal armed conflict, during which many people directly and indirectly experienced some form of political violence from the state or from armed groups.[36] Three legacies of this conflict are of crucial importance. One is that words such as *violence* and *terrorism* are loaded concepts that have a resonance with recent memory, carry a certain cultural weight, and hold a lot of power to remove public legitimacy. Second, as Cynthia Arnson has argued, internal armed conflict and state responses to guerilla insurgencies have decisive, detrimental impacts on the quality and possibilities of democratic governance in Latin America.[37]

Third, the state's counterterrorism apparatus is increasingly at the disposal of private companies. Peru's security forces, especially older generations and the people in positions of leadership, are likely to have undergone high-level counterinsurgency training by the state (and in some cases also by foreign militaries like that of the US). They can readily use intimidation, torture, and other tactics to neutralize internal enemies (from dissidents to guerrillas and terrorists). Research has found that, in Peru's postwar context—marked by a large, unregulated, and demobilized military apparatus existing alongside weak state capacity in the countryside—high demand from powerful extractive firms makes private security contracts a lucrative business for current and former members of the state's armed forces.[38] This threatens to blur the line between security forces' public duty and their responsibility to companies that contract with them.

INSTRUMENTALIZING LAW AND PUNISHING PROTEST

The extractivist reforms outlined above not only resulted in a vast expansion of mining investment, but also sowed an explosion of socio-environmental conflicts in the country. In 2004, when the total value of mining investment in Peru was about US$1 billion, Peru was beset by less than fifty socio-environmental conflicts. Six years later, when mining investment amounted to US$4 billion, the ombudsperson registered about 120 socio-environmental conflicts.[39] Successive governments adopted slow and uneven responses to these conflicts. One positive step was the creation of a dialogue and conflict resolution agency (the Oficina Nacional de Diálogo y Sostenibilidad, or ONDS), created under Humala. However, Humala's approach to protests remained heavy-handed. While carrying a discourse of "dialogue," his government reacted to rising levels of conflict by expanding police and courts' authority to punish and repress dissidents. In the words of a human rights attorney, the penal code was "instrumentalized" to prosecute protestors, delegitimize movement leaders, and facilitate police repression.[40]

A key example of this was the 2013 law 30151, known as the "license to kill" law, which gave police the right to use lethal force against protesters. Separately, many activists detained by the armed forces alleged that they were tortured while in custody.[41] But the less publicized forms of repression through courts, rather than through police violence in the streets, are equally problematic. Whereas the criminalization of protest under the Fujimori regime was already harsh, and often excused under the context of the internal conflict against armed groups (roughly 1980 to 2000), this was deepened by the García and even more by the Humala administrations.[42] García's judiciary added qualifiers to the penal code such as "extortion" and "hostile groups," both of which were used to crush resistance movements such as the Bagua Indigenous-led protests.[43] Despite promises to the contrary, García's successor, Ollanta Humala, escalated the government's repressive approach to mining protests. As of March 2016, as he prepared to leave office, more than three hundred activists were criminally processed in the Cajamarca region alone on charges ranging from disturbing the peace to support for terrorism.[44]

MEDIA BIAS AND HEGEMONIC DISCOURSES

A fourth factor that makes Peru a particularly contentious context is the insufficient regulation of corporate media. Namely, the Peruvian state has permitted the concentration of media into monopolies such as Grupo El Comercio, which controls about 78 percent of print newspapers as well as a large share of other broadcast media.[45] This allows the big players in the corporate sector to corner and dominate the public debate over politically salient issues, such as mining-related conflicts, around which they have entrenched a hegemonic but contested extractivist discourse that paints mining as obviously beneficial and its opponents as criminal, violent, and terrorist.

Out of many examples of this, a recent and exemplary case is the rhetoric adopted by the right-wing economist Hernando de Soto. In mid-2016, de Soto publicized the notion of mining-related activism as being a *Sendero Verde* or a "green" version of the Shining Path guerrilla movement. In his words, "they are former terrorists who have fulfilled their sentences. They are not armed. They are all ecologists." Hernando de Soto, a respected commentator and Peruvian economist with a pulpit on the mainstream press, has also often promoted the notion that there are two Perus: the pre-industrial country of Andean peasants and Indigenous peoples, and the industrial Peru of the urbanized middle-class and of corporations, where the former belongs in the past and is economically untenable, unable to develop new capital, and the latter represents the future. This same rhetoric has since been adopted by other media observers.[46]

In short, Peruvian media corporations are concentrated, economically entangled (because they belong to conglomerates that often have direct investments in mining), bought (because they receive advertisement revenues from mining companies), and ideological (almost uniformly probusiness). These conglomerates have reinforced the importance of mining for development and discredited its opponents. In political speeches, news media, networking websites, and public discussions, extractive capitalism is touted as beneficial and advantageous to the nation as a whole. Such narratives are contested, especially by left-wing politicians, activist groups, ecological organizations, and alternative media. However, these opponents' access to media pales in comparison with that of mining advocates, as can be measured through both large-scale public opinion polls and more specific speech events and interactions. Whether one analyzes everyday conversations, online commentary, or mass surveys, the prevalence of a pro-mining discourse becomes quickly apparent. These contested discourses may drive conflict escalation and erode resolution efforts, especially the dismissive and polarizing tones with which some state officials and media pundits portray mining activists as violent ideologues, corrupt manipulators, or ignorant and manipulated. This rhetoric constitutes a blatant rewriting of history, where environmental conflicts are remembered not by the extraordinary efforts of people defending their communities through overwhelmingly nonviolent means of struggle, but are instead marked by labels like "radical anti-miners" and "eco-terrorists." Their narratives not only miss the nuances of conflict, but also exacerbate distrust and alienation.[47]

Extractivist discourses pit those who would criticize mining projects as standing against the country and its people. Protesters become obstacles to the right of all Peruvians to progress and embrace modernity. Framed as threats to the public interest and enemies of the nation, they can be more easily treated as "second-class" (as Alan García referred to the Indigenous protesters at Bagua) and as "ungrievable" or undeserving of empathy (or basic rights).[48] This othering power has repercussions, blatant and subtle: it helps to justify repression, both through police violence and court sentences, but it also leads commentators to—strategically and sometimes unthinkingly—adopt blasé criminalizing tones (e.g., referring to protestors as violent and guilty before a court formulates a decision). In other words, they justify people's deaths as the inevitable cost of economic development. Such effects are harsh in Peru, where the recent and divisive experience of internal armed conflict gives terms like *violence* and *terrorism* a particular cultural resonance. Alas, due to ideological bias and economic interest in selling violence as spectacle, media have exaggerated the inflammatory and dramatic aspects of these conflicts, erasing their nonviolent aspects and prospects.

Beyond accusations and the physical punishment that they justify, the cases I studied demonstrate how discourses also influence the choices made by conflict stakeholders. Indeed, interviewees demonstrated how criminalization in media and in the public debate shaped how they organized, particularly in order to avoid this negative framing.[49] To be sure, contested and mainstreamed narratives, ideas, and discourses are central—but in uneven, not perfectly straightforward ways—to Peru's social conflicts, and perhaps especially its natural resource conflicts. Because of their varying levels of violence and the multiplicity of contested narratives that have emerged around them, Peru's resource conflicts have generated unique patterns in the links between discourse and material circumstances. The complexity of these conflicts cannot be captured if they are not analytically situated within Peru's post-conflict political context, economic model, institutional and legal framework, and public discourses.

One key aspect of Peru's political, cultural, and institutional context is the hegemonic influence of mining interests. Industrial-managerial groups, lobbies, and conferences are only some of the sites in which Peru's extractive economic model is reinforced as unquestionable. Discourse management takes place through media firms like Grupo DIGAMMA and public relations initiatives like its "I Want Formal Mining" campaign, which contrasted mining corporations with the threat of informal mining, portrayed as dangerous and irresponsible. Over time, their rhetoric sticks. The state is not an individual or rational actor, but clearly most state officials have largely internalized this model as a sort of official ideology that cuts across the country's main political parties. Peru is not the only Latin American country to have adopted an extractive economy, but its reliance on it has been critical, as is clear from the low tolerance it shows toward dissent to extraction.

Both the legacies of recent conflict, on one hand, and the hegemonic power of mining interests over legislation and public discourse, on the other, have vast repercussions on Peru's political institutions and everyday life. The former have granted Peru's governments the license to slowly expand the counter-insurgency state apparatus under the guise of persecuting enemies to national security, prosperity, and order. The latter has shaped Peru's economic model and institutional framework to accommodate mining investment (at the expense of alternative industries and of local concerns about water, for example). Together, they create a political, legal, and cultural environment that is favorable to the extractive economy, and unfavorable to anyone who may oppose extractive projects.

Conclusions: Situating Conflict in the Everyday

In the past we could hear the frogs every night. They were beautiful and happy! Now the river is poisoned, and you cannot hear them anymore.

ANONYMOUS WOMAN NEAR THE LA ZANJA MINE[50]

An extensive body of research has theorized the reasons behind the adoption of violent escalation in other contexts. However, an outstanding issue is that most of these studies focus on protesters as the source of violence, ignoring how other actors in these conflicts operate. Perhaps a substantive difference can be made by reframing research questions from "What causes violent protest?" to "What makes conflicts violent?" More profound problems entail the way research intervenes in recreating power relationships, oppression, criminalization, and exploitation. As this chapter has shown, it is important for analyses of these conflicts to be relational, participatory, intentional, self-critical, positionally reflexive, and contextualized in depth—not masquerading as impartial.

In a context wherein "violence" as a discourse is so blatantly politicized and so readily deployed, to adopt the term uncritically would be a fatal mistake for any study of conflict. The nature of violence cannot be captured without lived, everyday experience, nor without attention to language. This requires a bottom-up, contingent, micro-level approach to data collection and analysis. Various ways of framing violence can themselves make violence; yet at the same time, while there is "something mysterious about violence, which is never reducible to the explanations that the market of ideas" has offered, this does not mean one should shy from studying it.[51] Rather, to retrieve its juridical and analytical utility, the best way to study a difficult-to-tame concept is to attend to what it does, how it performs and is performed, how it is narrated, deployed, and perceived, and the everyday conditions it shapes.

The political, economic, institutional, and cultural context of post-conflict Peru is crucial to understand the strategic choices that people involved in mining conflicts have made. At the same time, localized conflicts over natural resource extraction are currently active in every continent, and studying them in depth holds the potential to unlock wider debates, relevant almost anywhere, about democratization, the role of the market, the viability of dominant models of social and economic organization, and the future of the planet. Although pitched as the most sensible route to economic development, extractive projects in fact threaten human rights and ecological sustainability on a global scale. This is why rhetoric about corporate social responsibility is so pernicious, in that it conceals and legitimizes a violent material reality without altering lived and embodied conditions.

While their benefits are concentrated, the promises of extractive development remain unfulfilled for the majority of people around sites of extraction. Instead, the immediate and long-term environmental problems associated with resource extraction, including the contamination of water and soil, can also generate and exacerbate other human well-being and security issues, including droughts, famine, mass migration, conflicts of different scales, and the multiplying crises of climate change. Thus, in addition to their relevance in preventing physical violence in their particular contexts, resource conflicts call to question the meanings of development, progress, and sustainability—critical matters as societies globalize and world temperatures rise yearly. More than ever, understanding conflicts related to resource extraction is of immense importance to the interdependent goals of human rights, sustainable development, and peace with justice.

CHAPTER 3

Tambo Grande

The Importance of Scaling Up

The fault must be of the anti-miners. A drought strikes the north of the country, the water reservoirs are historically low, and agriculture is endangered. . . . Even climate change surely is because of the anti-miners, according to the commentators on Hora N, two friends who are fortunate to have a television program where one invites the other to say, literally, whatever comes to their minds: "If mining had been allowed in Tambogrande, there would be no crime." "If mega-mining had been allowed in Tambogrande, there would be no informal miners." It doesn't matter that criminal organizations are settled throughout the whole country, in areas with and without mining. . . . How lucky some can be! They can say any nonsense on television, several times a week if they want to, and they even get paid!

JOSÉ DE ECHAVE[1]

This chapter describes a conflict between mining prospectors and the communities around the coastal-arid district of Tambogrande, Piura. It focuses especially on the period of intensified conflict between 1999 and 2004, when a mining concession was held by the Manhattan Minerals Corporation and the central state in Lima. The Tambo Grande project, as the mine was dubbed, is one of the most salient mining conflicts in Peru, and perhaps in Latin America.[2]

A direct result of the structural reforms of the 1990s—which opened an explosion of foreign investment to new areas, especially in the global South and most of all in Latin America—the case set the tone for subsequent mining conflicts in Piura (such as the Río Blanco project) and the rest of the country, and actually it influenced the strategies and tactics of actors in similar conflicts beyond Peru. It is therefore an appropriate case with which to open a study into Peruvian mining conflicts. The case is particularly interesting especially because of how its history and its lessons are imagined retrospectively in contemporary accounts, whether hailed as an example or diagnosed as the cause of this or that problem. Many people now believe the case was a failure which resulted from a political conspiracy orchestrated by environmental and foreign NGOs to prevent Peruvian economic growth, while others see it as a massive success for an underdog public concerned with defending its own preferred path to development.

Beyond that contested history, the conflict also showcased the key dynamics of external solidarity interventions, even despite a moment of violent confrontation. At the height of the conflict, riot police provoked an undisciplined response from protesters, leading to an arson and destruction of company property. The company—which relied on promises of development as well as some petty philanthropy—used an approach toward the locals that overall could be best characterized as coercive, and it exploited this confrontation to smear and criminalize its opponents, framing them as violent and terrorists. However, instead of abandoning the protesters, the movement's allies redoubled their efforts. The ties forged between local activists and supporters who represented organizations like Oxfam compelled the latter to lend their credibility and media access to the local movement against the mine. This helped activists reframe the debate away from the accusations of "inciting violence" and toward a clever media narrative based on portraying the valley's lime production as a necessary aspect of Peruvian identity. Thanks to the decisive leadership of the local movement and the support of outside allies—most of whom were women[3]—their cause scaled up, gaining more support from people who organized nonviolent disruptions and protests far beyond the district.[4] The local organizers thus drew strength from the confrontation, beat a state-backed multinational corporation, and set the stage for subsequent conflicts.

Agricultural Roots

Located one hour from the Pacific coast and less than fifty kilometers south of the Ecuadoran border, Tambogrande is a district of about one hundred thousand people spread across the San Lorenzo Valley. Its natural climate is dry forest, although it used to look much more like a desert. In the mid-twentieth century, the area's farmers organized to demand the deviation of rivers, to contribute to their production of cotton for the international market.

The valley's hydraulic infrastructure was constructed between 1948 and 1959, upon local initiative, state approval, and thanks in part to a World Bank loan. Promised a small parcel of land in return for their back-breaking work, thousands of farmers flocked to the San Lorenzo Valley and built the area's reservoirs. Watering the fields with their sweat, they transformed the valley and invested their future livelihoods into agriculture. Then, from 1963 to 1979, successive governments carried out a long process of land reforms that led to the redistribution of thousands of hectares from large haciendas to small-scale producers. This created a vibrant economy, and soon the San Lorenzo Valley became a thriving agricultural center. In the 1990s, the fifty thousand hectares' area had approximately 2.6 million fruit trees, which supported about seven thousand families.[5] The valley produced almost half of Peru's limes, and was a principal producer of many more products like mangoes and rice, meant for both national consumption and export. According to a 2002 study, the valley generated up to US$20 million in mango exports yearly. Furthermore, the agricultural sector employed an estimated two-thirds of town inhabitants.[6]

The area had no memorable history of metal mining. However, thanks to the advent of satellites and magnetic-testing technologies to survey underground resources, the district would become known for sitting directly atop one of South America's richest metallic deposits—containing high concentrations of gold, copper, and zinc. Because of the minerals' location, the construction of a mine would require the relocation of at least eight thousand town residents, or half the population, and the demolition of many parts of town—not to mention the threat it posed to the region's scarce water and therefore to the prosperous economy of export-based agricultural

FIGURE 2. Photograph of Tambogrande, 2015.

production.[7] These urban and productive conditions distinguished any proposal in Tambogrande from major mining projects in the north of Peru at the time, such as Yanacocha, which were usually installed in areas sparsely populated by self-sustenance farmers. Open-pit mining projects here would have to directly compete with both human settlements and the area's profitable (and more socially inclusive) agriculture industry, a situation that could make conflict especially acute.[8]

Over time, different companies expressed their interest in mining in Tambogrande. At the dawn of the 1980s, then Minister of Energy and Mining Pedro Pablo Kuczynski (who would serve as president between 2016 and 2018) and Congressperson Lourdes Flores were booted out of Tambogrande after they unsuccessfully promised jobs and modernity to locals if they would relocate from their city and allow the entry of mining projects. "At that time," according to community leader Luis Riofrío Crisanto, "people did not have a great deal of technical expertise, but they had profound feelings and expert knowledge about one thing: agriculture."[9]

Understanding this identity, cultural attachment, and consciousness is crucial. The French state-owned Bureau de Recherches Géologiques y Minières (BRGM) also entered Tambogrande to prospect in the late 1970s. They were "well behaved" and "had good attitudes," according to Riofrío, and when they realized that public opposition would not allow a mining project in the district, they politely left the area. BRGM's respect for their will, as they perceived it, made farmers realize their collective power. This newfound power would be tested again soon.

Elected in 1990, the increasingly authoritarian government of Alberto Fujimori promoted a mining boom, encouraging companies to seek concessions. The Manhattan Minerals Corporation, a junior company based in Vancouver, declared its interest in the concession as early as 1995, and it purchased the rights to the concession the next year, but the state did not approve exploration until 1999.[10] Manhattan secured investments and closed the rest of its operations in Mexico to pursue this single opportunity, promising to invest more than US$400 million on its open-pit mine, from which it hoped to extract $1 billion over seventeen years.[11]

Manhattan dubbed its mining project Tambo Grande, a twist on the district that would host it, and it arrived as if the Peruvian government in Lima would protect its project at all costs. In fact, the state had cemented its commitment to the project by retaining a 25 percent stake. And at that time, challenging the state was a dangerous thing to do. "If you opposed anything, they'd grab you, paint you as a terrorist, and throw you in jail," said Riofrío, now an elderly organic mango farmer. "This was a real fear—a risk" that prevented many from speaking up, but nonetheless, a grassroots movement called Frente de Defensa del Valle de San Lorenzo y Tambogrande was formed to oppose mining in the district once again.[12]

Rengifo and "the Manhattan Project"

The Fujimori government was so invested in the Tambo Grande mine that the president issued an executive order excepting it from a constitutional provision that prohibited mining within fifty kilometers of national borders. To see their project through, however, the government and Manhattan required the approval of the local district mayor, who at the time was Alfredo Rengifo Navarrete (1999–2002), a tall, wealthy, and light-skinned local. When I spoke with Rengifo in 2015, he invited me to his large estate, located right on the downtown square in Tambogrande, and he presented me his book manuscript about the mining conflict—an intimate collection that included his analysis, memories, and hundreds of appended official documents from his tenure as mayor. Rather than depicting the story of a "new conquest of Peru," his narrative painted a far more complicated picture: one of someone deeply rooted in his town, concerned with its well-being, and committed to propelling its social and economic development.

This was precisely what Manhattan promised. The firm's rhetoric to justify the project was crystalized in a report it issued in 2002, where it portrayed the district's economy as impoverished and underdeveloped, largely as a result of its dependence on agriculture. The report provided statistical information on high levels of child mortality, relatively low median incomes, and low access to hygienic services; it also commented on environmental factors, such as the poor conditions of the area's irrigation canals and eroding soil. Needless to say, it proposed mining as a silver bullet solution to these socioeconomic ills, as environmentally safe, and actually, as inevitable. To put it simply, the report attempted to portray Tambogrande as poor and in need of mining activity.[13]

Thus, when Manhattan came knocking at his municipal office's door, Rengifo used his executive power to authorize the company's investment and exploration in the area. As a few of my contacts made apparent, he became a polemic and unpopular figure for this decision. But when it became clear that his constituents overwhelmingly opposed the project, he responded to his democratic duty—albeit silently. Rengifo felt that to stop the project, the municipality needed to come across as impartial. "My advisors warned me that I might lose the elections if I didn't speak out against the company," he told me, "but were people better served by me showing up at the rallies, or by me remaining a credible opposition separate from the grassroots?"[14] In his official correspondence, Rengifo even denounced the company on several occasions, demanding that it cease its violation of his people's dignity. In the end, Rengifo would openly call for the project to be cancelled, but to the people organizing the Frente, he had shown his priorities and needed to be replaced.

Community Organizing

One day in May 1999, neighbors woke up to find a drilling machine the size of a semitrailer working on a perforation on their street. What had been fears and suspicions up to that moment had now materialized directly outside their doors. This physical encounter with the project forced locals to realize its severity; these holes would extend into multiple large open pits right where their families had built their houses, church, downtown square, schools, restaurants, and businesses.

The Frente de Defensa was spearheaded by well-organized, preexisting associations of agricultural producers and water users (*juntas de riego*), but it spread through local links among neighbors, extended families, and area residents at large. Members elected Francisco Ojeda, a young professional, school director, and charismatic farmer, as its president. As Luis Riofrío told me, Ojeda was elected because he represented a radical and incorruptible commitment to stopping the mine. The Frente began by convening local organizations to meet at least weekly, where they shared stories of their anger at daily interactions with Manhattan's people. Then they filed legal complaints against the company's incursion into their lands, and they issued formal and informal petitions to their representatives, demanding the company's withdrawal. They organized a massive rally with San Lorenzo farmers in Piura city, the provincial seat and regional capital. Within only a few months, the movement claimed that one of their petitions had gathered twenty-eight thousand signatures against mining in the district, out of thirty-seven thousand eligible voters.

At around this time, the mango farmer and president of the Association of Mango Producers, Godofredo García Baca conducted an economic evaluation of the region's agricultural production. He concluded that the benefits Manhattan was promising to the town (including sewers, three hundred jobs, and free repainting on houses that would not be demolished) were meager and incomparable to those the region was already producing through agriculture. García drew on his experiences opposing mining in the area since the 1980s, as well as the experiences of other communities affected by mining in Peru at the time—such as La Oroya, Cerro de Pasco, and Yanacocha. His assessment concluded that Manhattan's water usage could not coexist with the area's agricultural economy, and in fact it would directly threaten farming.[15]

As part of their community organizing effort, the Frente set up a technical roundtable with other local leaders, the regional archbishop, and NGOs including the Piura-based Agro y Vida, Cooperacción in Lima, Oxfam America, the National Confederation of Communities Affected by Mining (CONACAMI), and Friends of the Earth. These external allies did not arrive magically—activists had taken their arguments to the Congress, drawing attention from national media. Furthermore, one of the Frente's leaders had studied in Lima and used personal networks there to invite supporters. The roundtable was tasked with understanding the potential impacts of Manhattan's mining project on the valley. Each organization played on its strengths: they spread information to their national and transnational membership, provided financial support, and lent strategic and practical assistance on the ground. The deacon focused on legal assistance, CONACAMI transmitted knowledge among farmers in Peru, and Oxfam's people focused their attention on the technical and legal aspects of the project.

Manhattan planned to relocate 1,600 homes to construct several open pits, including one 1,000 meters long, 650 meters wide, and 250 meters deep. Among other things, the company also proposed to divert the Río Piura, the principal river in the district, and to consume much of it daily, causing concerns about the future of agriculture in the valley. However, company employees contended—in person, in publications, in law-mandated community workshops, and in media interviews—that the environmental risks of their state-of-the-art project were insignificant. Skeptical of these claims, locals worked with their supporters to commission an independent investigation. Oxfam, the Mineral Policy Center, and the Environmental Mining Council of British Columbia sponsored a study conducted by Dr. Robert Moran, an expert on the environmental impacts of mining and a hydrologist at the University of British Columbia.

In the first half of May 2001, Moran conducted a review of Manhattan's initial impact statement (its "baseline study" from July 2000), relevant publications, and interviews with Tambogrande residents and Manhattan executives. Moran concluded that this impact assessment failed to meet the standards of similar companies working in the US and Canada. His report provided a side-by-side comparison of Manhattan's baseline study with a comparable project in British Columbia, demonstrating the extent of the former's incompleteness and sloppy methodologies. Furthermore, it provided a sober and damning critique of the project based on the following: the state's conflict of interests as an investor in *and* regulator of the project; the El Niño cycle, unaddressed in the study, and how its typical inundations would affect the mine's heap-leaching and tailings dam; the risk of deforestation and subsequently the exacerbation of desertification in a vulnerable ecosystem; and other mining impacts ignored or understated in the baseline study, including the high risk of groundwater contamination, air pollution, and dispersion of toxic substances over agricultural land.[16]

The Frente hosted workshops to inform locals about their technical arguments against the project. At these meetings, organizers—predominantly Godofredo García, who was a popular and charismatic leader in the community—informed locals about four main points that formed the basis of their opposition to the project: (1) the higher and more evenly dispersed economic value of agriculture, which would be threatened by its proximity to a mine reliant on mercury, arsenic, and cyanide; (2) the technical and environmental conditions that made the project unviable on its own terms (for example, the lack of available water in the area that would force the company to use the irrigation reservoirs, or how the El Niño storms would inundate the open pit and flood the tailings dam, dispersing its poisonous chemicals into other water bodies and onto the soil); (3) the people's right to their land, which they had fought hard to acquire and which the state threatened to take by force (although it still offered landowners a reimbursement, via a direct deposit in the state-owned bank); and (4) the unjustified and underestimated risk of harm to people's health and livelihoods, due to the contamination and deterioration of soil and water resources. As Ojeda later summarized during an invited lecture at York University in 2002,

> This land is part of us; it has given life to our grandparents, our parents, and our children. Our life is here; our future is here. But all of this is threatened by the mining companies. . . . We reject the company's plans not because we disagree with mining investment outright, but because we understand that there are places where mining is appropriate, and places where it isn't.[17]

Still, local leaders noticed that the company was successfully purchasing loyalty from some of their neighbors and slowly gaining ground. Threatened, the Frente decided to raise the stakes and planned their first strike and roadblock, which paralyzed the town for twenty-four hours. The women members of the Frente were tasked with preparing the food for these events, and even to stand at the frontlines between protestors and the police sent to disperse them, in hope that police would not strike women. Refusing to be relegated as de facto cooks for protest activities, a group headed by Hermelinda Castro formed the Tambogrande District Women's Association (ADIMTA, in Spanish). Among other work, their organization began going around door-to-door—as the company had been doing to gather support—explaining to their neighbors why approving the project would be a mistake.[18] One mother's testimony exemplifies their rhetoric:

> I worked during all my pregnancies. At that time, we didn't give birth lying down—we crouched, hugging a cushion. Quickly, one, two, three pushes and the child is out. That's why I'm not going to hand this over to someone else, who comes and meddles in my papayas, in my farm, my fruit, my land. No, because I love my plants as though they were my children. I love my children. I have raised them alone. When they don't have anything, if I have one sol or two soles I say, "Take it son and work like me, so you'll have bread and life for your children. That's how I raised you." We'll struggle and struggle until god says, "Now your fight is finished." For my children and their spouses and my grandchildren. If I die the land will be there for my grandchildren, their children and so on, and that's something that lasts forever. Plants die, but they grow again.
> –Isabel Morales[19]

The social movement shifted from its origins in male-driven agricultural organizations to include a complex network of local women, the church, and outside allies armed with technical arguments.

Company Strategies

Just as the movement evolved, so did Manhattan Minerals during the course of the conflict. Its ways of dealing with locals and opponents moved through at least three discernable stages.

At first, it entered the town with an attitude of supremacy, arrogance, and impunity, according to Martín—a geologist who worked on its exploration team, who agreed to be cited on condition of anonymity. Martín believes that mining is rural Peru's best shot for development, but he regretted the way in which company representatives addressed locals in their first few interactions, which set the tone for what would come. He noted that part of the problem was that his team of explorers was not trained in corporate-community relations, but as the only people representing the company "on the ground," they had no choice but to act as such. Martín's team worked in Tambogrande almost every day, and between May of 1999 and May of 2000 they drilled more than four hundred exploration and feasibility holes.[20]

Martín recalls how, as he and his team were drilling for samples in the north side of town, a large crowd arrived to demand that they stop and withdraw from the area. (This anecdote appears in expanded form in the introduction to this book.) Feeling the pressure, Martín called the company's social relations director, Ricardo Samanez. Martín describes Samanez as someone who would show up in a town like Tambogrande wearing an expensive watch and new boots. When he arrived, Samanez demanded that the crowd disperse, argued with them, and even "rolled his sleeves up as if he were ready to fight all of them," Martín laughs. That night, after Martín and his team of geologists left the worksite, a crowd of locals set fire to the perforator.[21]

When the conflict escalated and its opposition mounted, Manhattan's strategy entered a second stage, when it wielded its economic power to influence the public debate through media. It paid a local tabloid newspaper to promote its agenda, began producing its own publication, and formed an organization of supporters in town. Its rhetoric was not only based on promoting the project, but also on discrediting its opposition. For example, Manhattan's supporters took to the airwaves to accuse activists of receiving salaries from outsider groups. Company officers assured investors and media that only a handful of people conspired against the mine and most of the population overwhelmingly supported it, and they falsified statements in favor of mining.[22]

Manhattan also opened legal cases against several of the local leaders, accusing them of obstruction, trespassing, and property damage. When the crowd set fire to its perforator, it exploited this to frame locals as violent and terrorists to discredit and delegitimize them. Even journalists who worked for Radio Cutivalú, the only outlet for the Frente in broadcast media, were targeted and framed as supporters of the Maoist guerrilla Sendero Luminoso.[23] Still, area residents could not be fooled—the accused were well known and respected. The spread of what they saw as lies only made them more resentful and distrustful of the company, not least because the firm's tactics were reminiscent of the Fujimori government, which was collapsing at the time.

In a third stage, the company ramped up its philanthropy, orchestrating a strong effort to purchase support with medicine and even doctors, hired to do domestic visits in town. For example, Manhattan paid for municipal festivals and handed out kitchen and school supplies in the town square. Additionally, Manhattan offered locals jobs as night guards of their perforation machines, thereby investing them in its agenda, and its operators offered money under the table to whomever would promise to publicly support their project. In this way, they bought off leaders and divided neighbors against one another. "They were going around offering money," said a member of ADIMTA and the Frente. "A widow with five children would have been very vulnerable to that."[24] Again, these small overtures were short-term and petty gifts, none of them oriented toward boosting local development, and they could not overshadow the company's predominant strategy of coercion and criminalization.

Around this time, Manhattan changed leadership and made public attempts to promote dialogue with the locals, setting up workshops. "But this was a double discourse because they were still trying to purchase people with gifts and cash," said a former mayor of a nearby district. "It was obvious that they were only holding workshops because they thought it might help their cause, rather than because they were interested in hearing people's opinions. So, things got heated."[25] When people boycotted their workshops around the district's localities, company workers allegedly transported their few supporters from other towns to each meeting they held.

Manhattan's operators also decided to show the town what their new homes would look like, if they agreed to its relocation plan, and built several model houses inside their brick-fenced compound in Tambogrande. They believed that seeing and visiting these would make many in their opposition change their minds in a heartbeat—but it was too late. According to Frente member Mariano Fiestas Chunga, "people already saw the company as their mortal enemy."[26]

Escalation and Confrontation

By this point Manhattan's presence in Tambogrande was characterized by heavy police backup. The Frente organized a second strike for February 27 and 28 of 2001. The strike began before dawn, drawing thousands of people. At around noon, there was a rally and a march from Tambogrande to Locuto on the same road where Manhattan's field operations were headquartered. Manhattan had requested state protection, and six hundred police were dispatched to surround its campsite. It is unclear if they acted on orders from company managers, but in obstructing the protest, these officers made "a fatal mistake," in the words of an organizer. "Had they let us pass, we would have gone down to Locuto peacefully, and then returned again, peacefully, on our way homes in the evening. But they didn't," he told me.[27]

Drawing only on the selective memory of actors involved makes it difficult to reconstruct the sequence of events during the confrontation. Thankfully, filmmakers Stephanie Boyd and Ernesto Cabellos were present to document the events, and their footage is useful to cross-examine and triangulate with other sources.[28] Overhead, a helicopter carrying police chiefs and Manhattan's country manager flew over several thousand protesters. As the protest converged outside of Manhattan's fenced headquarters, police took three protesters into custody within the company's compound, which provoked and infuriated the crowd. Police standing near the compound entrance fired tear gas across the moat, at the people who filled the streets. Frente leader Liliana Alzamora collected one of the exhausted canisters and took it to the police chiefs at the compound's gate. "You are launching these in an exaggerated way, right? And so this could be considered a form of provocation," Alzamora tried to reason with the police in charge. "As leaders, we do not want things to escalate further," she suggested. Tensions were high, and her request went unheeded.

After negotiations with Frente leaders inside the compound, the police released the detained, but only under the condition that both sides sign an agreement that essentially would end the strike. Agitated and angry, the crowd refused the proposal and demanded that Ojeda not sign it. Police then attempted to disperse the crowd with more tear gas, agitating younger protesters into throwing the canisters and rocks back at the police. The police's shields and the compound's brick walls were an insufficient defense, and company supporters fled. By the afternoon, the protesters had broken holes through the compound walls, and once inside, they burned down several of the model houses for relocated families, as well as offices and vehicles.

That evening, speaking to the thousands meeting in the town square, Ojeda said,

> We told you to leave in good faith. People are indignant, frustrated, and when this happens, they will react. Sometimes they react by harming themselves, sometimes they react against another person, and sometimes they react against objects. That has been the people's reaction today; they have overreacted against Manhattan's things. The population lost their nerve because there is no longer a way to be understood, we no longer have anyone who will listen.

When he finished, the crowd cheered and chanted, "Only through struggle will people be heard!"

Manhattan Minerals pressed its lawsuits against more than sixty social leaders, but it left Tambogrande for three months. Meanwhile, the media partners with which it had established publicity contracts, such as *Diario correo*, disseminated criminalizing accounts of the events. *Correo* asked its readers, "Who burned the mining company's compound? Who organized the pro-terrorist violent protest [*la asonada pro terrorista*] of February 27 and 28?" Its article is worth citing at length, at least for a different perspective:

> PRELUDE TO TERROR. Some 600 brigadiers of the Frente marched toward the miners' compound, which was being guarded by police under PNP Colonel Antonio Cabrera Sánchez. There the first arrests occurred, and the first scuffles between authority and the hooded vandals that attacked to rescue their detained.
>
> The confrontation was prolonged through the entire day, with resulting injuries on both sides, who could not be evacuated to

> hospitals due to the city's state of siege. By nightfall, there began rumors of taking the compound.
>
> Dialogue and mediation were useless. The Sullana police chief, the district attorney, and the deacon's lawyers were unheeded. The vandals attacked property and persons they believed were linked to the mining company. Several mango processing plants suffered this fate as well, and even the district attorney had to hide to avoid being lynched. The reporter for the *Correo*, Oliver Guerra, was attacked by the mob [*turba*], which destroyed his photographic equipment and material.
>
> A TAKE IN BLOOD AND FIRE. The second day of the strike, the robbery, the sacking, and the violence multiplied in the entire city. Hoodlums [*encapuchados*] destroyed with incendiary bombs the Manhattan offices on Lima Street. Furniture near the church was set ablaze, and the population, pressed with terror, had to flee toward the river. That night, the place where the company projected its social relations was burned.
>
> By morning, Tambogrande awoke in a state of generalized terror. After noon, the violence concentrated in the Manhattan compound, defended by about 300 police. It was assaulted and taken also, after blowing through the brick and concrete fence, reduce [*sic*] the agents and making them run or taking them hostage.
>
> When they entered, they grabbed what they could and set fire to what they could not. Thus, they destroyed six "pilot homes" built by the miners as a proposal for a probable relocation of city dwellers during the mine exploitation phase. The same fate was given to machines owned by the company Hermanos Britto, Diamantina exploration equipment, and other property of the Canadian contractor.[29]

Amid these kinds of accusations against them, leaders felt their movement slipping out of control and took time to regroup. The following month, on March 31, as Godofredo García of the Frente and his adult son, Ulises, drove to their farm, a gunman jumped in front of their truck and shot him in the chest. The masked attacker made sure he had killed Godofredo, but let Ulises go. The conflict had reached a peak of intensity: one of the most significant leaders of the resistance had been murdered. The murderer was later apprehended and identified as a former sergeant of the air force's secret service. Now serving a maximum sentence, he never revealed his motive.

Three months after García's murder, armed thugs abducted Ojeda's daughter from her university and dumped her in the street, the day before Ojeda was scheduled for a public debate with Manhattan. When Ojeda was invited to speak to a conference on Canadian mining, in the UK, his daughter received threats of being tortured, chopped to bits, and thrown in the streets if her father did not quit.[30] The movement read Godofredo García's death and other intimidation attempts as provocations, hoping to frighten or elicit a violent reaction from them. These events, alongside the accusations of terrorism and the legal processes leveled against its members, forced the Frente to reassess its positions. Upon deliberation, activist leaders committed themselves to a different framing —one that could leave no doubt about who was creating all of this violence.

Despite the unrelenting media rhetoric aimed at smearing them as violent anti-miners, their coalition expanded to include students and faculty at the regional university, youth in Lima, and other supporters from a variety of backgrounds, and their resistance grew. Together, their broad coalition created a public relations campaign that would echo with almost every Peruvian. Their slogan was simple: "Without limes, there is no ceviche [*sin limón no hay ceviche*]," and it seemed to resonate culturally. Ceviche is the national staple dish, a source of pride central to its increasingly globalized cuisine. The ingenious frame drew on Peruvian identity and juxtaposed it against short-term corporate profits. Posters with different takes on this threat to limes and ceviche were hung in Tambogrande, Piura, Lima, and many other cities.

In subsequent months, the protests in their region and in Lima were marked by young people playing instruments and dancing in lime and mango costumes, and by farmers wielding agricultural products instead of torches and machetes—a sign of the movement's explicit efforts to contest frames that criminalized them.

FIGURE 3. Poster against mining exploration in Tambogrande. Photograph by Payal Sampat, Earthworks, used with permission.

The movement's public rhetoric now emphasized frequently that their struggle was peaceful, and leaders often referred to their martyr, García, for guidance.

Conflict Transformation

One cannot overstate the agency of locals such as Nelson Peñaherrera, a journalist and movement supporter, who used his English skills and the internet to reach out to Peruvian and international media companies like CNN, Telemundo, Univision, America TV, and the BBC. While not every one of them responded or followed-up by sending journalists, some did. Peñaherrera believes that Hannah Hennessy's BBC report from December 2003 was "deadly for Manhattan Minerals," as it recorded the preponderance of local opposition to the mine.[31]

Capitalizing on their unprecedented international attention, the movement opted for a final gamble: they organized a referendum to weigh public support for the mining project. They announced their plans at a rally in the town square. Rengifo, who was still mayor, supported the referendum. However, the national electoral commission refused to approve the process, which was needed for the vote to be binding. The company also stated it would not recognize it. "It's quite surprising that the Tambogrande Defence would support a referendum prior to the availability of a study on the environment and the socio-economic impact of the project," Manhattan's CEO Lawrence Glasser told the UK newspaper the *Globe and Mail* in May 2002.[32] Manhattan's president in Peru, Roberto Obrodovich, also shared his distrust in the process:

> In other countries, there is [*sic*] very high levels of culture, levels of education among the population that are quite high, and probably in those developed countries a model of this type could be applied, more or less. However, in our country, where the population is so easily manipulated, I believe—personally—that if these kinds of referenda were to take place all over the country, I think the country would be paralyzed.[33]

Regardless, leaders of the Frente vowed to respect the wishes of the majority—even if it meant approval of the project. International observers and scholars were brought in to monitor the consultation process, which became highly formal: state IDs, thumbprints, sealed ballot boxes, and electorate lists were used to validate each vote. On the day of the vote, June 2, 2002, more than twenty-seven thousand people rode buses, in the back of pickup trucks, and even on floating devices on the river to cast their decision. Turnout was overwhelming for a nonmandatory election, with an estimated 78 percent of eligible voters taking part.[34] Valley residents wore their best suits to form long lines, where mothers breastfed as they waited and organizers distributed snacks to keep people energized. When all votes were counted, nearly 94 percent were cast against mining activity, seemingly sealing the fate of the project.

Manhattan's shares in the Toronto Stock Exchange fell by 28 percent during the following day alone.[35] Adding to its victorious mood, the Frente earned another electoral victory before 2002 ended; this time, its president easily climbed into the mayoral seat in Peru's regional and municipal elections in November. (Ojeda served as mayor again in 2011–2014.) However, Manhattan and the state proceeded as if nothing had occurred. The firm finally released its environmental impact assessment, or EIA—a multivolume, jargon-riddled, 4,500-page document. Manhattan had delayed the EIA's release repeatedly, circumventing legislation that required it and gaining extensions for this via executive orders from president Fujimori himself.[36] Legally, the last obstacle to the mine's approval was presenting their EIA at open meetings in the capital city of each level of government: municipal, regional, and national. Even though citizen's ultimate approval is not a mandatory aspect of these presentations, this legal requirement to hold multiple meetings gave social movements a lot of latitude, particularly as it offered a venue to flex their distant networks, which were stronger than ever by this point.[37]

The Frente de Defensa organized its third and final strike, this time of seventy-two hours, for the days in which the meetings were scheduled in November of 2003. In Lima, Luis Riofrío, students,

NGOs, and Tambogrande supporters held a musical vigil with so many supporters that Manhattan was forced to cancel its meeting. In the regional capital of Piura, ten thousand people arrived at the national university's auditorium; outside, their discipline was on display when everyone raised their arms to stop the chants so leaders could speak, and Ojeda reaffirmed their commitment against violent escalation. Their chanting as they entered the auditorium scared the company representatives, who exited through the backdoor before the EIA could be presented. In Tambogrande, the protests and chants began before sunrise; a general strike paralyzed the town completely, and roads were blocked for everyone except for ambulances and the press. Manhattan was unable to realize any of its token encounters, and protests turned to celebration.[38]

On December 10, 2003, Centromin, the state agency partnered with Manhattan for the concession, dissolved Manhattan's contract. The state claimed the company had stalled on the EIA for too long and that certain conditions in its contract had not been met, including the construction of a treatment plant and an equity investment of US$100 million; however, opponents of the Tambo Grande mine read this as the state's acquiescing to the public will. "We are very surprised by this decision," the company's chairperson and president, Paul Glasser, stated in a press release. "Manhattan presented a carefully prepared and thorough submission that would ensure, subject to community approval, the responsible development of the Tambogrande Project," he declared.[39] Manhattan launched an arbitration process against the ruling, but in one day alone during that December, it lost 41 percent of its value on the Toronto stock exchange.

By the same time the next year, Manhattan's luck had not changed. The company's new president and CEO, Peter Guest, threatened to sue Peru for damages, arguing to the international business press that his company had incurred a US$60 million loss. However, after five years of opposition, the company finally announced it was liquidating its Peruvian assets in February 2005. It withdrew from the country indefinitely and changed its legal name. Guest vowed resentfully that Manhattan would never invest in Peru again, but that it would consider other South American countries and "more mining-friendly" Turkey for future investments.[40]

Among environmental and social justice activists, the case is remembered an example. It encouraged movements against extraction to demand popular consultation processes in Esquel, Argentina, in 2003, in Sipacapa, Guatemala, in 2005, and beyond. In Guatemala, Godofredo's son Ulises García supported the consultation process in person. However, in Tambogrande, the struggle may have upended one mining project, but the district is still not clear from exploration. Since Manhattan was disbanded, mining companies such as Buenaventura and Arasi have overtly sought to explore the area, and many others surely covet the concession and the rich deposits below the town. Furthermore, informal miners prey in the valley's forest in Las Lomas, nearby. Their presence, however minor, has led people like Hernando de Soto to claim that,

> We must understand what people really want. Because in many cases, as with the Manhattan company in Piura, they rejected the mine—everyone has said, for ecological reasons—and now it is full of informal miners, who are the same locals. This means they are not against mining, but rather that they want the money going directly into their pockets.[41]

In his words appears the often-repeated trope that Tambogrande rejected formal mining only to let in the informal, "criminal," and presumably more destructive types of mining enter their area. This line of rhetoric is meant to portray ecologic concerns as false pretenses, delegitimizing and discrediting locals' diverse claims—some of which are environmental, even if many locals would more easily accept a project that actually benefitted them.

Conclusions: Theorizing Lessons from Tambogrande

Thinking theoretically about the case more than ten years after its conclusion, several factors appear significant: (1) the poor organization within the company, including its lack of a coherent strategy to address local concerns other than through coercion and petty philanthropy; (2) the strength of the local networks that formed around a lucrative agrarian economy in the valley, where they organized a resilient base that drew on their identities, histories, and kinship; (3) the support of NGOs and transnational networks, which lent legitimacy, helped transcend how regional and national media framed the town's struggle, and remained steadfast even after the movement's most difficult moments; (4) the movement's intelligent framing and decisive tactical transformation following the peak of violence in the conflict; and (5) the success of the popular consultation on mining, a democratic and nonviolent method to settle any doubts about whose interests the project represented. Many other cases of mining in Peru share some of these characteristics, but their combination in Tambogrande render it a unique case.[42]

The company's biggest error was thinking that with government support and the loyalty of some paid-off locals, it could push its project to fruition. It had imagined that any opposition against its project could be sidelined, bought, or discredited. When this did not work, it actively painted Tambogrande's farmers as ignorant, backward, and violent. Its strategic error was to cause indignation and desperation among people who refused to be ignored by an inflexible corporation and a compromised government. The arrogance of its operators gave the project a negative tone from the start, a path that was difficult to reverse even under new leadership. Activists and industry actors alike learned from the mistakes made in this notorious case.

Far more importantly, what is especially key about this case for the purposes of this study is the social movement's transformation —namely, after the provocation and confrontation at the company's campsite, and after Godofredo García's murder weeks later. Rather than letting themselves be provoked again, or be frightened into demobilizing, the local leaders of the social movement and their regional-to-transnational supporters moved to challenge violence itself, identifying the company's actions as one of its sources. Whereas Manhattan Minerals sought to convince the world that it was doing this town a favor and that whoever opposed its proposal was corrupt or violent, locals were decisive in making clear that the source of the conflict was the company's greed. Their smart framing juxtaposed the company's promises against Peruvian identity itself, and their networks ensured that this frame resonated widely by organizing creative and nonviolent protests that emphasized the importance of limes and mangoes.

Finally, a point that should not be missed from this case is the role of women in the conflict. They were key from the start in organizing neighborhoods, working across their social ties to persuade and mobilize the town. According to activists, witnesses, and journalists, ADIMTA and women professionals such as Liliana Alzamora were also the leading actors responsible for the movement's nonviolent framing. In the words of Nelson Peñaherrera,

> I have to underline that even the NGOs' officials who were training, advising, and helping us were mostly women, injecting us another way to say "no." Then, we used creativity, the arts, and rational arguments to fight. The women were who really turned upside down the violent destiny of the conflict: Sister Magdalena Tagliavini and the Sisters of Notre Dame of Namur; the Sisters of Fe y Alegría; El Tiempo's journalists Margarita Rosa Vega and Teo Zavala (and director Luz María Helguero); Marita Orbegoso and all Deacon crew; then the NGOs' Rocío Ávila and Janneke Bruil; Noticias Aliadas' team; [the filmmaker] Stephanie Boyd; [the NGO] Labor's Doris Balbín; [professor] Liliana Alzamora, [ADIMTA's] Hermelinda Castro, the late Lola Burgos, and the list continues. Is peace a gender issue? If so, why? . . . Women's participation in Tambogrande was a key factor that led from violent to creative protest. . . . Men are not good peacekeepers.[43]

Peñaherrera's arguments echo a large literature that has proposed similar arguments about the role of gender in violence, peace, and security.[44] Far beyond deterministic, overly simplified, and pseudo-biological arguments about female empathy and male testosterone, there is an undeniable toxicity built into dominant social constructions of maleness—not least in Latin America, which holds the record for the highest number of femicides per capita in the world. Peñaherrera's reflections remind me that interviewing the mayor was difficult when I arrived in Tambogrande. On my first day in town his municipality was busy preparing to host a Water Day event where townsfolk would be given free water filters and a presentation about how to use them. Meanwhile administrators were also working on preparing the town for an El Niño weather storm estimated to be stronger than any in the past one hundred years. At the same time, one of his municipal employees was embroiled in accusations of sexual assault against a minor girl. Environmental conflicts emerge upon a social fabric where different forms of violence are exercised and experienced every day but in different ways by people along ethnic, gender, and class lines. Even within environmental justice movements, tensions often emerge between women and men organizing protests, where the former accuse the latter of failing to recognize their leadership, undermining their labor, hogging the spotlight, lacking a gender analysis, and exploiting women's work.

The Tambo Grande mine proposal preceded and set the stage for a large wave of other conflicts over gold mining in the north of Peru. Given its preeminence in the national debate over mining and development, it doubtlessly influenced the behavior of actors involved in cases that followed. However, its lessons might not have been immediately apparent. As the next three chapters show, the extents to which states, communities, and companies adopted these lessons varied significantly.

CHAPTER 4

La Zanja

When and How Coercion Works

Political contestation around mining in Cajamarca is difficult to isolate by case. In this polarized region of northern Peru, conflicts around otherwise-distinct mines consist of similar political institutions and legal frameworks, as well as recurrent actors—even if individuals' positions may shift between state offices, civil society, social movements, political parties, firms and industry associations, media, and the broader population. These groups share information, members, and legacies from other cases in the region, the north of Peru, and beyond. Regional authorities are involved in various cases, and even individual municipalities become entangled in many cases simultaneously. For instance, key actors in the region's province of Bambamarca have participated in conflicts related to several distinct mines, including Yanacocha, Quilish, La Zanja, Conga, or Cerro Corona, and other extractive projects beyond mining, like the Chadín II hydroelectric dam, a project belonging to the construction conglomerate Odebrecth, which was found by the Operation Car Wash international criminal investigation to have paid nearly US$800 million in bribes across Latin American countries between 2001 and 2016. The investigation and its ripples implicated every Peruvian president during this period, from Alejandro Toledo (2001–2006) to Pedro Pablo Kuczynski (2016–2018). The majority party in the legislature, affiliated with the Fujimori family, nearly impeached the latter man twice during his abridged term, before he simply resigned on March 21, 2018.

For some of these actors, these project cases and their overlapping factors are signs that Cajamarca's story is that of a struggle between fundamentally opposing cosmologies: one motivated by land and water defense and another by the search for profits. Given the diversity of cases, of actors involved, and of the flexibility of their affiliations and positions, it would be misguided to reduce stakeholders' views and agency in issues related to mining to a dualistic choice between "in favor" and "against." Richer contextualization of cases is needed to better flesh out these dynamics and to draw actionable insights that may improve people's everyday lived experiences. Therefore, specific projects must be studied with an emphasis on four things at least: their idiosyncratic traits and dynamics, the heterogeneity of forces and actions, the fluidity of roles that actors occupy even at the same time, and their contextualized role in the region's broader politics and in macro-structural forces. Theoretically and comparatively, the chief factors among these are actors' strategic choices.

The case detailed in this chapter, La Zanja, is one of the least studied in Peru, despite its intense levels of conflict. To reconstruct its story, I relied on primary and secondary sources, including interviews, news reports, actors' publications and statements, technical reports produced by state and industry actors (especially from the ombuds office, Defensoría del Pueblo), media from events, academic studies, ethnographic fieldwork, and participant observation. Meaningful theoretical significance can be drawn from this case in a number of directions. For this research, La Zanja is worth inspecting and highlighting for the unbelievable odds that the company overcame to install its project, despite local opposition that seemed insurmountable. As I was told by many of the executives and officers in charge of the project (including one of the company's heirs and owners), the company achieved the impossible.[1] In this sense, the case stands in sharp contrast to the case of Tambogrande discussed in the prior chapter. The case study explores and traces some of the significant dynamics leading to this distinct outcome.

Mining Proposals and Small-Scale Agriculture

In the final decade of the twentieth century, farmers in the Andean region of Cajamarca in northern Peru entered what would become a heated, region-wide struggle against large mines. Cajamarca was already the home to South America's largest gold mine, Minera Yanacocha, which had drawn protests since the early 1990s.[2] The companies that owned Yanacocha (Denver-based Newmont and Lima-based Buenaventura) began exploratory drilling in the provinces of Santa Cruz and San Miguel in 2000 and produced a baseline study in January 2001.[3] The mine would be located in an Andean cloud forest, 3,200 to 3,600 meters above sea level, and removed from the regional capital by about 102 kilometers by road, which is only partly paved. Under the name Minera La Zanja, the joint venture purchased lands and installed a compound atop a mountain headwater—a water source for communities extending to the Pacific coast, including the valley leading up to and including Chiclayo, Peru's fourth most populous city.

The nearest districts include Pulán, in Santa Cruz, which had a population of five thousand at the time, most of whom were small-scale agricultural producers; and Tongod, in San Miguel, with about half of Pulán's population, similarly engaged in self-sustenance agriculture. Their livelihood predominantly depended on the area's rivers Pisit, San Pedro, Santa Catalina, and Chancay. Buenaventura claimed its concession area contained more than one million ounces of gold (in a concentration of 1.02 grams of the precious mineral per every metric ton of earth), as well as silver deposits.[4] Buenaventura and Newmont promised to invest US$35 million and to produce one hundred thousand ounces of gold per year. To meet such production goals, at these levels of mineral concentration, the company would have to remove 2,779,365 metric tons of soil and process them through cyanide lixiviation and heap leaching each year.

According to Freddy Regalado, who is one of Buenaventura's social relations directors and a regional representative of the corporate-interest alliance Grupo Norte, the project truly began in 1991, but the state's approval barriers (for which he used the pejorative *tramitología*) turned the proposal into a fifteen- to twenty-year process.[5] Along the way, La Zanja's managers continued buying land, preparing feasibility studies, offering work, and incorporating into the firm's payrolls some of the people who sold their lands. It was not until April 2003 that Buenaventura's explorations manager, César Vidal, announced company plans to begin the mine's construction by the end of the year.

Community Organizing

Locals in the mine's district, Pulán, began by registering complaints to municipal and regional authorities, even though their communities were divided. Up to one-third of people in the area supported the mining firm's entrance, according to one resident, but most were concerned about issues of water availability and quality, vis-à-vis the possibilities of scarcity and pollution.[6] Neighbors opposed to the project worked through the area's best established networks and most respected local leadership organizations: the rural vigilantes known as the Rondas Campesinas and Peru's public teachers' union (or SUTEP, in Spanish). Concerned locals and the Santa Cruz federation of Rondas Campesinas started out by forming local assemblies and informal meetings where they discussed their concerns about the company's exploration. They also sought to inform themselves about the environmental effects of mining, feeling that the information from the company was vague and that it purposely understated these impacts.

Their fears were motivated in part by knowledge of Yanacocha's mercury spill in Choropampa, also in the Cajamarca region. In the year 2000, a semitrailer carrying mercury from the Yanacocha mine—owned by Minera La Zanja's parent companies, Buenaventura and Newmont—spilled its contents on several miles of a road, including near the urban center of Choropampa. This caused widespread and serious deformities, birth defects, and chronic illnesses among the zone's already disadvantaged population. The scandal was aggravated by Yanacocha's deflections, slow admission of responsibility, and, as most people see it, inadequate and late compensation schemes. At the time of writing, residents continue to suffer from the health effects of mercury poisoning.[7]

Records show that early public protests were peaceful but included some arrests. A strong grassroots organization coalesced by 2003, adopting the name of Santa Cruz and San Miguel Defense Front. However, its rallies were localized and ignored. The area received little attention from the regional government—located eight hours away via muddy, mountainous roads—and even less from the central government in Lima. They also lacked contact with the then loose network of nongovernmental organizations that is active today in most of Peru's mining conflicts.

Escalation and Confrontation

Tired of being ignored, the movement escalated tensions. The provincial association of Rondas Campesinas organized a strike and a protest near the company's compound in November 16, 2004.[8] An investigation soon after the day's confrontation argued both sides had foreseen a confrontation. The Rondas had given and extended multiple deadlines, and they had announced for months their intention to take direct action to expel the company. Likewise, La Zanja had requested assistance from additional police from Chiclayo and nearby, had its own private security, and in recent days had also hired some locals as additional guards. Furthermore, company operatives invited state officials and hired a photojournalist to record the events.[9]

Hundreds of people walked the fifteen kilometers uphill from Pulán, and many more arrived from rural neighborhoods throughout Santa Cruz, San Miguel, and San Pablo provinces. Men and women from the Rondas Campesinas of Pulán, Ninabamba, El Cedro, La Chira, Calquis, San Lorenzo, Gordillos, and Tongod led the strike, having organized their communities for weeks. Some people used cars and motorcycles to shuttle others. Once atop the mountain, a large crowd of protesters gathered and surrounded the camp. Crowds chanted and issued an ultimatum to the company: leave peacefully or by force. Movement delegates were invited in to negotiate with company officials, but this dialogue was fruitless and ended before dusk.

Police began dispersing the crowd. Then, according to witnesses and peer-reviewed studies, the company's hired security guards opened fire at the protesters, killing Rondero activist Juan Montenegro Lingán. Many others, like Roberto Becerra, were shot but survived.[10] With cameras recording from the compound, the company's private security awaited a response, which was immediate. The enraged protesters advanced inside and set fire to vehicles, mineral samples, computers, and other property. Twelve people were arrested as riot police retook the camp by the next morning.

The company swiftly released edited videos from the event, and media outlets such as the Lima-based newspaper *La república* reported on the "extremely violent reaction" of these "attacks." Journalists' language is indicative. Under an inflammatory image of a burning vehicle and the headline, "Ronderos in Santa Cruz demand the withdrawal of Buenaventura," *La república* reported how "the attack that locals effected last night on the La Zanja compound left one person dead and various wounded," a characterization that is careless at best, and deceptive at worst: its passive language suggests that the death was caused by the protesters themselves. The same story even suggested, without any evidence other than a statement from Buenaventura, that the demonstrators "carried firearms," such as field hunting rifles.[11]

In my interviews, company officials and supporters made similar claims. However, one witness told me that activists only had sticks and stones.[12] One industry consultant suggested to me that the left-wing party Patria Roja was paying and arming protesters.[13] An executive from Buenaventura accused the protesters of firing weapons and throwing rocks.[14] And in separate interviews, several Buenaventura officers claimed that the protesters were interested in keeping out the project because they were "drug traffickers," who did not want the attention and progress that the mine would bring.[15] I investigated, but could not confirm the presence of drug producers in the area. On the opposite end of these arguments, some people sympathetic to the protests likewise drew on improbable, speculative, and even conspiratorial rhetoric about the events—for example, claiming that the company burned its compound down strategically, to legitimize repression.

Buenaventura issued a press release decrying the violence, estimating that only about 350 people were at the protests, and condemning that most of its property had been looted or destroyed. Buenaventura argued that Montenegro's body was not found any closer than eight kilometers away from its compound, distancing itself from the murder, and *La república* cited this company claim. In any case, killed more than three years after Godofredo García Baca in Piura, Juan Montenegro Lingán became well known as Cajamarca's "first" environmental martyr.

Peruvian news outlets were not the only ones interested in the events, nor were they alone in their criminalizing and paternalistic discourse. For example, the London-based financial weekly the *Economist* provided the following narrative:

> [At] La Zanja, a six-hour journey from Cajamarca, a mob of some 250 locals, stirred up by extreme leftists, burnt and sacked a prospecting camp run by Buenaventura; they destroyed ten years' worth of rock samples. . . . These events are widely seen as a turning point for Peru—in more ways than one. . . . The protests also pose some broader questions. Will Peru remain one of the world's top mining countries? Will an alliance of local activists and rich-world NGOs thwart investment in a crucial industry? . . . The riot at La Zanja prompted several NGOs to issue a statement condemning violence. The government sent police reinforcements to mining areas. "The state has drawn a line . . . (the threat to mining) is being seen as being as serious as drug-trafficking and terrorism," says José Miguel Morales of the National Mining [and Oil] Society, who is also Buenaventura's general counsel. The protests typically mix genuine grievance with ignorant fears that are whipped up by political extremists.

The *Economist*'s narrative mirrors that of the mining industry's fiercest advocates in a few ways: its criminalization of protest, its dismissal of local protesters as ignorant and violent, and its conspiratorial tone suggesting a manipulative plot by environmental NGOs. And as is characteristic of the extractivist discourses that circulate in Peru, in that same article, the *Economist* reminds its readers of the ultimate value of mining, adding, "While mining provides relatively few jobs, it is vital to Peru's economy in other ways. . . . Mining brings in 29% of total tax revenues. Of this money, the government last year returned $138m as a local royalty to mining areas, most of which are otherwise poor and remote."[16] Some of Peru's poorest neighborhoods host large mines, but this did not seem to matter to the author.

Five days after the confrontation at the campsite, local activists organized a forty-eight-hour strike, and a popular assembly was held in the provincial capital of Santa Cruz. In attendance were members of labor unions from across the region, as was Roberto Becerra Mondragón—at the time, the mayor of Tongod district, and one of twenty-six people wanted for arrest for allegedly burning the campsite. *La república* mentioned the strike, writing that, "The Court of San Miguel has issued arrest warrants for 26 locals who *were found guilty* of the fire in the mining campsite, damaging the Buenaventura company" (emphasis added). Perhaps the word choice, "were found guilty" versus *are suspects*, is a minor detail, an unconscious mistake attributed to lack of legal expertise, but it is still inaccurate and criminalizing. The same news story also included an interview with Buenaventura's CEO, Roque Benavides, who reminded the public,

> We have state authorization, [and] the deeds to the surface lands; our projects are developed according to law. Our country has its rules and laws, which we respect. However, we are conscious that we must respect the rights of locals, who decide to use force. We are against violence. We believe intelligent people do not opt for aggression. I opt for the development of Santa Cruz, Cajamarca, and Peru.[17]

It seemed that activists' perseverance had forced the project to be suspended, but those opposed to the mine were careful to not declare victory yet. The social movement opted for an institutional and electoral strategy, shifting from a predominantly protest-based movement into formal politics, which is reminiscent of what occurred during Tambogrande's struggle against Manhattan Minerals. First, in December 2004, they pressured the municipal government in Pulán to designate the site as a natural conservation reservoir, protecting it from extractive projects. However, this maneuver was undercut by an executive decree from president Alan García in 2007, which banned municipal authorities from demarcating conservation areas, overturning the Pulán municipality's decision.[18] Second, the resistance sought to take leadership positions through elections, in order to prevent the mine from gaining legal approval.

Meanwhile, another one of Buenaventura and Newmont's prospective mining projects in Cajamarca, at Cerro Quilish, had generated a conflict that escalated to violence and was suspended. Activists contesting exploration at Quilish argued that Cajamarca city's drinking water supply descended directly from there. Two months before the confrontation at La Zanja, those groups had organized an impressive two-week strike that paralyzed roads around Newmont and Buenaventura's prized Yanacocha mine, causing the mine's operations to slow down significantly and even forcing the company to send supplies to its mine by helicopter.[19] Reading the tense environment across the region, Minera La Zanja allowed for a period of cool-down. The miners left the area for a couple of years before returning with a new plan. Theoretically speaking, it is significant that the company's leaders saw their own strategies of approach and containment as a large aspect of their own failure, and subsequently chose a strategic reorientation.

Company Strategies: Overcoming the Odds

The price of gold skyrocketed during this period. Adjusted for inflation, the global price of one ounce of gold climbed from under US$400 in April 2001 to above US$2,000 in August 2011. There is therefore no doubt that in the period between 2004 and 2007, Buenaventura and Newmont were not prepared to discontinue their investment in projects like La Zanja, as they had been forced to do at Quilish. Companies and the state—now headed by president García (2006–2011, and previously 1985–1990)—were under great pressure to maximize the bonanza while it lasted.

Minera La Zanja reorganized its approach. First, the project managers hired the Lima-based development organization FADRE, a CSR (corporate social responsibility) partner to companies including Buenaventura, to win the hearts and minds of the communities in the area.[20] Additionally, La Zanja hired consultants including academics from the regional capital, Cajamarca city, to work in Santa Cruz and San Miguel to understand the development needs of the population. Minera La Zanja's employees in the Santa Cruz office also set their minds on a "divide and conquer" strategy: they used local supporters and company funds to create the *Asociación* de Rondas Campesinas (emphasis mine), a parallel organization to compete for local authority against the established Federación de Rondas Campesinas, which was decidedly opposed to the mine proposal.[21]

As the mining project regained steam, Peru held regional and municipal elections on November 19, 2006. The organizing efforts of the Rondas and the Frente de Defensa paid off: that night, they celebrated the election of Salatiel Romero Malca, president of the Pulán Rondas, as the district's 2007–2010 mayor. Voters overwhelmingly supported Romero and his slate's campaign pledge to promote sustainable development via agriculture and to defend the area's water quality. In addition to the mayor's seat, the slate won four of the five municipal legislative posts, while the party that had pronounced itself in favor of mining received 5.8 percent of the votes. This gave a committed opponent to the mine the authority to prevent it, at least for three years. Romero Malca's signature was now legally required for the mining project to move forward.

On April 26 of the next year, local organizers held a general assembly in Tongod, San Miguel province, where about five hundred people agreed to give Buenaventura and Newmont five days to abandon the area. The attendees included the Frente de Defensa activists from Santa Cruz and San Miguel; the mayor of Pulán,

Salatiel Romero Malca; Idelso Hernández, the president of Cajamarca's regional federation of Rondas Campesinas; the regional legislator representing San Miguel province, Desiderio Mendoza Zafra; representatives from the Tongod municipality; the Pulán general secretary for SUTEP, the teachers' union; the Cutervo provincial federation of Rondas Campesinas president, Porfirio Medina Vásquez; and many other men and women.

In addition to this ultimatum, the assembly agreed to organize a march on May 10 to verify Minera La Zanja's exit, and otherwise, they would take matters into their own hands to, as they said, "take justice and recuperate the land." According to an attendee, they also demanded that the police in Tongod be replaced, as they thought these state security forces had worked actively to divide the Rondas Campesinas on behalf of the mining company. The assembled agreed to organize a two-week strike in July, and they approved a resolution to work on the long-term goal of forbidding mining in Chota, Bambamarca, San Miguel, or Santa Cruz.[22]

A large crowd of protesters showed up at the company's compound on May 10, as promised, and representatives from the Ministry of the Interior waited inside. Police officers were dispatched to invite a delegation of activists inside, to discuss the terms of their mobilization and notarize their claims. Salatiel Romero Malca and a few other leaders refused to enter the compound, citing reasons of personal safety and fear of legal persecution, but they made their claims to the Peruvian National Police officers outside, with several journalists recording the conversation. Pulán's mayor then said to the police chief,

> On behalf of our population, we ask, please, that this project is not allowed, because it is located in a headwater, which provides water for all of us, the population of Santa Cruz, much of the Cajamarca region, and the whole Chancay-Lambayeque valley. We really are an agricultural zone with agro-industrial and ecotourism potential, and we must conserve our environment if we will bet on sustainable development. We do this thinking about the humble population of the zone who live from agriculture, because if we were in

> this for our self-interests, we would have already negotiated with the company, which has been pestering us about this for a while. Now they repress us with legal charges, one after another, but our recourse is God and our dignity.
>
> This is why we're here: to dialogue mutually. If last time some certain inconveniences were generated and certain destruction happened at the company's compound, this really was fostered by the mining company and was not our fault. As proof of that we have a dead Rondero partner, killed by a gun fired by a company employee. And it is worth noting that the Ministry of the Interior will not place itself at the service of the people. This is truly discomforting. After all, they can paint us as agitators of the masses, whatever they can, but in the end, we are defending the right to life. Because if the La Zanja mine is built, it will pollute the water, air, and soil. There is no place on earth where open-pit mining has brought progress, development, or well-being to the populations nearby.

Romero Malca called on the police officers to follow their conscience instead of orders, adding,

> You are not to blame for being here, but we ask you and your humanity to carry this message—to heed the decision of the people of Santa Cruz, San Miguel, and the Chancay-Lambayeque valley—that Buenaventura please leave and not exploit a mining project here. If they own lands, let them use and exploit these, but agriculturally, with fish farms, reforestation, cultivation, or I do not know. . . . Why don't they come out and dialogue? Why do they hide behind the government officials, the judicial authorities, and the police? If they're doing a good thing for the population, why not show their faces?

The police commander answered that police were there to prevent violence. Romero Malca responded to this emphatically, "I guarantee you, boss, that there will not be any violence, because we are tired of violence, which only generates more violence. On the contrary, we came here to dialogue in tranquility, and we are met with police tear gas." As the police chief insisted that they enter the compound to continue the dialogue, another one of the protest leaders interjected, "We cannot go up [to the compound] because we have suffered repression, our leaders have suffered persecution." The police commander replied, "Just like you have a right to fear that if you go up there you will be repressed, the commission from the Ministry of the Interior also can fear that out here they will be subject to repression." On those words, at least two protesters in the delegation replied in unison, "That is what the police are here for!"[23]

Police did remain in the area. On May 15, the Cajamarca-based newspaper *Panorama*, a favorite for mining advertising, interviewed the regional police colonel Rommel Pérez Arráscue, who claimed that the protesters in Pulán and Tongod intended to burn the La Zanja compound again. The colonel also stated that "a strong contingent" of the National Police's Division of Special Operations (DINOES, in Spanish) remained in the area to prevent these threats.[24] Even after Peru's return to democracy in 2001, DINOES has a marred human rights reputation, especially among mining activists in the north of Peru. In 2005, leaked photos and an investigation revealed an operation by which DINOES kidnapped and tortured twenty-eight protesters who were opposing the Majaz mining project in Piura. The operation was conducted by DINOES in conjunction with the Majaz private security contractor, Forza—which incidentally was also Buenaventura and Newmont's private security provider. The DINOES and Forza operatives had raped the kidnapped women. One of the protesters, an elderly man, died while in their custody. The survivors were released within three days and were subsequently charged with terrorism. An investigation into the events was launched, but never concluded.[25] Forza was also investigated by the central government, the Inter-American Human Rights Commission, and the United Nations the following year, in 2006, for conducting illegal surveillance and harassment of environmental activists leading protests against Yanacocha.[26]

While the negotiations at the La Zanja compound in May yielded no noticeable result, it was a show of the movement's organizing capacity, which was stronger now than in 2004. This would not last. The next month, in the afternoon of June 25, 2007, the area's Rondero activists received notice that Romero's truck had been found after falling to the bottom of one of the cliffs along the dirt road that connected Tongod and Pulán. Romero had been attending the town anniversary in Tongod, on invitation from the mayor there, where both mayors played in a soccer match between the two towns. In the early afternoon, Romero drove his truck on the mountainous road back to Pulán, taking with him a few passengers, including a five-year-old girl. Although Romero knew the road well, the weather was fair, and that particular curve was wide enough for safe turns, his truck fell some sixty meters down the cliff. Romero and the child were found dead inside his destroyed truck, and the other passengers were rushed to the hospital.

Ronderos and opponents of La Zanja interpreted this as a signal of the risk they faced as social leaders. Romero Malca increasingly had told his acquaintances and media of the pressure he was under to provide his signature for the project—in the form of both bribes and threats. Furthermore, his organizing capacity from the mayoral seat was formidable. In only a few months, he had begun a coordinated effort to provide employment opportunities to people who were otherwise begging for work at the mine; he had moved to decentralize the municipality's development planning; he used his pulpit to convene frequent assemblies; and he was constructing a cross-provincial alliance with the Tongod municipality. In all, Romero's actions were perhaps even more proactive than those taken by Francisco Ojeda when he adopted the reins of the Tambogrande municipality. These factors added to the strange circumstances of the crash to sow doubt and distrust, which in turn fueled rumor and conspiracy theories. For example, the crash survivors alleged they were unconscious during the accident, and that a smell in the truck had forced them into sleep soon after getting in the car. Citing recent death threats against the mayor, but producing no proof, the Rondas vowed to investigate his crash.[27]

Responding to allegations of foul play, La Zanja issued a statement expressing its condolences, demanding an investigation, and warning people against politicized defamation attempts against the company. The Cajamarca-based newspaper *El clarín* published a report boldly claiming that Romero crashed due to inebriation. Its story, headlined "Human flaw would have caused Pulán mayor's accident," stated that the "celebrations motivated the ingestion of alcoholic beverages."[28] Regardless, this was a lucky strike for the company; as one local La Zanja operator described the event, this was a "godsend" for them.[29] The key leader of the resistance—a charismatic organizer who had a natural ability to articulate its claims and inspire farmers—had died just as the company completed its environmental impact assessment (EIA). Without tangible evidence, the conspiracy theories circulated and helped characterize tensions thereafter.

Hundreds of people attended Romero Malca's funeral on June 27. Local musicians Darwin and Oswaldo Villegas wrote a commemorative song for Romero, which was performed by a local band during the funeral procession. The song lyrics vowed to continue the fight and alluded as well to the movement's earlier martyr, Juan Montenegro Lingán.[30] Romero Malca's second-in-command at Pulán's municipality, Celso Santa Cruz Izquierdo, took over as mayor, and the movement kept its promise to hold a two-week strike in the second half of July. Both Santa Cruz and Romero belonged to the Nationalist Party, which resolved, in its Cajamarca convention in June 2007, to "decolonize" the country—in part through mine expropriation.[31]

Minera La Zanja proceeded along and presented its project in Cajamarca city, in a public meeting mainly meant for regional legislators and other regional government authorities. Among others, the meeting was also attended by affected locals, members of the regional MINEM office, and Buenaventura representatives. This was not an EIA presentation, although the firm's representative in charge of the event, Luis De La Cruz, stated that the EIA would be ready within months, using the event to persuade the audience about the sustainable development that the project would generate. *El clarín*'s coverage of the event cited De La Cruz at length, including his claim that this was the second such public presentation in this renewed stage of the project, "after the regrettable events of 2004, when [the company] was attacked at their compound by some groups of locals who radicalized their measures against mining exploration activity and who frustrated all advances that had been made for this opportunity." *El clarín*, a newspaper typically sympathetic to mining projects in its coverage, argued, "The event relied on the participation of representatives from various sectors in the vicinity of the project, who expressed their predisposition to favor the mining proposal as long as it complied with all legal exigencies and it used high technology to avoid generating environmental problems." Further, in one sweeping sentence, *El clarín*'s story also assured that locals supported the mine:

> Locals and representatives from the districts of Pulán, Saucepampa, the neighborhoods of La Zanja, and the provinces of Santa Cruz and San Miguel were also present, and the majority expressed their support for the project, recognizing some of the actions that the mining company has already undertaken in their jurisdictions, among which they highlighted the rural electrification project that benefits various neighborhoods that were forgotten for some years.[32]

Farmers' fears about pollution seemed to be confirmed in September 2007. Locals and the Peruvian environmental organization EcoVida documented the deaths of five thousand trout in the river Pisit, which descends from the mine's operations area—allegedly due to lead poisoning from the miners' exploration activities. EcoVida's analysis affirmed in October that the fish had been killed by large concentrations of heavy metals, especially lead, although it did not explicitly ascertain whether this was caused by the company's explorations in the site of the proposed mine.[33]

The following year, the company arranged to have a mandatory public audience to present its EIA to the communities in the mine's vicinity. After a meeting scheduled for the rainy season in March was prevented by protesters, a meeting took place in the early morning of July 3, 2008, in the La Zanja neighborhood's sports complex. The Frente de Defensa organized more than three thousand people to attend, but when they arrived, they found a metal fence and a perimeter of hundreds of police—a barrier between the meeting and its supposed audience. The thousands of farmers were not allowed to enter the meeting, and they scuffled with police.

As a journalist present told me, the company "had bused people in from their other mines. They removed everyone who had gotten there early, then only let in people who had an invitation—and only their employees had invitations."[34] The clamoring of the protesters outside made it impossible for those inside to hear the presentation, and the company left in less than an hour, but it declared the meeting a success. An official statement by the Pulán municipality, signed by leaders of local organizations, unions, and the Frente de Defensa, denounced the meeting: "instead of a solemn and legally mandated meeting, this was a reunion of hungover company employees who remained from a party organized by the company the night before." The statement also expressed "gratitude, admiration, and respect" for the protesters' "civic, noble, and dignified behavior before the grievances suffered publicly at the hands of government representatives, such as the Ministry of Energy and Mines, which in disloyal collusion with the mining company Buenaventura has trampled our constitutional rights." Of particular importance to this study, the municipality also pronounced,

> This trampling of our faith in our governing authorities constitutes a psychosocial conflict, the consequences of which are distrust in law, and it attempts against our dignity and self-esteem, which will only bring more violence, more rebellion, and more distrust among the younger generations, who we are obligated to guide through a path of righteousness, respect for authority, and lawfulness. Our transcendental behavior has demonstrated that in Peru the only violentist [*violentista*] is the government, which stigmatizes social leaders and democratic authorities as Chávez-affiliated subversives.[35]

In Lima, the paper *El comercio* relied on secondary sources to issue the headline "La Zanja Mining Project Was Approved by the Cajamarca District of Pulán."[36] The mining advertiser and news agency Andina produced a similar byline, "Cajamarca Locals

Support Start of Operations of the La Zanja Mining Project."[37] However, *La república* published a contrary view, shared by most people I spoke with in the areas near the mine, which claimed that,

> Close to three thousand farmers from districts and neighborhoods of Santa Cruz province were impeded from participating in the presentation of the La Zanja mining project's environmental impact assessment, despite being convened by the Ministry of Energy and Mining's Environmental and Mining Issues Office. They refute that outsiders gave the rubber stamp [for the project's approval].[38]

Unrelenting, the provincial and district mayors and the Frente de Defensa blockaded the road from the regional capital to Santa Cruz in November, demanding the EIA's nullification.[39] In early December, they organized a massive march in Chiclayo, capital of Lambayeque region. *La república* reported that the march in Chiclayo drew five thousand protesters, organized by the irrigation union of Chancay-Lambayeque. A city resident threw a rock at the protesters and injured the head of fifty-five-year-old José Cruz Torres Vega. Then the crowd arrived at the Lambayeque regional government to meet with its general manager, and they delivered a message for president Alan García and prime minister Yehude Simon. The Lima-based paper cited the president of the irrigation association, Genaro Vera Roalcaba, who argued that campesinos were out on the streets to defend their water and to prevent its pollution by mines. According to *La república*, "When the march concluded in Workers' Park, he said that if the government does not heed their demands, blood could be spilled in defense of water."[40]

Carrots and Sticks

The company's new interest in corporate social responsibility investments was overshadowed by its infamous legal persecution of mining opponents. In comparative perspective, whereas La Zanja provided a lot more compensation and pacification overall than Tambogrande, its strategy should be characterized as much more "coercive" than "persuasive." (Lagunas Norte, the case studied in the following chapter, could be treated as a mirror opposite, where the company used coercion but to a lesser extent than it used persuasive approaches to the communities in its impact area.)

For example, the president of the Rondas Campesinas provincial federation in Santa Cruz, Estinaldo Quispe Mego, was detained by Peruvian National Police on December 29, 2008, and subsequently taken via helicopter to Chiclayo. Fellow Ronderos from the province, Santa Cruz, and other parts of Cajamarca organized a large demonstration to fight against this "arbitrary arrest," and they drew close to a thousand people to the provincial seat, Santa Cruz de Succhabamba, on January 11, 2009. They marched through town and chanted, for example, "Down with yellow journalism! Down with the sold-out press!" When they arrived in the downtown square to rally, speakers claimed that their leaders were under surveillance and "tenacious persecution" simply for "defending life and opposing the pollution caused by the mining company." Quispe was released on January 8 and arrived in Santa Cruz on the eleventh to provide a public statement on his arrest. At this rally, the organizers announced a region-wide day of action, scheduled for four days later, with marches in Cajamarca, Chota, Santa Cruz, and others to protest the repression faced by rural leaders in the social movements against mining. One speaker at the rally also stated,

> Do not sell your conscience for a crumb. I want to leave you this reflection: that money will end. . . . Comrades in Santa Cruz, you must know that in this city, there are media that are mistreating us daily, each day, us leaders and Ronderos. They call us this, that, and the other thing, a whole bunch of adjectives. These men that have no roots in Santa Cruz. They do not care if Santa Cruz dies.[41]

According to the National Human Rights Coordinator's 2011–2012 yearly report, Quispe Mego would become "an emblematic case" of "the criminalization of Indigenous and rural leaders" in the country's conflicts. A report published by the Judicial Branch in 2014 also referred to Quispe Mego and Alejandro Izquierdo

Torres—who spent two years in jail after being accused of beating a mining supporter—as "social leaders who have been systematically accused by people affiliated with a local mining company in Santa Cruz," and as "representative cases" of "how environmental conflicts are transported into the judicial arena, generating a loss of legitimacy for the Judicial Branch and the Ministry of the Interior [Ministerio Público]."[42]

Leaders from the Santa Cruz provincial federation of Rondas Campesinas, the Cajamarca regional federation of Rondas Campesinas, and the irrigation association of Chancay-Lambayeque rallied in Cajamarca city and delivered a memorandum to the regional government on November 9, 2009. Signed by almost ten thousand people, including diverse social leaders from San Miguel, Santa Cruz, and Hualgayoc, the memo denounced grave environmental damages caused by mining, and it demanded the indefinite annulment of the mining concessions to Minera La Zanja, Tantahuatay, and Sinchao. Reiterating the importance of their cross-regional union "in defense of life," the activists announced that they would take their same petition to the regional government of Lambayeque on November 16, and then to the central government in Lima on November 18. "Cajamarca is not alone," said the president of the Chancay-Lambayeque irrigation association Genaro Vera, adding, "it is time that we the poor understand we are more numerous. Only united will we self-govern and stop being trampled."[43]

Just as the company pursued legal strategies to finalize its project, activists similarly sought a policy strategy to prevent it, alongside its massive nonviolent protests. On October 2, 2009, Pulán mayor Celso Santa Cruz Izquierdo submitted an official plea to the country's highest court, the Tribunal Constitucional, arguing that the mining project should not be built on the vulnerable headwater, as it threatened the right to a safe environment. On January 2, 2010, the tribunal found the plea "unfounded." The mayor appealed but was denied again.[44]

The protesters took their message to Lima the following month. Celso Santa Cruz (Pulán's mayor), Estinaldo Quispe Mego, Oscar Romero Malca (Salatiel Romero Malca's brother, a Rondero leader from Pulán, and president of the Santa Cruz defense front), and a few other Ronderos had travelled to Lima to talk to congressional representatives about their reasons for opposing the mine, on grounds of the threat it posed to the headwater and to all the ecosystems, economies, and societies it feeds along its hundreds of miles trajectory to the Pacific Ocean via Lambayeque. Their objective was to request intervention from the central state to monitor the impact of mining in their area. Specifically, they sought to form a "high-level commission" under the auspices of the Ministry of Energy and Mines and the Ministry of the Environment to verify the project's viability.

The Ronderos' first day in the Congress was relatively successful, as they had a chance to speak with members of the Nationalist Party. However, on the second day of their meetings in the national legislature building, February 2, 2010, Peruvian National Police officers arrested Oscar Romero Malca when he tried to enter the Peruvian Congress. Romero was apparently wanted on charges pressed by Buenaventura against him and thirty-seven other local activists, for the events at the compound in November 2004.

Celso Santa Cruz denounced the persecution of local leaders and stated to media how, in November of 2009, a study by the Pedro Ruíz Gallo University and the central government's toxicology service analyzed water samples from the San Pedro river (which the company refers to as a creek), and its results registered cadmium (a carcinogenic element) and lead pollution.[45] That morning, when interviewed on news radio, Quispe Mego denounced the lack of response to their communiqués sent to the president and several cabinet members. Quispe also decried the "abuse and arrogance of controlling the national police and the judicial branch to repress and smear the Ronderos."[46] Romero's arrest at the door of Congress was a symbolic moment, a literal denial of entry that was also a denial of a space where stakeholders could find their representatives and safely resolve their problems. This was the state's security forces acting upon a private company's interests to arrest Romero as he sought intervention, mediation, and a nonviolent resolution from his democratic representatives in the Congress.

Returning to my theoretical argument in this book, the process described in the account of this case demonstrates how activists contesting La Zanja dealt with a combination of criminalizing and favorable media. Furthermore, even when they astutely activated media attention and had a moment to express their positions, the protestors were mostly unsuccessful at framing themselves favorably (as explicitly nonviolent and waging a righteous struggle against an unjust opponent) in order to solicit outside support for their movement, as activists in Tambogrande had achieved.

Waves of Conflict

The state approved Minera La Zanja's environmental impact study in 2009, and construction was swift. Amid more protests, including another one in Chiclayo in June 2010, the mine began producing in September 2010. Organizers in San Miguel and Santa Cruz partook in a region-wide strike two months later, but their mood was noticeably different, as if they had lost after all. However, they continued organizing, shifting efforts from preventing the mine to demanding benefit redistribution, environmental safety, and no mining expansion.

Since the La Zanja mine was built, conflicts over work, contracts, and water quality have sparked again in 2011, 2013, 2015, and 2017.[47] Some media covered the confrontations with police in 2013, but focused on how protesters threw rocks at police. The tone in reports of the events is surprisingly partial, defending or failing to mention how police fired at protesters.[48] When an activist was shot in the leg in a similar strike in 2015, this also received little attention. Most activists with whom I spoke were acutely aware of the criminalizing, delegitimizing language that had been used against their movement. They reported their rejection of all forms of violence, and some turned this narrative on its head, accusing of "terrorism" those who impose extractive projects against the will of locals. In the words of an activist leader in Pulán, "We want to organize and not fall in acts that may seem violent, because they'll paint us as terrorists. We want peaceful demonstrations, etc. We hope international NGOs will get interested in helping and that we can do all of this."[49]

In 2013, Estinaldo Quispe Mego was given a sentence of four years in jail, allegedly for disrupting the public order. In jail he was beaten and tortured, denied medical treatment, and threatened with death. Meanwhile, his partner back in Santa Cruz was also subject to intimidating calls.[50] Then another prominent environmental leader and the head of the opposition to La Zanja, Carlos Vásquez Becerra, was found dead on June 26, 2013. According to *La república*, his body was found one day after he "coordinated a meeting in the district of Ninamamba to organize local bases there against mining expansion planned by La Zanja and other mining projects."[51] A member of the mothers' club in Pulán remembered this as the second mysterious death of a resistance leader in the area, alluding to the suspicions about the former mayor's car accident.[52]

Testimony from both activists and regional company operators provided evidence that the threat of harsh repression played an important role in activists' thinking during this time. Their opposition did not end. Instead, they found ways to resist the mining project while minimizing their risk, such as through noncooperation, false compliance, and foot-dragging. A women's group in Pulán noted how they refused to provide food to mining workers or affiliates. Other interviewees said the Ronderos detained a woman working for FADRE, the NGO hired by Buenaventura to "work on development projects" in the region, and forced her to drink from the water stream that descends from the mine to their town. She became very ill and never went back.[53] The women who told me about this act against FADRE's employee framed it as a shameful act of spite or revenge, but they said it was motivated by their fear, and the company's repeated denial, of water pollution. Despite these nuanced and everyday attempts at resisting nonviolently, the fundamental outcome of the case is that the movement was unable to stop the project.

Water quality remained the subject of ongoing conflict. One controversy entailed the state's 2012 authorization of Minera La

Zanja's request to redirect more than 1.7 million cubic meters of treated water, used in the mine's industrial processes, into public waterways.[54] Another issue stemmed from a state-conducted analysis of human blood samples in the area, especially after the executive cabinet of the central government withheld the publication of the results for three years.[55] Between May 14 and 18, 2012, the National Health Institute collected six hundred blood samples from 309 randomized volunteers, including many children, in three districts in the central Cajamarca region: Querocoto, in Chota province; Granero, in the province of Hualgayoc; and Pulán, in Santa Cruz. The regional government paid the national health office for the results, expected for release the next month. However, the Peruvian Vice Ministry of Health held onto the results until early 2015, when protests—including a forty-eight-hour strike in Hualgayoc—media attention, and legal complaints successfully pressured for their release.[56]

Cajamarca regional officials suspected the release was withheld most likely because the executive cabinet feared the destabilizing effect these results would have in a region engulfed, at the time, in its most serious conflict to date, over Yanacocha's proposal to expand into the Conga lakes. The study found that most of the samples contained dangerous levels of lead pollution, among other issues. Multiple interviewees told me that the San Pedro river was toxic, but that they could still rely on the Santa Catalina river for their crops and daily water use.[57]

Locals' narratives demonstrated awareness of these scandals and hostility against the negative impacts of the mine. Many people said they felt betrayed by the promises of development and economic assistance, and bitter about repression and pollution.[58] However, the resistance seems to have slowly become powerless, especially as La Zanja contained residents' distrust and anger with jobs and philanthropy, such as an optometry campaign, a scholarship program, a reforestation initiative, and support for a local soccer club.[59] Furthermore, compared to other cases, the people who resisted La Zanja were subjected to harsher repression. At least one person died protesting, and two other key resistance leaders died under suspect circumstances. Many protesters were criminally prosecuted and even jailed. This may explain the movement's ultimate failure to prevent the mine's construction. Still, as of 2020, conflict was still latent in the districts near the mine, with the company facing legal disputes over land ownership as well as strikes from its workers. Activists reported the difficulty they faced in mobilizing their communities, although resentment against the company among area residents was widespread.

The social movements in Santa Cruz and San Miguel provinces appeared deflated, but many continue to organize. Local leaders were conscious of their need to exercise self-control against police provocations. Moreover, when public activism and organizing became dangerous as a result of repression and criminalization, locals found creative ways to resist the mine's operation. The partial but noticeable change in strategies as the conflict developed suggests perhaps a learning process resulting from a violent confrontation and subsequent repression. All of this was occurring within a context of broader tensions in Cajamarca as a whole, so in many ways the movements that formed against otherwise-isolated projects gradually learned from one another. This kind of information sharing happens also across regional boundaries; for example, one interviewee mentioned how a delegation of activists organizing against mining in nearby Tambogrande in fact attended a meeting in Cajamarca hosted by anti-Yanacocha protesters.[60]

Still, activists in more recent confrontations against La Zanja have continued using property damage as part of their repertoire of resistance, which several interviewees attributed to the company's similar persistent use of violent repression, even in these more recent waves of conflict. This case therefore illustrates how repressive company strategies best explain movements' use of violent collective action. In this case, as in the next, the final outcomes are characterized by a routinization of conflict, due mostly to the company's combination of persuasive (e.g., CSR investment and petty philanthropy) and coercive (repression, intimidation, defamation, etc.) strategies.

Conclusions: Success, Demobilization, or Routinization?

Among people whose discourse could be classified as sympathetic to mining, La Zanja is "an exemplary success," the lessons of which should be shared.[61] The clearest factor to explain the movement's demobilization is the company's mix of strategies, including heavy repression alongside NGO partnerships and corporate social responsibility programs. However, the recurrent waves of conflict related to La Zanja suggest that this combination has had the effect of not resolving conflict, but in fact incentivizing it—both by building resentment through repression, and by pacifying escalation with investment "rewards." In other words, the company provides a motive and a recompense that galvanize anger and resistance—sometimes undisciplined, such as in the case of arson and rock throwing. Replicating this might backfire.

The forms and structures of movement organizing set this conflict apart from others. For example, although both cases were set in areas not previously known for open-pit mining, one difference between the La Zanja mine and Manhattan Minerals' proposal in Tambogrande is that, in the latter, the farmers were organized not through the Rondas Campesinas but through economic associations that included large- and mid-scale agricultural producers. That stronger base in Tambogrande also built upon the district's experiences rejecting mining proposals, which they had been doing since the 1980s. By comparison, Santa Cruz province was relatively new to mining exploration.

In contrast to the La Zanja case, where the company leaned more heavily into repressive strategies, the company in the next case adopted strategies that, while similar, tilted in the opposite direction (see Table 3). Like in La Zanja, the social movements in the Lagunas Norte case also organized primarily through the Rondas Campesinas instead of through agricultural economic associations. On the other hand, in contrast to La Zanja, the next two cases, Barrick's Lagunas Norte and Gold Fields' Cerro Corona, were installed in provinces with a recent history of mining, with active mines in the area even employing many local farmers as seasonal workers. As scholars like Moisés Arce have explained,

FIGURE 4. Photograph of a school and street in downtown Pulán, 2016. Years into being host to a large open-pit gold mine, the district of Pulán still lacked pavement.

this structural, economic, and coalitional difference in the movements' respective organizing bases is a significant factor in understanding the trajectory of conflict and the different outcomes of each case. However, ultimately, one cannot overlook the role of company strategies, which affected dynamics more immediately and more forcefully, and therefore were a significant factor in the cases' differences.

CHAPTER 5

Lagunas Norte

What Does "Corporate Social Responsibility" Do?

When I woke up, it was early and freezing cold. Even in November, the global South's spring weather had been reluctant to arrive in our elevated part of the Andes, in the northern Peruvian region of La Libertad. However, I had an invitation to drive to the lakes near the town where I was staying, Quiruvilca, and I could not miss the chance. I made my way from my rented bedroom to downtown, where I met my friend—a local farmer and seasonal worker at Barrick's mega mine, who asked to remain anonymous in this study. I will refer to him as Arturo in this narrative.

We had first met in Santiago de Chuco, the provincial seat, a few weeks before. At that time, I was waiting for an interview at the mayor's office, in a long line of other claimants. The two people sitting to my right, an elderly man and his adult son, struck a lively conversation with me, inquiring first about what brought me to this office in this town. Their interest was piqued after I introduced my study, and they asked me who else I was hoping to interview, so I shared with them a few names from my list. Upon hearing me calling out each and every name, both men reacted audibly and visibly, clearly recognizing all of them and not feeling at all bashful about sharing their opinions regarding the people I was mentioning. Both were taken aback by the list of names I had compiled, even before I had arrived in the area, and they decided to help.

The younger man, Arturo, asked me whose phone numbers I still needed, and pulled out his phone. "Write this down," he said, and he added the names and contact information of several others. "We are Ronderos, miners, and community leaders," they told me. Drawn to my research, Arturo and his father invited me to stay with them at their farm near Quiruvilca. When it was finally their turn to talk with the provincial mayor, we exchanged contact information and I promised I would reach out to them soon, when my research schedule would take me to their district.

Weeks later, in Quiruvilca, we had already shared meals and talked at length when they invited me to see the lakes they sought to protect from mining expansion. At that early morning hour, downtown Quiruvilca was already busily trafficked by miners in uniform, coming and going in small groups as the night shift ended and another began. I met up with Arturo as we had agreed, and he introduced me to another Rondero, who had also been involved in the protests against the mining company. After asking taxi drivers for fare estimates at the corner of downtown where the taxis are usually parked, we remained unsatisfied with this option, so Arturo decided to ask the municipality for a truck. He ran into the municipal building, and while he was gone his friend agreed to be interviewed for my study; he explained to me that, as leaders in this small town, they knew the mayor, who would agree to lend us a truck for our expedition. Soon, Arturo came back with truck keys and another Rondero, a driver who joined us for the trip. The four of us got in the truck and headed north, curving upward on a road around an active underground mine, around which the town had been built over the past centuries.[1]

We stopped at the San Lorenzo lake to talk about the cultural, ecological, economic, and everyday importance of this water, which they said sourced their city and many others. The San Lorenzo and Callacuyán lakes are the origins of the Chicama and Moche rivers, which descend toward La Libertad region's coastal capital and Peru's second largest city, Trujillo, as well as the valleys north and east of it. The Ronderos said the area and its lakes are coveted by Barrick, which operates an open-pit mine just a couple of kilometers away, for its underwater mineral resources and plentiful water.

Arturo takes up seasonal work in the nearby mines to supplement income from his family's small-scale farm, and he did not want to be interviewed on camera, so I asked the two other Ronderos if they would like to sit down for a video interview. Both agreed and we sat next to the lake. "We lack the liquid element [water] in our community, Quiruvilca. We lack water there, so we need these lakes," one of them said. "We need, above all, the help of authorities and NGOs that help out, so we can have water in Quiruvilca, and maybe with more competent authorities this will be possible."

I asked the other if he concurred, and he replied that the problem was blurred jurisdiction, so the central cabinet in Lima should get involved in resolving these issues. "We'd like the president to make an appearance here, to see what kind of reality we live in Quiruvilca. He makes his presence felt through aides, but we want him to come in person," he replied. "We want him to show up in person so he at least says, 'Yes, I will help you.' Because when they send a delegate, all we get are momentary commitments," he decried. Before we finished talking, I asked them if they believed their conflict had become violent, and if they identified as "anti-miners" (as the Lima-based conservative media pundit Jaime de Althaus referred to the area's protesters two years earlier).[2] This stirred the Ronderos. "We are not *violentists*," one of them declared. "We only claim our rights as any citizen—who whenever they are offended, have a right to respond—but not through violence."[3]

Those words rang heavily in my thoughts a few months later when I woke up in my apartment in Lima to news of a confrontation leading to the death of two police officers who drowned in that very same lake, the Laguna San Lorenzo. A protest had been organized in response to a road construction project leading into and passing through the area with its several lakes. Ronderas and Ronderos rejected the road construction, led and financed by Barrick's regional corporate social responsibility initiative, the Fondo

Social Alto Chicama (FSAC). Barrick has repeatedly marked this particular lake as containing rich mineral deposits and identified it as a "target area" into which it wished to expand its extractive operations.[4] While the FSAC claims that this road had nothing to do with mining, the road could doubtlessly provide anyone with convenient access to a lake that Barrick considered "of interest" and of "exploration potential."[5]

The FSAC directive board consists of two Barrick managers and the mayors of six nearby districts (the three nearest districts and their respective provincial seats: Quiruvilca and its seat Santiago de Chuco, Usquil and Otuzco, and Sanagorán and Sánchez Carrión). Together, they develop projects that are funded by Barrick in order to fulfill its "voluntary contributions" scheme in exchange for tax reductions.[6] The area's activists committed to protecting these lakes perceived the road construction as a step toward mining there. Worse, they expressed feeling offended at the company's attempt to veil this as an unrelated act of generosity to its local host communities.

Videos and witness testimonies provided evidence that police fired live bullets and tear gas canisters indiscriminately at the crowd, but well over two thousand Ronderas and Ronderos responded with their bodies, stones, and cow whips—often used in Rondas justice, which involves corporal punishment.[7] Despite the heavily armed police forces, the injuries of those within their ranks only committed the protesters further. Their masses soon overpowered the police, cornering them near the edge of the water and threatening them with retribution. Fearing this fate, many police tried to escape by swimming across the water (although many of them stayed and were only disarmed and yelled at, but not harmed). On the other side of the lake, some police also recorded the events on video while others screamed, pleading with their partners to keep swimming. Some of the police officers made it all the way across; however, some turned around and swam back to the protesters, perhaps realizing the distance was unachievable in those cold temperatures. Two of them died while trying to swim out of the freezing water in this Andean lake, situated roughly four thousand meters above sea level. The day's events also left a toll of thirteen injured police officers and at least nineteen farmers wounded by police bullets.[8]

Because of the deaths of police, this confrontation reached the front pages of Lima-based newspapers for days, but the attention seems to have been mainly negative for activists. *RPP Noticias*' report characterized the protestors as a "mob of 2,000 locals" that, "with violent attitudes and equipped with overwhelming weapons, threw rocks at police and ambushed them." *RPP* named every police officer injured and the two disappeared, but only estimated in passing that thirty-nine people were injured in total, including thirteen police.[9] *La república* dedicated its front page to the story, following the police's rescue teams and uncritically quoting Barrick spokespeople, who emphasized that the company was not involved in this road project.[10] However, some local and independent media related the conflict to Barrick. Radio Chami, out of Otuzco's provincial seat, centered in its narrative how Barrick's corporate social responsibility arm, the FSAC, financed the road. The online blogs *Tomate colectivo* and *Lucha indígena* went further, tracing the nature of the conflict to the company.[11] The recently formed youth activist group Colectivo Alto Chicama also linked the protest to Barrick in its reports.[12]

Finger-pointing aside, a few things became clear to me. First, these issues were not resolved and actually had become resurgent or routine in the terms of engagement between the communities and the company. Second, the case was, once again, not about a conflict between mining opponents versus supporters (as almost all activists I interviewed for this case study said they supported mining or were even seasonal workers at one or two mines). Third, local leaders were unable to contain and redirect people's rage and discontent through nonviolent action. And fourth, state institutions faced the greatest challenge in learning to effectively channel conflict through deliberative mechanisms that could help to resolve these nonviolently.

In terms of the theoretical framework built by this book, the Lagunas Norte case is an excellent illustration of how company

FIGURE 5. Photograph of the Los Ángeles Lake and Lagunas Norte Mine, 2015.

strategies of community engagement—which in this context have been predominantly persuasive but still significantly coercive—can explain both social movement's tactical responses and the outcome of cases. The movement has organized resistance on legitimate environmental and redistributive claims, to which the company has responded with state repression and alleged intimidation, directly provoking escalation and violent collective action. Furthermore, Barrick's mix of coercion with investment (in philanthropy and public works projects) have provided two forms of incentives for conflict: both angering people, on the one hand, and encouraging them to escalate conflict as a way to draw outside attention, embarrass the company, and extract concessions from it, on the other.

This chapter ethnographically explores the reasons behind these recurrent effects. It retells this history, as in previous chapters, multi-vocally—as I learned it from my diverse hosts, as well as through a critical assessment of countless secondary sources. While I explicitly want to highlight the histories told to me by local actors who are typically ignored in academic studies (for example, women, people of color, and people who are poor, gender nonconforming, or disabled), in this chapter as in the others, I aim to focus on the actions and the generative effects of the people variously involved in these conflicts, rather than on my own assessments of their morality or intentions. My aim is to avoid rather than contribute to the polarized discourses of mining and development—a polarization that has also percolated into the academic literature on these matters.[13] Therefore, I strive to provide a complex narrative critical of my normative assumptions of whether actors—especially when lumped into heterogeneous groups such as "the social movement" and "the company"—are being altruistic, malicious, or something else.

Background

Barrick Gold—which has topped (or closely contested companies like Goldcorp and Newmont Mining for the top position in) the list of the world's largest gold-mining companies during the past decade—discovered deposits in La Libertad region's highlands in the late 1990s. Barrick proposed to build its mine in a headwater zone containing dozens of lakes, the source of rivers spreading both toward the Amazon and toward the Pacific Ocean via the port city and regional capital, Trujillo. At the time, there were other mines operating in the area, considered a "historical mining district"—rhetoric that Barrick's public relations efforts echo euphorically.

The area is rich with pre-Inca settlements, including especially those of the Huamachuco civilization, and an Inca road passes through the area, connecting the San Lorenzo lake and Quiruvilca to the capital of the empire in Cusco. Archaeological evidence seems to suggest that people in the area actively practiced mining in pre-Inca as well as Inca times.[14] The name Quiruvilca itself can be roughly translated from Quechua as meaning "silver tooth." During the time of Spanish colonialism, the first modern mines settled into the "Monte Quiruvilca" in 1629, using indentured day laborers (under the *mita* system of Spanish feudalism in the Andes) to produce silver for the crown. By the late twentieth century, Quiruvilca's existing mines were under the state-owned mining entity Minero Perú, which was created in 1970 and privatized in 1992.

In 1998, Barrick Gold declared its interest in the Alto Chicama property. Named after the Chicama river and its valley downstream, the property contained an old carbon mine where Barrick's Lagunas Norte open-pit mine now lies, as well as a number of other large lakes in the Lagunas Sur area (including the Lagunas Verdes, Laguna Los Ángeles, Laguna El Toro, and others). Although fourteen other companies also formally declared their interest in the concession, Barrick was the only one to make a bid. Its geological assessment estimated the mineral to be concentrated at about 1.54 grams per metric ton (or about .045 ounces per US short ton) of soil, and projected production levels at 535,000 to 560,000 ounces of gold per year. The company also forecast production of high quantities of silver from the mine's extraction and processing. Furthermore, Barrick promised to invest US$340 million during the mine's lifespan, which it estimated to be about ten years. The Ministry of Energy and Mining (MINEM) granted the concession in 2001, and deep drilling explorations began immediately.[15]

Company Strategies

At the time, the proposal drew small protests from nearby Andean communities. Most of the people in the company's impact area practiced subsistence agriculture, but many also worked seasonally in one of the region's few mines. Local concerns centered on water, which they identified as a source of identity, of ancestral heritage, and of life. Much of the water in the concession area's lakes descended toward both the coast and the Amazon, supplying farmers, small towns, and cities along the way. However, Barrick already had experience establishing a large mine in Peru—its Pierina project, in nearby Áncash. The company's Latin American and Peruvian managers in its Lima-based subsidiary, Minera Barrick Misquichilca, understood the political context of mining in Peru at the time, one in which the town of Tambogrande was becoming a household name. Thus, the company acted quickly: it offered petty cash and jobs to many local families, and the protests largely ceded. In the meantime, it took advantage of reforms to mining law that accelerated the project approval process.

In 2002, the international mining industry consultant Golder Associates conducted an environmental impact study for Barrick's Alto Chicama property. The area was estimated to be "the zone with the greatest potential in Peru" for the carbon industry.[16] Barrick's environmental impact assessment (EIA) estimated the mine would use 10 to 20 liters of cyanide per cubic meter of soil per hour. The company declared its requirement to hold public audiences complete in 2003. The following year, it announced to investors that it expected its EIA would gain final state approval by mid-2004, and that it expected to pour its first gold bar before the end of 2005. Unlike what Newmont and Buenaventura faced in La Zanja, where the company's estimates would be delayed by five years, Barrick's mine began operating on schedule by mid-2005.[17]

In the meantime, the company also opened offices from where it began negotiating the contract of local service providers. Initially, its offices were in Quiruvilca and the provincial seat, Santiago de Chuco, although it temporarily relocated its Quiruvilca office to Huamachuco, the capital of the Sánchez Carrión province, in 2004.[18] Alongside hiring local workers and service providers, part of the company's plans involved satisfying both its own operations' needs and the needs of locals by constructing roads, bridges, and an electricity grid to connect its operations to the coast. For example, in August of 2004, it concluded a US$11 million investment in roads and bridges upgrades along seventy-one kilometers. This construction employed seven hundred people and connected Barrick's mine to Otuzco, halfway between the coast and Quiruvilca, where the paved road from Trujillo ended.[19] Framed as part of its social responsibility, these moves were essential to meet the operation's needs and at the same time to solidify its reputation as a "different" kind of mining company. In the words of a former Barrick Misquichilca officer at the Lagunas Norte project, "Barrick fulfilled local expectations and knew to satisfy a local need. It was very intelligent."[20]

The Lagunas Norte project would soon become one of the largest gold mines in the world, second in Peru only to Newmont and Buenaventura's Yanacocha mine. It would also raise La Libertad's standing as the second largest gold producing region in Peru, with 29 percent of total production in the country—after Cajamarca's 38 percent.[21] In contrast to the land use size of La Zanja and Cerro Corona (only the parts where it is currently concentrating activities, and not their entire respective concession areas), Lagunas Norte is about five times larger, from a bird's-eye view. The region's total gold production over time also helps to illustrate the Lagunas Norte mine's productivity and economic importance. The entire La Libertad region produced 9,235 kilograms of gold in 1996, 14,922 in 2000, and 18,460 by 2004. Gold production in the region grew slowly but steadily, doubling over those eight years. Barrick began producing gold one year later, in 2005, when La Libertad produced a total of 35,924 kilograms of gold; and in 2006, the region produced 55,924 kilograms of gold. In other words, gold production in the entire region more than tripled between 2004 and 2006, mostly thanks to Barrick's operations.[22]

Community Organizing

Because the mine was located near a district with a long tradition of mining, organizing resistance to this economic activity was diffi-

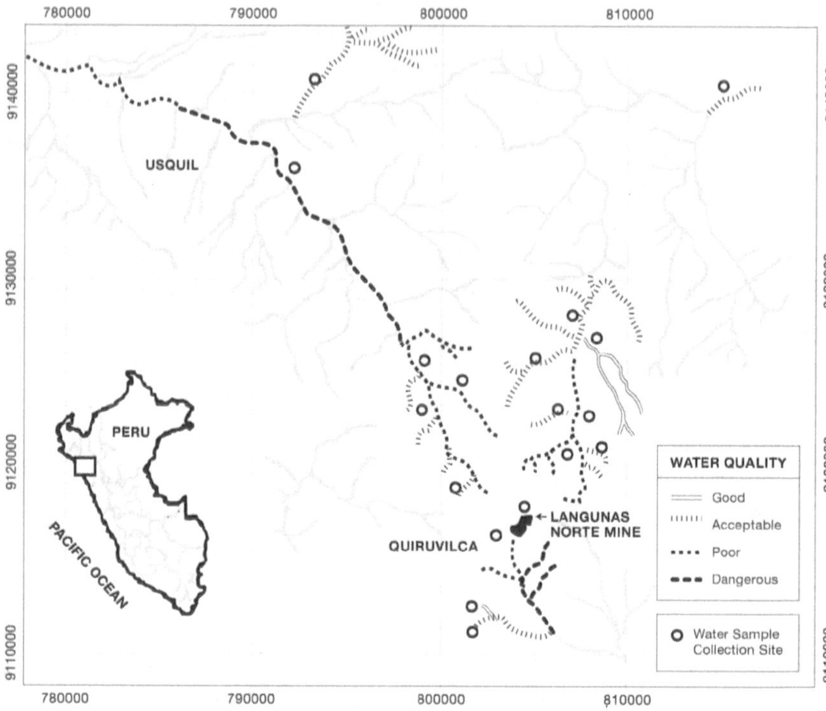

FIGURE 6. Alto Chicama water quality, 2008 (*left*) and 2009 (*right*), by Medina Tafur et al. ("Calidad del agua en las cuencas del Alto Chicama," 2010), modified and reused here with permission.

cult. While most people in the area are small-scale farmers, many of the people who would become protesters were also incorporated as contractors or seasonally employed as miners in one or more of the area's several mines—among which Lagunas Norte is by far the largest and most lucrative. Furthermore, Barrick had incorporated the Rondas Campesinas through institutional and informal mechanisms. It reached out and recognized their authority, which was a significant departure from standard practice by other mining companies in the area at the time.[23] Still, contestation started as early as 2005, when the National Coordinator of Communities Affected by Mining (CONACAMI, in Spanish) issued a communiqué claiming that "the adequate procedures for the approval of the environ-

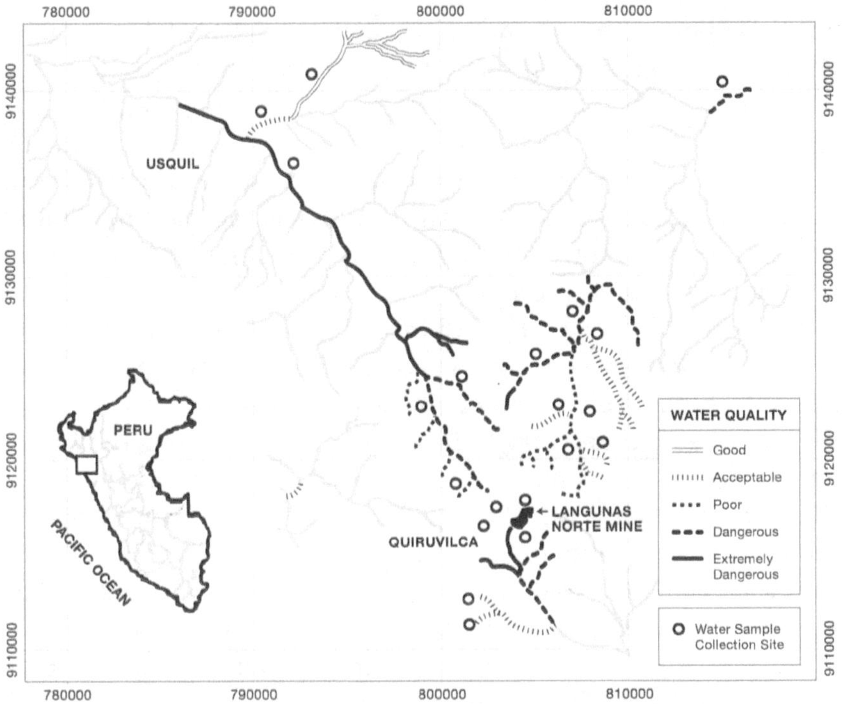

mental impact study have been unfulfilled, constituting a violation by Barrick of the rights to prior and informed consent."[24] (To be clear, Peru did not ratify the right to informed consent until 2011.)

Multiple interviewees said the first signs of discontent emerged because companies "abuse the locals' ignorance, offering much less than their better-educated neighbors."[25] Concerns over water also appeared relatively quickly: requests from area farmers prompted a team at the public Universidad Nacional de Trujillo (UNT) to conduct water monitoring evaluation of the rivers descending from the mine's area of operations. Under leadership from chemistry and biology labs at the university, as well as from the Otuzco-based religious and environmentalist organization Asociación Marianista de Acción Social, a group of participants were trained and formed into monitoring teams starting in 2006. The results of the participative study were published in 2010 via the UNT journal *Sciéndo*. Its comparative analysis of macro-invertebrates in water sampled in eighteen different points, including control points, concluded that water descending from Barrick's mine was being impacted negatively.[26] UNT researchers had data collected from many of those points even earlier, in 2006, which provided more contrast to the data they collected in 2008, and again in 2009. Comparing the results across time allowed the researchers to corroborate their finding that mining was having a negative impact on the area's rivers (see Figure 6).[27]

The UNT biologist and lead investigator for that study, César Medina Tafur, showed me photos of Barrick's security guards, who he said would often arrive when his team was taking water samples, to question and "try to intimidate" them, and take photos and videos of his team. Medina joked while telling me about it: "They would *inspect us*! While we were trying to inspect *them*!"[28] Another biologist and university professor involved in water monitoring activities also told me that her research—which used similar methodologies focused on invertebrate populations to determine water pollution levels—was conducted under a context of constant surveillance, "harassment," and "intimidation" by company employees and security.[29] More importantly, Medina alluded to the pseudoscience and the methodological dishonesty of the reports created by the company in response to their water monitoring study. In his own words,

> Mining companies use the "Surber" sampling method to say that this area is not so polluted. "Dip net" is a multi-habitat methodology which finds more problems. There is a *huge* difference in the biodiversity results each method finds. I use the D-frame dip net method, which finds less biodiversity, and it is multi-habitat, so its sample is more representative. They just want to measure PH levels in the water. What I do is measure the population of invertebrates in the water.

At this point, Medina criticized how companies often add crushed limestone to the water to raise the PH levels, "but even with that, the results point to high levels of conductivity. They are just trying to hide all the aluminum, iron, and cyanide in the water." He added,

> The company reports are what we [in the field] refer to as "grey literature"—they have no peer review, and often they are not even made public. They don't follow a consistent and adequate methodology, and they even plagiarize studies. Sometimes you find internal reports about animals that do not exist in their areas! Why? Because they just put a stamp and their own name on some other mining company's report from elsewhere. They are also not inspected to make sure that the author ever visited the field. They could have sent a couple of students and that's it. It hurts me. It affects me that the poor, my friends in the highlands, lose their lands. We lack political organization and are too easily driven by money.[30]

In the perspective of a Trujillo-based public defendant, who seemed optimistic about the role of mining and who reiterated his doubts over the motives of the environmentalist groups, the study's publication was the spark that ignited the local movement against Barrick.[31] Other interviewees told me that water pollution was not the most serious source of conflict in the area. In general, several people said, locals there tend to care less about pollution, to which they were presumably accustomed, than about benefitting economically and fairly from mining.[32] Residents in the towns around the mine also mentioned their perception that their communities were changing negatively. "We have lost our identity," reflected a young woman who worked at one of the area's municipal buildings. As we ate during her hometown's anniversary, she and her cousin proudly guided me through the many products on our plates and through details about the area's agricultural wealth and diversity. "We would not be poor without the mine," she concluded.[33]

The study of mining's impact on local water supplies coincided with two events. First, in 2009 locals denounced, and the National Indigenous Association as well as the National Coordinator of Human Rights corroborated, the deaths of thousands of trout—allegedly due to mining pollution.[34] Second, Barrick attempted to modify its original EIA starting in 2010, including a plan to expand to the Lagunas Sur area just south of its open pit. This area includes the Laguna El Toro, Laguna de Los Ángeles, and Lagunas Verdes, which source Quiruvilca's water for human consumption, as well as that of numerous other communities further downstream. Thus, in 2010, a movement with broad support from the provinces around the mine (Santiago de Chuco, Otuzco, and Sanchez Carrión) was formed.

Barrick was required by law to hold meetings in the area regarding its EIA modification request. It scheduled "participatory workshops" in various locations. In the neighborhood of Chuyugual, in Sánchez Carrión province, hundreds of people marched toward the meeting and held a protest that prevented Barrick's scheduled workshop.[35] Videos of the march, recorded by a Lima-based university researcher, show that a majority of the marchers are women. Wearing traditional garb and holding signs, they set the tone and the route of their march. The core complaints were captured by a sign that read, "First keep your promises, then we'll dialogue."[36]

Many interviewees in this study cited anger stemming from unfulfilled promises, overpriced and useless corporate social responsibility programs, and health concerns as the reasons behind this conflict wave.[37] Others reported that their initial indignation resulted from realizing that the company had "taken advantage" of those who sold land to the company—locals persuaded to accept a fraction of their lands' worth.[38] And during this second stage, the movement was larger than the initial opposition. It had the support of at least one district mayor, as well as urban and rural residents, farmers, young activists, women, and even the area's seasonal miners. The words of one company employee summarized what many interviewers expressed; he said that his community supported mining, "but these lakes are untouchable."[39]

Conflict as Routine

The way the company handled this conflict is key. First of all, Barrick availed itself of police repression to quell strikes that paralyzed its operations. On February 8, 2007, only months after these agreements became constitutionally allowed and formalized, Barrick Misquichilca signed a private security agreement with the Peruvian National Police's Directory of Special Operations (DIROES).[40] It renewed this contract in 2017. More interestingly, Barrick adopted a well-funded corporate social responsibility strategy. Noting the economic costs caused by the strike, Barrick quelled the protest by offering private contracts and cash to opponents and by staging a "dialogue table" in which it verbally agreed to finance various construction projects.[41]

Many of these investments were channeled through Barrick's "Obras por Impuestos" legal option—product of the 2008 Peruvian law 29230—which can be translated as paying for "public interest projects instead of income taxes," and specifically entails companies' right to deduct the cost of building or operating these public projects from the taxes it owes the state.[42] For example, in 2012 Barrick concluded road construction connecting various neighborhoods in Santiago de Chuco province, for which it invested $2,331,217 (in 2012 USD). In September 2013, it committed to a partnership with another mining company, Poderosa, the plastics company Backus y Johnston, and the Banco de Crédito del Perú to construct a technical police school for the Peruvian National Police in Trujillo over the next eighteen months. Under the partnership, Barrick, Poderosa, and Backus would each invest a little over $2,500,000 (in 2013 USD), and the bank would invest just over $3,845,000. Then, in March 2014, Barrick approved a budget of $5,613,000 (in 2014 USD) to build a hospital in Santiago de Chuco, its host province, in partnership with the transnational bank BBVA, which matched Barrick's contribution.[43]

In addition to the tax-substitution option, mining companies were bound to a five-year executive decree known as the Mining Program of Solidarity with the People (PMSP, in Spanish), passed by the García government in 2006, which demanded their "voluntary, extraordinary, and temporary" investments in projects, programs, and works aimed at improving social well-being.[44] For both of these reasons as well as its intentional efforts at being a different, more socially responsible mining company, Barrick founded its FSAC in 2009. Since then, it has also executed small projects such as an artisanal textiles workshop, a math program, an optometry campaign, the restoration of the poet César Vallejo's home in Santiago de Chuco, and others.

However, the combination of carrots and sticks established a pattern of conflict that would reignite again in 2013, 2015, and 2017, as well as more frequently at the neighborhood level. In each of these major conflict waves, the company responded to physical disruption, such as strikes and roadblocks, with a combination of police repression—leading to serious activist injuries each time[45]—alongside the usually slow, state-mediated, and nonbinding process of installing a dialogue table. Because the processes dragged sluggishly and the promises reached during these negotiations were not binding, these dialogue tables appeared to be a strategy of conflict avoidance rather than of resolution, in the words of many interviewees.

"Roadblocks are the only way for [protesters] to be heard, but then the company makes promise after promise, and it all stays in paper. This is how they shut the people up," said a man in the natural resources department of a local municipality. "They make promises, get people drunk, and that's it."[46] As a result of this approach that both feeds and pacifies conflict, strikes and road blockades have been recurrent in the conflict surrounding Lagunas Norte, just as in the La Zanja case. However, one important contrast between the outcomes in both of these cases is that Barrick has been slightly more persuasive and slightly less coercive than Buenaventura, which might be why the movement against Lagunas Norte is stronger, whereas in La Zanja it is partly demobilized (see Tables 2 and 3 for an analytical summary of this contrast).

The strike in June 2015 was violently dispersed by police. Barrick's lowest-paid workers and their families, including women and children, were demanding higher wages and more opportunities for the area's mine employees. Their strike involved withdrawing their work as well as blocking access to the mine's entrance, which they did for two weeks before national and regional police were sent to break up the blockade. Police opened fire, and younger activists responded by throwing rocks and setting fire to company vehicles and equipment.

The flames acted as a vindicator for the use of force, and police injured dozens of protesters. The limited media coverage of the event focused on the confrontation, barely mentioning the movement's goals.[47] Afterward, the movement's leaders agreed to no longer allow youths to their actions, realizing the cost of these activists' reaction. They instituted an innovative rule for their protests: they ensured that only people who had been debriefed on their rules of engagement could attend their actions by requiring to see their state-issued ID cards.[48] This is an impressive type of innovation, which demonstrates leaders' process of learning not to play into the trap of provocation, and then adapting their tactics accordingly. It is likely that this "movement learning" is tied to the strength and representativeness of local organizations.

However, this internal learning process bears qualifying, because many interviewees also said that the lesson of these rounds of conflict was that only violence could help make their voices heard.[49] Their thinking lends support for my argument in this book that a lack of favorable attention and, by extension, a lack of support from NGOs and outside allies have increased the movement's propensity to adopt violent collective action as forms of waging conflict, making claims, and forcing the company into negotiation spaces. Almost every interviewee who mentioned the appeal of violent tactics directly stated this dynamic and its efficacy as their justification for it.

Finally, it is also useful to interrogate what the activists who felt violent tactics were necessary truly meant by violence; certainly, property damage is not on the same analytical level as attacks on human beings, even if it does carry a symbolic aggression and causes physical damage. And whereas I have focused on violent confrontations, other things like the deaths of thousands of low-income farmers' trout—the source of livelihood (as in direct nourishment and economic income) for their families—must not be lost in this narrative as a form of violence also.

As illustrated by the June 2016 events I mentioned in the opening to this chapter, where a Barrick-funded road construction near the San Lorenzo lake led to a deadly confrontation between thousands of people from the Rondas and riot police, recent evidence suggests that further escalation is well within the protesters' repertoires.

Conclusions: Learning the Meanings of Violence

Media and outside attention played interesting roles in this case, even in their absence. It is noteworthy that some of the people with whom I spoke and spent time seemed to believe that violence was not only a way to get attention from others, but also a tool to legitimize themselves and to mobilize locals. Repressive laws, the trigger-happy behavior of police actors, and Barrick's combination of conflict management strategies pushed actors in multiple directions, even among the groups involved in this conflict. Therefore, some interviewees' claim that violence is the only way to garner attention illustrates that, although many people described their intentions and efforts to shift to disciplined activism and to avoid provocation, the lessons drawn by local social movements in the upper Chicama river area seem to have been mixed. It is useful to question whether resources or attention from outside allies could alter this. Several contacts within NGOs in the global North intuited this during our conversations, but previous research has shown that neither is a sufficient explanation for the shift in movements' tactics and means of waging conflict.[50] For the time being, it does not appear that the lessons learned by key movement actors uniformly pointed toward nonviolent resistance in this case.

Similarly, another theoretical point this case highlights is the importance of the company's strategies. Barrick seems to fuse a propensity to rely on police and court repression (as well as private intimidation, which perhaps is not organized at the corporate level, but was still widely reported), with discourses of openness, philanthropy, and their will to engage in state-mediated dialogue. While conducting my fieldwork at the Lagunas Norte case, a lot of people complained to me that conflict was easily suppressed by company strategies, and this meant the underlying conditions of conflict were never addressed. Grief was silenced with token gifts and public investment projects.[51] This sort of "depoliticization" has created a sense that escalating conflict—by any means necessary—was needed to attain concessions from the state and from the company.

Confrontations surrounding the Lagunas Norte mine have grown in intensity from one campaign to the next, an intensification that may be an even worse outcome than (presumably stable) "routinization." It may be that some activists place greater importance on getting the state's attention than on the means to do this. To be sure, Peru's legal and institutional framework bears a lot of the responsibility for the extra-institutional escalation and entrenchment of conflicts within its territory. While local activists as well as company actors have learned much about avoiding violence, the onus of preventing violent conflict is on the state, which has largely doubled down on repressive responses to protest and, despite some agencies' work, has failed to provide credible spaces for democratic resolution.

CHAPTER 6

Cerro Corona

Dialogue and Depoliticization

The fourth case I selected for the focus of this book is quite different to the previous three. To answer the first of this study's two main research questions (why do some mining conflicts become more violent than others?), it was crucial to analyze null cases—contexts in which conflict had not escalated noticeably, despite the circumstances they may have shared with other cases that did intensify. Gold Fields is a Johannesburg-based corporation that operates projects worldwide and enjoys a reputation as a modern and responsible mining company, globally and perhaps especially in Peru. Its Cerro Corona mine in Cajamarca is exemplary among mining projects because, while there are serious complaints among the nearby communities, it is one of the few in which conflict has remained entirely nonviolent. From an analytical standpoint, this is especially significant and puzzling given that the mine is situated in Cajamarca region, infamous for its often-violent mining conflicts. Cerro Corona is only miles away from the largest gold mine in South America, Yanacocha, and nearby to La Zanja. Indeed, Gold Fields began developing its mine as conflicts over the La Zanja and Quilish projects intensified between 2003 and 2004.

This chapter explores the reasons why protesters whose claims and grievances center on the Cerro Corona mine have largely kept to low levels of organizing, and why their tactics have never escalated beyond symbolic demonstrations and sporadic, nonviolent disruptions. Among the cases in this research, Cerro Corona is

FIGURE 7. Map of Cajamarca, Santa Cruz, and Bambamarca cities. This map shows the proximity and relative size of cities like Cajamarca against the Cerro Corona, La Zanja, Yanacocha, and Tantahuatay mines (courtesy of © Google and © Landsat, 2018).

the smallest mine (although not by far—see Figure 7), and it operates in a "traditional mining district," but the ethnographic study below will argue that, far more importantly, it is the company's community-engagement strategies, at the corporate and everyday levels, that explain its relative success in avoiding or preventing conflicts. However, this study also posits that the company's strides toward building amicable relations with locals have been insufficient to build durable and mutual relationships. The everyday tone of friendliness and openness that most company actors have built with locals does affect the levels of confrontation and has been effective at avoiding explosive conflict. However, these interpersonal efforts do not diminish, and sometimes reinforce, the material inequities that surround mining operations, particularly the uneven distribution of their benefits and burdens. In other words, treating locals with less arrogance and having larger budgets for corporate investments in local projects has pacified, but not resolved, the serious tensions and complaints that locals expressed.

Background

Under the name of its brand new (at the time) Peruvian subsidiary, Gold Fields La Cima, the South African mining firm bought the Carolina mine from the company Sociedad Minera Corona in the Cajamarca region's small district of Hualgayoc in 2003. Despite the fifteen years of mining conflict that have plagued Cajamarca since then, the renamed Cerro Corona mine has kept a low profile, and in fact it was rated as Gold Fields' "most productive" operation worldwide in 2011—when a huge and deadly conflict over Yanacocha's Conga project was quickly escalating just a few miles away.[1]

It is not that Gold Fields' executives knew, from the moment they bought and took over the mine, that Cajamarca and adjacent regions would soon concentrate such a great number and intensity of conflicts around mining. At the time, Tambogrande had just held their popular consultation process in the adjacent region of Piura, and the La Zanja project was merely a proposal, a latent conflict. Still, Gold Fields had to file an environmental impact assessment before it could begin expanding and modifying its purchase, which gave its managers time—about two years—to learn about what was going on in the region. The state approved the company's environmental impact assessment in December 2005 and the company began constructing its Cerro Corona mine, directly on the former mine, in May of 2006. By then, Gold Fields had witnessed the processes of conflicts nearby at Tambogrande and Cerro Quilish, both of which were scrapped, and the arson at La Zanja. New to Peru, experienced elsewhere, and seeking a different trajectory, Cerro Corona was deeply strategic about its community relations.

Peruvian census data from 2007 portrays Hualgayoc as a 17,425-person district. Among 5,653 people registered as "economically active," 3,367 were farmers and 1,317 were miners. More than 70 percent of people in the entire province were poor, over half of them in absolute poverty. According to a Gold Fields field manager, they found a "very distrustful" community: "And we understood that this social context was generated through long historical relationships between the state, them, and mining companies. But at the same time, there was this hope—they were so unwell that they saw an opportunity to develop themselves."[2]

His team studied these relationships with the help of hired sociologists. "Before we entered, we started with social responsibility projects—before anything else, because we saw the culture of distrust that existed," he said. As its many representatives interviewed for this study retold the story to me, the company managers committed themselves to studying and working through that deeply rooted distrust. "Our treatment was intentional at the social level as well as in the land sales," said the officer. In my assessment, this everyday intentionality is one of the most significant factors that led to Cerro Corona's relative success in preventing the outbreak of violence, which was hugely surprising especially given the cultural and political context in which the project exists.

Community Organizing

Cerro Corona's operations are of a similar scale as La Zanja's, as are its methods of gold extraction. From the stadium in Hualgayoc's south side to the houses and stores on the three roads leading north from town, the size of the Hualgayoc district capital city (which is more a small concentration of buildings near the mine) pales in comparison to the 1,264 hectare mining project that looms over the hill, only one kilometer away. Gold Fields' own environmental impact assessment and subsequent reports indicate that it sought to produce 1.9 million ounces of gold and 369 kilotons of copper by 2024. To do this, it would dig an open pit, then remove and process 94 million metric tons of soil and rocks through its concentration plant, which was designed and equipped to process

17,000 metric tons per day.[3] Thus, for a project of this size, concerns about ecological and economic redistribution were foreseeable.

The Peruvian ombudsperson first reported local concerns regarding water pollution and scarcity in 2006. The area is known to have more than 1,286 mining-related registered environmental hazards, including dozens of ponds polluted with heavy metals.[4] Companies in the area claim this is related to centuries of mining there, but the several large-scale, cyanide- and mercury-intensive mining operations in recent decades are also partly responsible. Hualgayoc also hosts the Tantahuatay mine, owned by Coimolache (Buenaventura), since 2009.

On October 24, 2006, *Perú21* reported that Gold Fields had suspended its work due to a strike that had, since October 12, blocked the road leading to its operations. The strikers were area miners who demanded job opportunities and the mediation of government authorities. However, according to the report, Gold Fields already had 768 people from the Hualgayoc area in its seasonal workforce, which was more than twice as many as its operators had promised earlier.[5]

Then in September 2007, two impoverished farmers, Felicita and Amelia Celis Guevara, filed a legal complaint to judicial authorities in San Miguel province against Gold Fields for usurpation of lands and aggravated damages. The Celis Guevara sisters said the company was operating in, and had appropriated, growing parts of their land without any authorization since July 2007. *El clarín* cited the sisters' plea for the authorities' assistance against this "illegal act" also accompanied by "abuse and arrogance from company representatives." The two farmers said they were unwilling to cede any part of their land to the company, and vowed that they would resort to "all necessary means" to stop the abuse being committed against them and to prevent other farmers in the San Miguel and Hualgayoc provinces from being abused as well.[6] While this type of claim seems to have been common, and a small strike accompanied it in 2007, more organized and collective forms of resistance were picking up speed as well.

A couple of years later, on August 12, 2009, some activists in Hualgayoc organized a march through town and then to the site of the

FIGURE 8. Photograph of the Hualgayoc Municipal Stadium, 2016.

mine. At around 10:30 a.m., they also forcibly entered the location of the electricity transformer meant to provide electricity to parts of Chota, Santa Cruz, and Hualgayoc provinces. The protesters were aggrieved because, at least in their perception, the town of Hualgayoc was excluded from these benefits. They scheduled their protest to coincide with the transformer's inauguration ceremony, which they interrupted, taking advantage of the public attention on the event to demand the integration of the town of Hualgayoc—which had gone without electricity for three months. Two days later, on a Friday afternoon, the Hualgayoc district municipality organized a public meeting between locals and Gold Field officers, held at the town's soccer stadium, in which the agenda would concentrate on water availability, electricity, work opportunities, and damage to houses from mining explosions. The meeting appears to have been unsatisfactory to both the protesters and the company. Municipal leaders and company officials met again the following Monday morning in the mayor's office. In this closed meeting, company representatives offered services and investment, and—although the terms were much weaker than what the majority assembled in the stadium had demanded the previous Friday—the mayor and lieutenant mayor signed onto the offer.

By August 18, social leaders from the area—most of them members of the Rondas Campesinas—had already held two meetings to strategize a strike against Gold Fields. A few days later, locals from Hualgayoc, San Miguel, and Cajamarca provinces began their two-day strike against Gold Fields, in the words of a strike organizer, "for being a liar on the offers and agreements it made to this population."[7] Protesters claimed that the company distributed pamphlets throughout the town of Hualgayoc aimed at smearing protest leaders. At 11:00 p.m., protesters arrived to block an entrance to the Cerro Corona mine. Three hours later, they ignited firecrackers to symbolize the start of the strike, blocking the road that connects Cajamarca and Bambamarca (the larger city and capital district of Hualgayoc province).

In the morning of August 19, 2009, at seven o'clock, the Rondas detained Gold Fields' Community Relations Director, with whom they negotiated throughout the day. At eight they marched through Hualgayoc, announcing an indefinite strike against the company and encouraging others to join. The mayor joined the protests by around nine o'clock, apologizing to protest leaders for his delay in arriving and promising to support the measure. The protesters then marched to meet their friends who were blockading the mine's entrance, where they were met by about twenty police. The hundreds of protesters soon overpowered the small police presence, which withdrew, and protesters had all mine entrances entirely blocked by noon. Representatives of the regional district attorney and of Defensoría del Pueblo then arrived and allegedly told the protesters of the legal punishment and economic damage that protesters and Hualgayoc would face for their blockade. A few hours later, the company made several offers to the protesters, but the latter remained in place and were even joined by delegations of Ronderos, for example from Cobro district in San Miguel, throughout the afternoon.[8]

The next morning, at around seven, police shot tear gas at the protesters, fired bullets overhead, and confiscated all the food and kitchen supplies that the protesters had brought. Two protesters and one police officer were reportedly injured during these confrontations. About thirty more people joined from Vista Alegre to support the strike, and by noon, a high-level negotiation commission arrived from Lima, including representatives from the Ministry of Energy and Mines, the regional government, and the regional office of the national police. The negotiations lasted several hours and ended on a five-point commitment from the company to (1) provide free electricity to Hualgayoc within twenty-four hours, using first a temporary feed and then quickly building a permanent integration with the broader electric grid in the surrounding provinces; (2) provide water to the town of Hualgayoc through two cisterns and other long-term water initiatives including sewage and treatment systems; (3) replace its outside workforce with local hires and invest in training programs and related infrastructure; (4) set up a commission to determine whether Gold Fields was responsible for damages on the more than forty houses with infrastructural cracks; and (5) to fund a local environmental monitoring committee, which would be institutionally created by the Ministry of Energy and Mines.

Four days after the two-day strike against Gold Fields, Wilmer Delgado Fernández of the provincial environmental group Asociación Civil Vida Verde en Hualgayoc [roughly, Green Life in Hualgayoc Civil Society Association] made the following public statement:

> Four years after the arrival of this mining company, Hualgayoc didn't have electricity until three months ago and didn't have water until two months ago. There are forty homes affected by open-pit mining explosions only half a kilometer away in direct distance from the population, with dust and polluted water as products of the company's work. And as if this was not enough, with a population totally divided as a product of the mining company's community relations work. So, what happened? Hualgayoc awakened suddenly, two years after the previous strike, and said, "in this house I am the boss," and with over one thousand locals this struggle was initiated against this fierce mine. Whatever was attained may be

> minor, but it is the base to continue fighting and accomplishing the development of this town, which is why we became united, and every day there are more of us in this struggle to save Hualgayoc from this mining company's claws.[9]

In 2010, Walter Barboza Villena and Napoleón Gutiérrez Anticona, who headed the Hualgayoc Socio-Environmental Struggle Committee, traveled to Lima to demand the executive cabinet's attention to what they said were grave environmental issues in their district, naming especially the socio-environmental effects of Gold Fields' operations since 2007. The two Hualgayoc leaders claimed that the Tingo-Maygasbamba headwater was "totally nullified for irrigation and animal herding, according to a report from DIGESA [an agency of the central government's Ministry of Health]." They also denounced that Gold Fields was currently under protection from over two hundred police. As *La república* reported it, the men complained that the mine's tailings dam was at risk of collapsing and flooding, and that company representatives had told locals to "run uphill" in such an event. The two men concluded by issuing a warning: "If we are not heard now, then do not try to point the finger at us when there are consequences."[10]

The consequences, although tragic, were not quite what was expected from this warning. To avoid some concerns about pollution, Gold Fields transported its copper concentrates via road to the Port of Salaverry, where they were shipped for processing elsewhere. It also employed a regional subcontractor to manage the transportation (although, on September 20, 2010, one of these industrial trucks drove off the road, turned over, and spilled the concentrates it carried).[11]

The Peruvian Ministry of Health conducted an evaluation of water quality on the Llaucano River and its main tributaries in 2011. Among the evaluated sites were the Tingo and Maygasbamba rivers, both of which had been the subject of activists' claims for some time. Most locals I spoke with expressed their often-regretful notion that mining was their town's only or best economic activity available, even though they sensed that their rivers were facing negative impacts from Gold Fields' activities. The government's water quality study confirmed that water bodies near the areas occupied by Yanacocha, Minera Corona, Minera San Nicolás, and Gold Fields La Cima were acidic, polluted, and a high risk to local populations. It identified dangerous environmental hazards due to high amounts of cyanide, copper, iron, manganese, mercury, zinc, and lead.[12] However, in the words of the Cajamarca-based analyst Teresa Santillán, the legal definition of "environmental hazards" in Peru (as set by Law No. 28271) is weak. Constraining its operative (or actionable) definition to only residues by "abandoned and inactive" mines, this law "cannot encompass everything that environmental hazards may mean, as it is limited to some of the damage left by abandoned mines, but not the losses to the state, the population, and the environment." Santillán adds that these restrictions ignore the "loss of territory which jeopardizes people's right to health, and to live in a healthy environment, as the Constitution demands."[13]

In addition to work and economic opportunity claims, and to environmental and health concerns, a third major and recurrent source of conflict in this case regards the damage to houses caused, allegedly, by explosive activity at Gold Fields' mine. While it had already been highlighted in protests years earlier, Hualgayoc social leaders, professionals, and residents held a large public meeting on April 3, 2012, in which about 150 participants shared their preoccupation with damage caused by dynamite explosions at the mine, which they said had damaged at least 437 homes. The municipal attorney Jorge Salazar said to Noticias SER that he had technical proof of the damage the company was causing to local homes and infrastructure. Also citing water pollution, locals agreed to demand economic compensation from the company for these damages.

The company responded via its external affairs officer, Rafael Sáenz, who told Noticias SER that Gold Fields had requested that the Ministry of Energy and Mines' environmental supervisory body investigate the matter, and the results of that study had absolved his company of the damages to housing, which were within the "maximum permitted levels in international standards." Sáenz added, "None of them found us responsible." However, the Gold

Fields representative promised to convene a dialogue table between the company, the Ministry of Energy and Mines, the municipality, and the population to find solutions to any issues.[14] A few months later, Gold Fields La Cima's environmental issues director, Luis Alberto Sánchez, expressed to the media emphatically that Gold Fields had never dumped, nor would ever dump, its mine's waste into the Maygasbamba or Tingo Rivers.[15]

The heaviest conflict wave that Gold Fields faced was probably in 2013. The previous year, three of the provinces in central Cajamarca—including Bambamarca—were placed under a "state of emergency" and martial law, including curfews, during the heated conflict over Yanacocha's plans to expand to the Conga lakes. Five protesters had been killed during all of this. This was followed by a massive, nationwide "water march," during which communities from across Peru marched all the way to Lima and held an enormous rally. To be sure, there was an intense air of conflict in Cajamarca, which scaled up and spread to encompass projects even outside the region, like Lagunas Norte. Perhaps inevitably, the Gold Fields mine also got wrapped up in this. First, the Cajamarca federation of Rondas Campesinas approved and organized a region-wide strike that drew more than three thousand people to paralyze several roads for a few days starting on March 10.[16] In its aftermath, on March 23, more than one hundred of its workers shut down activities at Cerro Corona.[17]

In April, *La república* also reported that locals in Hualgayoc rebuked their provincial mayor, Hernán Vásquez Saavedra, for his "duplicitous" posture against Conga while acting as a hired contractor for Gold Fields, to which he had also sold his lands.[18] This illustrated how the atmosphere of distrust and region-wide mining conflicts had seeped into local politics. Then in August, about six hundred protesters blocked the road between Cajamarca and Hualgayoc until 250 riot police dispersed them, arresting the young Rondera leader Yanet Caruajulca and three others.[19] This is especially significant because this same dynamic—protest followed by police dispersal—occurred in every case considered in this study, and yet the Gold Fields conflict is the only one where it did not trigger a turn toward violent collective action by the protesters.

FIGURE 9. Photograph of Gold Fields' Cerro Corona mine, 2016.

The same inter-provincial organizations repeated their 2013 methods in 2015, months after Gold Fields announced plans to expand its operations by 213 hectares, or 13 percent.[20] Furthermore, Defensoría del Pueblo's reports from August and September mentioned Gold Fields as one of fourteen mining companies that had "failed to fulfill its pacts and agreements" with the communities that surround them, leading to renewed conflict.[21] This time around, the Hualgayoc province had just elected a new mayor, Eddy Benavides, one of the most recognizable faces of the Rondas Campesinas' resistance against Conga. From his office in Bambamarca, Benavides and the Rondas organized cross-provincial "monitor and protest" delegations that were charged with visiting all mines located near headwaters in the region. They did not block roads as in 2013, but Hualgayoc protesters organized two more general strikes specifically regarding pollution in the district, which paralyzed the region in June 2015 and May 2016.[22]

The international press largely ignored the massive strike against pollution in 2016. Instead, newspapers such as the *Economist* referred to Gold Fields' Peru operations as an example of multinational mining companies that take "environmental and social responsibilities much more seriously than in the past" and strike "mutually beneficial agreements" with communities, "provided there is trust and goodwill." According to the *Economist*, Gold Fields,

> began by holding many meetings with local people, at which managers explained the project and listened to concerns, . . . promising to employ some locals and train others to use the money they received from the sale of their land to set up service businesses. It brought in an NGO to work with herders to improve pastures, dairy cattle and cheese production. It worked with local mayors to install electricity and drinking water.

The *Economist* cited Miguel Incháustegui, Vice President of Corporate Affairs and Sustainable Development for Gold Fields in Peru (2012–2017), arguing that people protest "because they want things rapidly, they fear missing a golden opportunity," and that "the keys to achieving social consent were to listen more than talk and to ensure that living standards improve."[23]

Company Strategies

Gold Fields' corporate strategy was intentionally devised to start on a different footing. Of course, recognizing this is not meant to erase any mistakes it has made throughout its history in the area. But besides its heavy CSR investment policies, there is a qualitative difference here that is worth noting: company discourses are centered on principles of openness and mutuality. Participant observation in Hualgayoc confirm this sentiment; Gold Fields' provincial managers know people in the town by name, approach them to ask about their families, sit down to eat next to them, and treat people with a great deal of dignity and respect. This may seem minor, but Andean communities are believed to have retained traditional norms and values that place a lot of importance on everyday rules of engagement, courtesy, and deference. Gold Fields has picked up on and intelligently adopted these norms, as is noticeable not only in the relationships of company and community members, but also in Gold Fields rhetorical and discursive practices outside of the community. While other companies are quick to use their access to media to disparage and delegitimize opponents, Gold Fields has an open policy of recognizing opponents' claims as valid. In their media relations, Gold Fields' strategy seems to be to highlight the added, "shared value" that they bring to the town, instead of disparaging or criminalizing detractors.

A crucial and remarkable aspect of this openness is that, while Gold Fields has a private security contract with national police forces since at least 2010,[24] whenever there are conflicts, these officers are usually briefed on the importance of not using physical force against protesters.[25] This has had significant results that make the case distinct from the others in this study (see Table 3). There have been at least three strikes, each accompanied by road blockades, and several demonstrations aimed at the company since 2006, but no property damage has been registered, although some injuries have been reported. During the 2009 two-day strike, a company representative was detained by authorities from the local Rondas Campesinas, but these groups are legally empowered to detain suspects temporarily, so whether this is framed as a kidnapping or not is subject to debate. The fact is that the strike led to serious concessions from the company, which understood the importance of acceding in order to lift the blockade.

Dialogue, Discourse, and Material Conditions

Although perhaps unrelated, Gold Fields *did* face a more violent conflict, in which multiple people died, but only indirectly—by partnering with Buenaventura in a joint venture as Minera Consolidada. Operated by Buenaventura as the senior partner, Consolidada sought to explore mineral deposits near Hualgayoc, in the more elevated and isolated Linda Vista communities. About half of the people there had been opposed to the mine's proposal since 2006. Their resistance grew, and by August 2009 they staged demonstrations and road blockades. However, many people living closer to the site of the mine had already sold their lands, found the offer of jobs alluring, and supported the mine, so during a strike in September, they arrived to confront the mine's detractors. A large contingent of police was dispatched to the area. I cannot confirm the sequence of these events, but the confrontations were lethal. Many were wounded, and police shot and killed a young girl from the area and a young adult protester.[26]

These events bear mentioning because they involved Gold Fields, even if not as the operating partner in the joint venture; but they are also analytically interesting because not even the fiercest of Gold Fields' opponents in Hualgayoc hold them against the company. Many local interviewees, including its two most outspoken opponents, said that this particular firm's relationship with their town had been largely respectful.[27]

At the same time, mining opponents in Hualgayoc have serious claims. One crucial point of conflict has been the damage that controlled explosions at the mine are causing on nearby houses.[28] The closest houses are only about one kilometer away from the epicenter of explosions within Cerro Corona. Their inhabitants have documented their fractured walls and complained to local authorities. However, the mayor at the time of my stay there seemed to have a favorable outlook on mining in the district, and no urgency to address these complaints.[29] More broadly, Cerro Corona and the other mines in the area have left more than one thousand open environmental hazards, which dangerously jeopardize the town's water and more.[30] This is not the work of Gold Fields alone, but it begs the question of who is responsible for cleaning it. And while Hualgayoc has been patient, most of its populace seems to be painfully aware of the immediate and long-term effects of the pollution and is sick of waiting for answers. District activists have organized widely popular strikes in 2013, 2015, and 2016 specifically around these concerns—and around others in 2007 and 2009—but the state has dragged its feet in responding. The "slow violence" of poor peoples' blood poisoning through pollution in the local waterways does not attract the same level of attention as the burning of company machinery did in other cases, but nonetheless the people of Hualgayoc have remained steadfastly nonviolent in their claims.[31]

A sharper criticism of Gold Fields is that, while its large corporate social responsibility budget could help it evade conflicts, its investments into community programs do not reduce the mine's environmental impact and water consumption. As one environmental movement leader told me, the company's openness to dialogue spaces and its investment programs were meant to depoliticize conflict and keep people complacent.[32] This may be significant, as Gold Fields' strong corporate social responsibility programs may actually prevent local groups from mobilizing, making claims, and finding the institutional mechanisms to seek resolution. In the absence of accessible, deliberative, and participatory avenues to resolve conflict nonviolently, resentment is dangerously forced to boil under the surface.

Conclusions: Repackaging Mining and Avoiding Conflict

Toward the end of the Mining Program of Solidarity with the People policy—an executive order from the second García presidency (2006–2011) that exempted companies from taxes on extra earnings made from the boom on mineral prices—the debate about how to tax and distribute mining rents reignited in Peru. Chiming in, Gold Fields La Cima's general director, Juan Luis Kruger, suggested to *Mining Press* that if the rising prices of metals in the world market were to be taken into account in the state's decision to tax these extraordinary profits, then the state should also account for the rising cost of gold production, which he claimed had risen from US$300 per ounce of gold in 2007 to "more than $1,200" by 2012. Kruger encouraged others to share his faith in companies doing the investment work that the state was slower to accomplish.[33] However, the central claims made by protesters in the company's impact area exactly contest this poor distribution of benefits.

Companies are legally responsible for one primary goal, the maximization of its investors' bottom-line economic interests. Therefore, however altruistic their desire to bring local development may be, this economic responsibility to their investors dampens any argument that companies dedicate themselves to the work of service provisions that—at least in the traditional conception of the social contract in liberal democracies like Peru—is the purview and responsibility of the state. Justified by efficiency and "cutting out the middle-person" arguments, the privatization of service provision is antidemocratic. This point is further strengthened by the company's reticence to take responsibility for, or actions to, clean up the thousand environmental hazards in the area or to economically compensate the victims of blood poisoning, both of which would be hugely expensive. In sum, the image of corporate social responsibility might be touted as doing virtuous work with the state to fund and improve local development; this may be beneficial for companies' public relations and economic bottom lines, but firms get this benefit without facing any risk or responsibility for the regular duties of the state.

Far more interestingly for the purposes of this study, Gold Fields' attempts to form amicable relations interpersonally in their everyday interactions with locals—described, in the words of one company officer, as "on sincere grounds from the very first impression"—have been effective at rebuilding trust between the company and a community affected by centuries of mining exploitation.[34] Another Gold Fields officer went further and framed these relationships as "reciprocal" and "horizontal."[35] The "openness" discourse and everyday relationships that are at the heart of Gold Fields' explicit community relations strategy signal that the aggressive policies and discourses in the mainstream of the country are not immutable or inexorable. For example, Gold Fields officers repeatedly mentioned that they welcomed conflict as an opportunity.

Companies' agency—including their strategies of engagement as well as their discourses—may be a crucial variable that makes the difference between violent conflict and nonviolent civil resistance, and the difference between this case and the others. However, these efforts merely occlude an ongoing and largely unaddressed environmental tragedy. Through heavy investment in local contracts and development projects, and by fabricating the illusion of friendliness, equality, and reciprocity or horizontality in everyday relationships, the company renders locals' complaints delegitimized, denied, framed as unnecessarily adversarial, and harder to mobilize around as demands for better conditions. These practices are subtle and unattended forms of manipulation, power, discipline, and control, which reify and yet occlude the unbalanced relationships between impoverished locals and a profit-driven transnational corporation.

Finally, Gold Fields' actions in Peru cannot be entirely abstracted from the company's actions in other places. For example, although well known for its social responsibility in Cajamarca and throughout Peru's mining industry, the firm responded to a workers' wildcat strike (conducted by rank-and-file union workers, against union leadership seen as collaborating with the company) at its South African gold mines KDC East and KDC West by firing ten thousand of the mines' employees after the strikers refused a company ultimatum to return to work. The Associated Free Press noticed how Gold Fields' competitors (some of the top producers in the mining industry, AngloGold Ashanti and Harmony) learned from and adapted this ultimatum strategy to address similar strikes at their own mines. Moreover, Gold Fields was also entangled in a similar struggle near its Abosso mine in Ghana in 2018, when it fired 340 striking workers.[36]

Studying this case is useful, whether reading it from the perspective of a mining company looking to resolve strikes or improve corporate community-relations strategies, or from the viewpoint of an activist interested in what makes resistance effective. For conflict mediators, drawing various lessons from the Gold Fields case is productive especially in the quality of its conflict response (with a tame form of police repression), deliberation and negotiation spaces (and large investment budgets), and its practice of actually following up on its commitments. This is particularly interesting in contrast to, for example, Barrick's style of transactional negotiation, which seems to have locked Barrick into a pattern of recurrent conflict, a routinized means of forcing the company and the state onto a negotiation table.

What else explains these differences? This case study helps to highlight that a part of the answer to this question is both in the way its managers publicly frame their community conflicts and in their everyday relationships with community members. Gold Fields engages in a different discourse. Not wholly unproblematic (especially insofar as they help to conceal various forms of mining-related environmental and structural violence while legitimizing the mine's operations), the company's strategies and discourses are a lot more open and less repressive and criminalizing than those adopted by other companies I studied. It is perhaps this difference that has shaped the nonviolent character of their local conflicts. Especially in contrast to the process of conflict in the other cases, Gold Fields' behavior appears to reinforce the idea that discursive contestation is crucial to understand the reasons why some protests against mining are more violent than others.

CONCLUSION

Extractive Effects, Violence, and the Role of Outsiders

It is not the tyrannized who initiate despotism.

PAULO FREIRE[1]

I opened this book by noting the high risks faced by land and environmental defenders today, especially in Latin America. To be clear, there are good reasons to question assertions such as "Latin America is the deadliest place in the world for environmental activists." For starters, the data is underreported and incomplete. Additionally, there are competing definitions of who counts as an environmental and land activist; for example, were not most of the people who fought against the invading US army in Vietnam defending their land? Databases and coders also differ in their definitions of violence; for example, most consider only deaths. It could be that this "rising trend" refers simply to the growing popularity of these issues and is but a reflection of increasing reporting about it as well as the unavailability of data from earlier periods. Moreover, it is possible that violence against environmental activists in some places is merely a function of overall growth in the general homicide rate in those areas and therefore not an ecological-only problem.[2]

Despite these detail-level disputes, there is widespread agreement that this trend of violence against environmental defenders is undeniable and critical—however one defines and measures such concepts. Names such as that of Chico Méndes (in Brazil), Ken Saro

Wiwa (in Nigeria), and Berta Cáceres (in Honduras) are recognizable among cases used to represent this issue. However, there is also a risk in personalizing the problem around a handful of known martyrs, who are among possibly millions of others who have suffered similar fates; for example, at least two other activists from Berta Cáceres' organization have been also killed: Lesbia Yaneth Urquía and Nelson García. Furthermore, while these kinds of killings —and the inspiring lives of those few we know about—have been the impetus of this work since I began thinking about it in 2011, conducting this study has forced me to realize how an overemphasis on murders can both highlight and obscure the many other forms of injury, harassment, intimidation, and coercion that environmental activists face more broadly and much more routinely. This research seeks to expand understandings of environmental justice and violence. Beyond attention-grabbing events such as confrontations with police, arson, property damage, and assassinations of leaders, this study centers on, and is motivated by, countless stories of hope, suffering, uncertainty, and survival that I heard and witnessed during my research.

This final chapter returns to my theoretical arguments in light of the evidence presented in the previous four case studies and their comparison. In these closing (but not necessarily conclusive) reflections, the chapter summarizes this study's insights in direct response to the following questions: What causes conflicts to escalate into violence? What does violence do, and how does it shape the outcomes of conflicts? Finally, how can it be prevented or channeled? Then, the chapter also zooms out to consider the implications, contributions, and limitations of this research in the broader task of understanding and preventing violent conflicts over natural resource extraction.

What Causes Escalation into Violence? Company Strategies and Resistance

First, this research contributes to a rich literature on natural resource politics by demonstrating the little-studied importance of corporate strategies in explaining protesters' use of violence. It is not that companies operate in environments or among cultures pre-disposed to certain repertoires of collective action that immediately include violence. Rather, the agency of company actors in their approaches and responses to community actors—at the level of corporate decision making as well as in everyday interactions—is key to understanding why some conflicts over mining in Peru become more violent than others.

My within-case process-tracing and the cross-case comparison shows that companies that are more repressive, and whose local agents treat their host communities with arrogance, encourage anger and provoke escalation from opponents. Likewise, the opposite is true: it is much harder for social movements to justify any use of violent tactics against companies that pacify locals with heavy investment and train their employees to address locals with respect. This counters the dominant narratives I heard, especially from people sympathetic to mining, that the presence or absence of outside agitators like NGOs feed the escalation of social movement tactics. Movements adopted tactics that could be framed as violent, such as property damage, whether or not they counted on outside supporters. In actuality, as I have argued, they may be doing so precisely because they seek outside attention and the opportunities this may bring.

In each case that experienced acts of violence committed by actors within social movements, this was directly triggered by coercive, repressive, and arrogant behavior from company agents. The company that refused repression and was most open, Gold Fields, has fared most successfully, whereas the company that used little pacification (petty philanthropy, like pencil and notebook giveaways) and relied mostly on arrogance and repression, Manhattan Minerals, fared by far the worst in terms of both encouraging violent escalation and in the project's ultimate defeat.

Additionally, the responses and agency of local groups help to explain, in combination with company strategies of engagement, the ultimate outcome of each project. Company strategies have a strong influence on social movements' choice of tactics, but not a determinative one. Internal characteristics of the groups contesting mining projects can make the difference in the result of each case. These factors include groups' modes of organization, preferences (e.g., whether they support, reluctantly accept, or refuse mining, and why), power constructs like race or gender, composition and decision-making processes, and their learning over time—from their own histories, through various campaigns or waves of conflict, and from other cases.

Two cases illustrate this well. In Tambogrande, where a widely representative movement used its outside supporters and overall favorable media attention to scale up its resistance, and where it decidedly and persuasively shifted to a creative and nonviolent strategy, the mine's opponents won an uphill battle against state-backed transnational capital. In the case of Cerro Corona, where the multinational company used a strong corporate social responsibility effort to dissuade and incorporate its opponents, and where media coverage of the social movement has been minimal, the protest organizers had little means to scale up, encourage resistance, and gain leverage. Therefore, despite serious claims shared widely by locals, the company has skirted its opposition, for now.

This study shed light on the public relations and corporate social responsibility strategies that effectively depoliticize conflict, allowing companies to postpone and avoid local tensions without having to seriously alter their fundamental governance structure, their extraction processes, or their budgets. Companies like Gold Fields, Barrick, Buenaventura, and Newmont deploy such strategies to permeate their economic goals into the most intimate human spaces—interpersonal relationships, identity, memory, and everyday encounters. (In fact, Minera La Zanja produced an illustrated children's book, titled *Our Identity*, about Cajamarca's myths, legends, and folklore. Buenaventura heir and vice-president Raúl Benavides Ganoza gifted me a copy when I interviewed him at the company's headquarters.) One could perceive this as an insidious, hidden-but-purposeful way of disciplining behavior and establishing a politics of domination by other means.

Similarly, one of the most interesting findings of this study is that the companies that used strong CSR investment alongside repressive strategies to stifle opponents—a mix of coercion and persuasion—generated a pattern of recurrent conflict in their vicinities. I have referred to this as a routinization of conflict, where a cycle of intensification and pacification becomes a part of the relationship and modes of engagement between companies and local groups seeking some benefit redistribution. In the two cases that showcased this, La Zanja and Lagunas Norte, conflict has intensified roughly every two years in a similar cycle: tensions escalate; confrontation and repression ensue, followed by dialogue, negotiation, company promises, and unmet expectations; then, as may be expected, tensions rise again. This offers important lessons to companies and the state, as well as conflict mediators and reconciliation advocates, for it challenges the assumption that repression is a useful or effective method of waging conflict.

These findings also contribute to the literature on repression, especially arguments that it can backfire, because they show how repression interacts with its opposite strategy, concessions—something generally undertheorized in extant studies of repression and backfire.[3] This study shows that repression feeds resentment and distrust; when combined with concessions and pacification as rewards, it not only backfires (which is taken to mean that it encourages further resistance) but also institutionalizes conflict into the routine life and fabric of community and company relations, rendering attempts at durable resolution extremely difficult.

What Does Violence Do? Media, Attention, and the Roles of Outsiders

The second major theme in this thesis is what I have termed the politics of attention, which I have argued is a crucial factor to understand why conflicts escalate to violence. Social responses to conflict have an overwhelmingly immediate, event-driven, and sensationalist bias. Whereas violence excels at grabbing public attention, there is generally a lack of attention to structural sources of conflict, procedural issues, and everyday aggressions and relationships, which therefore remain unresolved. These mutual dynamics can be explained using Henri Lefebvre's idea of the "double construction" of social space—a process always manipulated and contested through power relations—which creates narratives of "reality" based on experiences and subconscious actions that structurally highlight what is desirable, convenient, and expedient, while simultaneously ignoring or occluding what is not.[4]

This discursive construction of mining spaces in Peru was illustrated in my interviews as well as through the dynamics I observed in the field. For example, the mining industry is heavily involved in public relations and discourse-shaping, promoting the idea that mega mining is "new"—to distance itself from the reputation of the "old" mines—as well as technologically advanced, socially responsible, environmentally safe, and so on. This helps to give cover and legitimacy to their activities' negative impacts, environmental, social, economic, and political. Politicians of various stripes and at all levels, municipal to national, also become invested in these narratives, because they can rely on mining to boast about rising revenues, public budgets, and gross domestic product (GDP) rates, and they can mobilize incoming investment into their pet projects, which may help them and their factions win reelections. When the hegemonic discourses in favor of mining are so powerful, companies gain cover and legitimacy, and their opponents are more easily discredited as corrupt, ignorant, or manipulated. More generally, company strategies are aimed at avoiding and concealing conflict in the short term. This is successful most of the time—that is, until an outbreak or spectacle can disrupt that semblance of peace. Therefore, these understudied aspects and dynamics highlight the importance of corporate strategies of conflict management in shaping what gets categorized as violent, nonviolent, and not-violent.

Most people involved in and affected by Peru's mining conflicts disapprove of violence. However, my field research and the materials I collected demonstrated clearly that actors on different sides of conflict "use" violence in one way or another. Especially as a discourse, violence is used strategically to generate symbolic and material benefits. Violence is, in other words, an instrument to leverage opportunities at least rhetorically, thanks to the attention generated by events classified as violent.

The favorable attention that companies work hard to cultivate (e.g., through CSR and other media strategies) is disrupted by violent protest, which draws attention, forces state intervention, and pressures companies to renegotiate. Violent protest may serve to break the seeming stability and upset the status quo. It is often adopted as a means of protest when people perceive that institutional mechanisms will be ineffective in addressing their grievances, and when the stakes are high enough for them to risk willingly the repression that will likely follow. They thus engage in acts such as property destruction, because they have more to gain from upsetting the status quo than companies, whereas the latter bank on avoiding and silencing conflict. Furthermore, this status quo is not nonviolent until spectacles of violence break out—rather, the violence contained in the everyday, as I have detailed in this study and I will summarize below, is selectively and unconsciously unnoticed by media, the state, civil society actors, academics, and would-be spectators.

Where local movements use violence to draw attention, outside actors tend to reinforce this dynamic. Because they are usually reluctant to get involved, but they quickly respond to explosive moments of confrontation, outsider actors—including media, the state, and conflict mediators—and even company agents end up adding credence to the idea that violence is necessary to bring attention, to reframe the narrative and show that not all is well, and to extract some sort of compensation or benefits. In the end, the results are mixed: despite various forms of retaliation that ensue—such as state and private violence, intimidation, repression, and criminalization—protesters sometimes get tangible results from rupturing the status quo through their conflict escalation tactics and dangerous forms of contestation.

How Can Violence Be Prevented? Discourse, Affect, and the Everyday

The third thematic focus of this study borrows from the concept of "everyday" politics, developed at length predominantly by Black women, women of color, feminist, and postcolonial authors over the past four decades especially (and even earlier).[5] Understanding the politics of attention described above carries conceptual and methodological implications in the study of violence. These findings call to question the overreliance on events as opposed to processes that are more routine and quotidian. They challenge those interested in conflict and its resolution to expand and criticize taken-for-granted definitions of violence.

Event-driven logics are analytical obstacles that lead to problematic conclusions. Interrogating the event-bias of the literature, of state and media reactions, and of mediators can help direct efforts toward ordinary complaints and tensions. If focusing only on explosive events is part of the problem that leads to violent outbreaks—limiting analyses of conflict, leading to erroneous conclusions, and weakening responses to it—then questioning how violence operates beneath the surface will increase the potential to understand and prevent it. Quotidian interactions, everyday relations, and routine processes matter. Understanding everyday violence can help to deliver better results in channeling conflict before it breaks out into open, physical violence. Doing this well requires immersive and reflexive methods of analysis. Methodologically speaking, this means privileging subtle processes traditionally unattended by aggregate data, distant coding, and superficial analyses, and instead foregrounding the voices and experiences of those closest to the problem. It means doing in-depth, qualitative, critical, and engaged research, wherein the use of violence as a discourse and its representations, including by researchers and our interlocutors, are suspect and not taken for granted. Furthermore, gaining deeper understandings requires reading official sources between the lines, or "against the grain."[6]

Violence should be conceived of as a quotidian process, a phenomenon that precedes and outlives explosive confrontations. What violence is, what it means to people, how it is contested, and how it can be prevented, are contingent and contextual. Violence is both a structural occurrence (constructed over time through institutions as well as unconscious actions) and a phenomenon embodied in micro-politics and people's material conditions. Just as it is material, it is also symbolic and discursive, part of the contested creation of "what is" through narratives, stories, and representations. Finally, it may manifest for various rational as well as affective reasons: it is provoked by anger, deep-seated resentment and distrust, feelings of inequity and injustice, arrogance, hatred, and love (e.g., for one's land or way of living); likewise, it is also adopted for reasons of expediency, self-interest, and political machination.

Everyday life in Peru's postcolonial and post-conflict context is marked by lingering and unresolved issues of historical exclusion and systematic discrimination, especially racism, colorism, sexism, classism, heteronormativity, ableism, ageism, and more.[7] Understanding these aspects of life and politics, understated in traditional analyses of mining conflicts, is crucial in addressing the escalation of violence. Discursive othering—the creation of exclusive social categories through narratives—serves to build the impression that violence is legitimate: for example, state and corporate violence against protesters is argued as necessary because the victims are framed and treated as evil, dangerous enemies of the national development project, worthless, criminal, irredeemable, and either ungrievable or, worse, worth eliminating. Hegemonic notions of development are not separate from these forms of exclusion and violence.

Legitimizing and delegitimizing discourses are also mediated by contested perspectives about what "is real," which in turn are clouded by doubt, distrust, rumor, and conspiracy. For example, mining supporters often repeated their belief that outside agitators, European environmentalist organizations, and Chilean mining companies were profiting from conflict and actively working to stop mining projects in Peru. Similarly, some distrustful locals and activists made conspiratorial claims—some more believable than others (especially because cases of private security operations against activists, as well as US embassy involvement in Peru's resource conflicts, have been documented[8])—about how secret police, the US Central Intelligence Agency, and companies' private security actors were orchestrating operations to infiltrate, intimidate, and murder dissidents. Without giving unverified conspiracy theories any credence, they matter in this analysis because it is precisely out of these internalized animosities, these rumors and distrust, that extra-institutional and violent forms of conflict grow. Even half-truths, hyperbole, and empty rhetoric, when they resonate with our socialization, prejudices, and preconceptions, can be internalized into our thinking, altering our values over time.

Contested scientific knowledge was similarly crucial in each case: health indicators and reports of pollution clearly contributed to activist fervor around La Zanja, Lagunas Norte, and Cerro Corona. In Tambogrande, a technical study of the impacts of mining, conducted by a mining expert and hydrologist from a Canadian university, became an organizing instrument for the people opposed to the mining project. On the other hand, mining companies produced and disseminated pseudo-science to discredit opponents; for example, Barrick created water-monitoring reports arguing that contamination was below levels of accepted risk, but their methodologies were challenged as dubious and misleading by biologists at the regional capital's universities.

Furthermore, just as claims to scientific authority and corporate responsibility are part and parcel of mining supporters' strategies, discourse is equally important in resistance movements. One of the main lessons that activists can take away from this analysis is that altering hegemonic discourses through creative means that resonate with the broader population can be the most productive way to turn scrutiny to their favor. Some concrete ways in which this was manifested, especially in Tambogrande, include playing protest cumbia music during road blockades and disruptive events, which kept people engaged and in good spirits, or dressing up in colorful costumes during direct actions, drawing overall on cultural identity symbols (e.g., limes in ceviche).

In short, language contestation factors into how state, corporate, and civil society actors conceive of and promote ideas such as development, citizenship, conflict, and justice. As long as rhetoric emerges from and reinforces exclusionary biases, distrust, and structural animosities, which are built historically and reproduced in everyday life, the likelihood of violent escalation will hardly be reduced. This is especially troubling and significant in terms of building durable solutions and mechanisms to transform conflict, given that preventing violence and channeling conflict nonviolently require the direct engagement of institutions that are credible, impartial, and effective. Institutions are built on trust; institutional strength is dependent not only on their much-emphasized availability of resources, but also on the public's faith in them. Therefore, distrust makes democratic institutional building very difficult. Relationships built from fear, misinformation, duplicity, bait-and-switch, and everyday antagonism are powerful obstacles to the goals of preventing violent conflict and building peace. Without trustworthy and active mechanisms to redirect disputes, build mutual recognition, and ensure participatory negotiation, the resort to violence will endure.

Likewise, dialogue is inherent in peaceful conflict transformation and social reconciliation, but the language of dialogue has been subverted to conceal the claims at the root of conflict, papering over them. Dialogue spaces meant to pacify conflict in the short term (involving excessive foot-dragging and intentionally exhausting the claimants in the process) tend to exacerbate the perception that violent direct action is the only way to resolve unequal power relations.

Conflict has the potential to unleash conversations and practices to resolve tensions, and to arrive at alternative models of organizing societies and conceiving of their progress. The ability to hone these opportunities greatly depends on how states and companies respond to conflicts. They may seek to quell these conflicts through institutional half-measures, attempts to buy off the population, or the use of repression to force compliance, but in order to truly appreciate and take advantage of the potential of resource-based or other socio-environmental conflicts, it is necessary to hear the voices of those engaged in them, instead of assuming their self-interested motives. As long as actors see conflicts as events in need of short-term extinguishing, not reflections and symptoms of structural causes and ways of thinking, they will continue to deny themselves the transformative opportunities that emerge from the outbreak of conflict.

Concrete institutional design proposals that may be drawn from this study include at least five points. First, serious consideration should be given to strengthening plebiscite or popular consultation processes, although these are vulnerable to corruption and cooptation. Second, another valuable option, already underway in many Peruvian regions, is land-use planning, known in Peru as the interrelated instruments of territorial ordering and ecological and economic *zonification*. These participatory processes demarcate areas that could and should (if locals demand this overwhelmingly) be reserved from mining activities, at least open-pit mining. In Cajamarca, I noticed how they were feared by mining lobbies, which aimed to delegitimize and subvert these zoning mechanisms. Third, companies would do well to train their employees not only on company-community relations, but also basic human rights. Fourth, a possible reform involves restrictions on the use of cyanide, mercury, and similar poisonous substances in the gold refinement process. Finally, countries like Peru can go beyond seriously revising open-pit mining laws, greatly increasing taxes on it, and revamping participatory methods of benefit redistribution, to considering a ban on it altogether, as lawmakers in El Salvador and Costa Rica achieved in 2017 and 2010 respectively.[9]

Contributions, Limitations, and Future Research Agenda

How does this matter? How are people outside of Peru implicated in the broader ecology and economy of resource extraction and the many lives of gold? What are the roles of local-to-international actors in these conflicts? This study analyzed two different outcomes: first, why conflicts escalate to violence, and second, what leads each case to its current status or results. The answers found here for both of these questions can be useful to residents in Peru's mining communities, activists organizing against oppression in other contexts, and especially people resisting extractive projects; to civil society beyond those localities, especially as consumers and participants of globalized economies and societies; to people working within the state in its various levels and agencies; and to extractive industry actors. There is much to be gained from studying these patterns.

This research expands and complicates our understanding of the forms of violence that environmental defenders face, it illustrates how people are responding to these, and it interrogates the practices that lend greater attention to some forms of violence over others. In tracing causal mechanisms leading to violent escalation and to resolution, this study also assists policymakers in the design of effective institutions that can channel conflict, gives international actors the understandings to best direct resources toward preventing violence, equips companies with tools to protect their investment by understanding how to build durable and mutual community relations, and helps civil society in promoting forms of development that match well with local needs and aspirations.

In addition to dispelling some of the myths surrounding discourses of mining in Peru—including criminalizing notions that portray protesters as "inclined to use violence" whereas in fact their self-restraint, pacific actions, and patience against the violence levied upon them is far more prevalent[10]—this theory-building study has generated a number of hypotheses that I hope will be useful. For one, international solidarity might have an effect on cases' outcomes and movements' victory, but not necessarily on the capacity, willingness, or likelihood that protesters use violent tactics, contrary to the speculations of many interviewees and the expectations in extant literature. In the Tambo Grande case, international solidarity was present before the escalation to the violent confrontation, and rather than abandoning the local movement, outside allies held on steadfastly to their support for the movement even after this outbreak. In fact, external solidarity increased after repression triggered an undisciplined response from the protesters, and after the killing of a leader. Second, media attention might help movements scale up and succeed, but it does not determine their choices to engage in or eschew low-level violent tactics like property damage. For instance, cases where media was totally criminalizing also exhibited movement attempts to transform tactics away from violence. Third, the strongest and most direct explanation for the adoption of violent tactics are the corporate strategies of community relations—of approach, persuasion, reaction, repression, and co-optation.

These insights are also applicable in other cases, especially in Peru, where there is no shortage of new conflicts to analyze and address—many of them involving the same companies and regions that I investigated here. I especially believe that the lessons drawn from this study can be applied to understanding and confronting other cases of conflict over gold mining in Peru, such as Cañaris, Shahuindo, and Michiquillay. Companies should learn to refrain from repression, train employees in human rights issues, and redistribute wealth.

Through my reading, travels, observations, and conversations, many themes and separate cases arose as potential avenues to branch out from this research in future analyses. In this study I have focused on very specific research questions: why mining conflicts escalate to violence, and what explains their ultimate outcomes. In answer to these questions, I have found ultimately the importance of dynamics that accompany company strategies and conflict routinization, the politics of attention, and the various forms of unattended violence that surround extractive conflicts. With due caution not to overstate this, these questions of resistance tactics, the escalation into violence, conflict resolution, and the task of building sustainable development may also apply beyond Peru, and beyond extractive conflicts. The theory built through this analysis can and should be tested against more cases to measure their application. My own future work will also expand this research, building on the partnerships I built during the course of this study to continue examining forms of violence in Latin America's extractive sectors, mining and otherwise. Overall, this book moves forward a broader research agenda on political ecology, violence, resistance, and social justice.

Zooming Out: Lessons for Environmental Justice Everywhere

All over Latin America, the legacy of Chico Méndes and Berta Cáceres remains alive through the thousands of people who have taken up their mantle and are risking everything to preserve their environments, such as the three Garífuna women leaders murdered in Honduras in September 2019, or the Indigenous Amazonian peoples who are resisting state-sponsored violence meant to displace them from their lands, which are coveted by transnational capital, cattle-ranchers, illegal loggers, miners, and soy bean corporations. And their fight is intimately linked with that of others well outside of the region: the thousands of farmers who commit suicide each year in India as a result of getting pushed aside and into debt by the encroachment of transnational corporations that have created monopolies on food, the farmers in Central Africa who are fighting back against elephant poachers, and the grandmother in the Philippines who was gunned down for organizing her community against a toxic coal stockpile.

People refer to environmental activism nowadays as a suicide mission, particularly in countries that emerge from colonialism with export-dependent economies and weak institutions. These tend to be areas where powerful actors can silence their opponents with impunity. However, violence over natural resources is not limited to these places. Furthermore, these localized dynamics are increasingly tied to globalized commodity chains, and so conflicts over natural resources challenge traditional formulations of distance and space. They engage and link people in various spaces, from the places of extraction to those of retail, consumption, and waste. For example, there is gold in almost every electronic device, and millions of these end up in the world's waste piles every year. Therefore, the idea that extractive sites are remote, or somehow removed from this book and its readers, should be suspect.

Ultimately, this is a global and pressing matter—not because of political or even economic reasons, but because unsustainable resource governance threatens the entire biosphere. Resource

FIGURE 10. **Photograph of protests against extractivism in Lima, October 2015.**

conflicts involve everyone and impact everything, no matter how far away those places of extraction and those conflicts may seem to be. Through participatory research, my work documents, describes, and theorizes lessons from those struggles. Studying resource conflicts in depth can help to unlock wider debates, relevant across the globe, about democratization, the role of the market, the viability of dominant models of social and economic organization, and the future of the planet.

At the same time, the full complexity of these conflicts cannot be reduced to a good and evil story, which would contribute only superficially. Learning the intricacies of these conflicts, in their particular contexts, is much more useful, as it produces actionable knowledge. This is what my work aims to do. It contextualizes the localized dynamics of structural forces, and it highlights the agency of people traditionally undermined by the academic mainstream. Their theorizing and their actions can be invaluably instructive for people involved in similar struggles for sustainability, peace, and justice.

Appendix 1: Theoretical Underpinnings

The recent, tremendous expansion of extractive industries in the global South has fed and enriched theoretical debates about the causes of extraction-related conflicts. Common explanations, from within as well as outside Peru, can be roughly classified according to their focal points: institutions, structures, and agents. These are worth unpacking briefly here.

One strand of research points to the negative impacts of resource abundance on democracy and development. These negative impacts are not only ecological, in the form of pollution, nor only social, in the form of healthcare, but also political and economic, in forms such as corruption, diminished democratic confidence, decreased scores in human development indicators, and anemic state institutions.[1] A large body of works has elaborated these outcomes as different aspects of the "resource curse," a theoretical framework that describes these negative effects in resource-wealthy states with weak and exclusionary institutions, which is especially the case in former colonies. Scholars have drawn on these frameworks to explain conflicts specifically within the Peruvian context,[2] and practitioners of conflict mediation confirm the important role played by the state's eroded credibility as an impartial mediator of company-community relations.[3] However, resource curse literature sees violence merely as one of the possible side effects of institutional fragility and has paid little attention to the specific ways that social actors choose among the full range of strategies and tactics available.

Structural explanations center on the unequal distribution of the benefits and burdens of extraction[4] and on social and economic dislocations.[5] Meanwhile, studies of agency highlight competition among local factions,[6] environmental ideologies,[7] and claims about autonomy and identity. [8] Literatures on collective action and subnational conflict are also instructive. Explanations for the general incidence of collective or political violence draw attention to the importance of historical and contextual factors,[9] social and economic structures,[10] leadership, emotions, and meanings,[11] institutional exclusion and unrepresentative political systems,[12] a desire for self-determination,[13] the perceived efficacy or rationality of violence,[14] and environmental factors such as resource scarcity—but scarcity-based analyses are over-deterministic and often racist, providing cultural assumptions and generalizations instead of explanations.[15] Finally, some scholars have also suggested that the nature of the resources at stake, their value, and the cost-benefit of their extraction and transportation affect conflict dynamics.[16]

Alternatively, literature on nonviolent or civil resistance merges the ground between structure and agency, presenting a ground-up framework to study the ideas, conversations, learning environments, institutions, practices, and symbolic systems of non-elites who are moved into political action, even despite their cultural or political differences and regardless of the risk of violent repression or authoritarianism.[17] Civil resistance literature suggests that attention to social movement's internal processes—including leadership structures, cohesion, decision-making, and collective learning—may explain their transformation from violent and spontaneous actions to organized, sustained, "disciplined," and intentionally nonviolent resistance.[18] For instance, Wendy Pearlman has argued that activist groups can sometimes build cohesion and discipline to remain nonviolent, despite intensifying political pressure and even violence from actors with more influence or firepower.[19] As broad as the bodies of literature on subnational conflicts and on resource conflicts have become, each field and the spaces between them remain incomplete in important ways, as I write in Chapter 1 and in Appendix 2.

Appendix 2: Notes on Methodology and Methods

This annex examines critically what it might mean to conceive violence as a subject of study. The pages that follow unfold in four sections. In the first part, I draw on my research and anchor the chapter on epistemological and conceptual reflections about the study of violence, and I offer some critiques of traditional approaches. Next, I question my position and ethics as a researcher, an "outsider" in Peru, and a student of conflict in other peoples' lives, and how these are reflected in all these choices—for example, my choice to scrutinize actors in the mining industry, as opposed to only social movements, is informed both by the lack of attention to them in extant studies and by my position as a white-skinned, non-Peruvian male, which granted me unprecedented access to interviews with numerous players in the corporate sector.

Departing from this discussion, I propose a qualitative and participatory logic that may guide this and future inquiries, and that may hold greater transformative potential in its approach to understand and prevent violence. In a nutshell, the methodology I propose consists of a balance between, on the one hand, an in-depth, specific, and thick understanding of cases, and on the other, a comparative and explanatory look at patterns beyond one site. Then I zoom in to specify the methods by which I collected the data for this study and the methods I used to analyze it systematically.

The final section summarizes the analytical advantages of this methodology, and it provides some closing remarks on the social, ethical, and humanitarian commitments generated by these epistemological choices.

Human Conflict and the Social Life of Violence

Concepts are malleable objects, constructs perpetually in motion across times and spaces, and contested sites of power. The same concept is articulated and positioned within the logic of widely diverse ideologies and worldviews. From general understandings to situation-specific uses, their performances—that is, how they act through the meanings imparted onto, perceived from, and mis-transmitted by them—richly vary, even within the same cultural and historical context.[1] For example, *freedom* means different things to members of the same group of investment bankers collaborating on an oil pipeline, and their interpretations may also differ from those of a member of the Wet'suwet'en nation on whose land the pipeline is being proposed. Likewise, sustainability and even the discourse of peace are often appropriated by neocolonial actors who hope to promote their so-called universal values through the same process of domination that interrupted local visions and understandings of sustainable peace.

Perhaps no concept is more morally and emotionally confusing than the label "violence" and its cognates.[2] Such confusion is conceptual, ethical, and quite common—perhaps understandably, given the politicized nature of a term such as violence, which sells so well, entertains so easily, and can mean so many things. The categorization of events as violent is often used to delegitimize certain groups, practices, and actions. On the other hand, the use of the label can help to bring attention, moral outrage, and action against violations of human dignity. Therefore, toward the goal of transforming and preventing violence, there is an important use of the term, for in order to correct an injustice, societies must have the language to recognize it. Despite its politicized nature, it holds important analytical and juridical utility. To retrieve and reanimate this utility, it is necessary to disentangle the concept, take as few things for granted as possible, and critically assess its "social life."[3]

Explanations of violence cluster around either macro-structural or idiosyncratic factors. Among literature that has explained patterns of human violence in diverse settings and through multiple approaches, the strongest explanations treat violence with skepticism, rather than assuming universal interpretations of the concept. These works attend to the contextualized, contingent ways in which the word is constructed and deployed, as well as to the political, economic, and social relations that it generates.[4] However, such studies are a small minority within the literature. What dominates instead is an objectivist approach to violence—a paradigm that is either intentionally or unconsciously problematic, for at least a couple of reasons. First, a common problem is the propensity for over-determination. For example, while attention to peoples' grievances is useful, these have existed in much of the world, at various times, but they have rarely led people to violence.[5] Second, most of these kinds of works mistakenly conceive of conflict as equivalent with violence, and thus ignore how resource conflicts might escalate and intensify in nonviolent ways.[6] A third and more fundamental problem in dominant studies is that they see violence from the sterile and unreflexive lens of positivism, an ontological and epistemological stance centered on the firm belief in objective scientific authority.[7] Positivism, in its preference for detachment as opposed to commitment to the people and life under scientists' microscopes, is often unreflexive about the politics of research and knowledge.

These potential issues do not mean that the term *violence* is any less useful, or that studying it is any less important. Rather, they challenge us to realize that, through serious reflection about the construction of violence in both its material and discursive manifestations, we may develop greater leverage against these obstacles to social justice and sustainable peace. Although undervalued and discounted in mainstream social science, careful and reflexive analysis may be far more productive than obsessing about treating every argument as if it had an equally valid counter-position. Alongside requiring a complex conceptualization of violence, these alternatives call for positional and engaged methods, rather than distant and statistical coding. More than simply a matter of choice, this critical framework may provide greater analytical and practical tools to understand and dismantle various forms of violence.

Despite the richness of literature on violence, its over-prediction, narrow conceptualizations, and detached analyses thwart the potential of studies to understand, transform, and prevent it. Interviewees shared with me a complex picture of what violence meant in different contexts and to different people, which requires reconceptualization and re-theorization. To understand violence, it is important to ask not only where it originates but also what it *does*. How do people experience, perceive, and give meanings to it? How do its various forms shape their broader practices and their rules of conflict engagement? Knowing how it manifests symbolically and materially can help develop new tools to prevent it from flaring well in advance of its eruption.

Methodology

If studies of this complicated phenomenon are to move beyond event-driven foci toward a process-based analysis, then they must account for its contexts, its construction, and for the relationships, networks, and legacies it generates, none of which should be taken for granted.[8] It is therefore necessary to conduct immersive, thick, and in-depth analyses that can trace these processes and dynamics in a grounded way.[9] However, the sheer number of active resource conflicts in Latin America and the rest of the world demonstrate common patterns that deserve inspection. Comparison across cases can be helpful in drawing insights and explanations that may be transported to and useful in other similar contexts. This study therefore merges ethnographic within-case analysis with a controlled comparison of four cases, as I detail in this section.

One-third of the world's mining investment concentrates in Latin America. For Peru, where mineral commodities represent about 65 percent of the country's export income, the global mining boom and the influx of foreign investment have transformed it into one of the world's fastest growing economies. Given the large number and variation of Peru's mining conflicts, it is a prime context in which to study these issues, especially at the subnational level.[10]

As a result of two processes that Peru and many Latin American countries have adopted (to different extents) in recent decades, liberalization and decentralization, subnational politics are of increasing importance. The slow devolution of power to Peru's municipal and regional governments means they have growing autonomy to administer local needs and budgets, attract foreign investment, and respond to local conflicts. And in addition to their growing political importance, subnational units offer unique strengths methodologically: to borrow a term from Richard Snyder, the "scaling down" of comparisons to local levels promises a more grounded and accurate analysis, which can produce finer inferences about complex processes and causal mechanisms.[11]

A comparison that is not guided by careful case justification will fall short of its potential.[12] To narrow the case selection, I began by focusing on conflicts over gold extraction in the north of Peru, and on conflicts that were active between 2000, when Alberto Fujimori's authoritarian regime unraveled and Peru began transitioning to democracy, and 2015, the year when I began my fieldwork. These choices helped to control for a number of factors and center my attention on the key mechanisms driving these conflicts' different outcomes. For instance, dynamics of conflicts that have taken place since the return to democracy might have been different under authoritarianism. Also, there is good reason to believe that conflicts over dams do not develop in the same ways or through similar mechanisms as conflicts over logging, natural gas, or mining, all of which, although related (e.g., dams are often built to provide electricity for nearby mines), are governed by different legal regimes, discourses, cultural values, and often, state agencies.[13] Finally, none of the cases are located within communities explicitly identified as Indigenous (nor recognized by the state as such, a struggle for which would entail another layer of complexity and contestation). The selection of cases in Indigenous communities would also entail different rights regimes such as the International

Labor Organization's Convention 169 on "free, prior, and informed consent," ratified by Peru in 2011.[14] All of these potential differences would be further amplified across different legal, cultural, and temporal contexts, which would be nearly inevitable through a cross-national comparison.

Case Selection

I specifically survey conflicts about gold given this commodity's highly contentious nature. The likelihood that gold mining projects in Peru will be socially controversial is mainly due to two factors. First is the touted importance of gold for Peru's export income and macro-economic growth. One-fifth of the country's export income derives from gold alone. Peru is the sixth largest gold producer in the world and has been the largest gold producer in Latin America since 1996.[15] Another factor that makes gold particularly contentious is the disparity in the distribution of its benefits and burdens—for example, while gold extraction is hugely destructive to soil and water in the areas of extraction, its monetary gains are highly concentrated. Gold carries an additional symbolic salience historically, in which it is associated with Pizarro's conquest of the Inca; physically, as a highly malleable, durable, and convenient superconductor; and economically, as the expensive mineral is associated with power, wealth, prestige, victory, luxury, treasure, divinity (and the sun), and—literally and figuratively—brilliance. For these reasons, gold embodies an epicenter of symbolic and material contestation.

Broadly, all gold mining projects in Peru between 2000 and 2015 could be classified according to their levels of violence, as indicated by death and injury statistics (see Table 4).[16]

To understand how corporate-community conflicts in the gold mining industry reach different levels of violence, it was necessary to study not only explosive conflicts but also medium- and low-intensity ones. Additionally, given the proportional dominance of conflicts in the middle category, I selected two paradigmatic

TABLE 4. Intensity of Corporate Gold Mining Conflicts in Peru, 2000–2015

	Low (some local organizing)	Medium (sporadic protests, public mobilization, arrests, injuries)	High (mass mobilization, violent confrontations, deaths, injuries)
Projects	*Cerro Corona* Antapite TROY Las Palmeras	*Lagunas Norte* *Tambo Grande* Cañariaco Afrodita-Dorato Quilish Yanacocha Kimsa Orcco Sulliden	*La Zanja* Conga Chumbivilcas Pierina

NOTE: "Intensity" assessment is based on Defensoría del Pueblo's conflict database, the Environmental Justice Atlas database, and media reports. Mining projects such as Las Bambas and Tía María, which contain gold but are mainly copper deposits, are excluded from this list. (Italicized names are cases discussed in this study.)

cases from it; this choice keeps the study representative, and it further enables me to systematically conduct "paired comparisons." Through a methodical examination of two cases with similar outcomes, in contrast to two cases that differed, I can refine my observations and develop theory even more precisely.[17]

The four cases I selected are the most representative of each category: Tambo Grande, owned by Vancouver-based Manhattan Minerals, proposed (but never constructed) in Piura region; La Zanja, a Buenaventura and Newmont joint venture in Cajamarca; Lagunas Norte, owned by Barrick Gold and located in La Libertad; and Cerro Corona, owned by South Africa-based Gold Fields and located in Cajamarca. The inclusion of four cases also allows for paired comparisons between cases owned by mining companies of different and similar sizes; for example, Tambogrande was owned by a small company, in contrast to Lagunas Norte and La Zanja, which are owned by two of the largest gold producers in the world (Barrick and Newmont, respectively).

Despite their shared demographic and contextual backgrounds, a crucial factor that varies across the cases is how corporations responded to pressures from their communities of influence, and

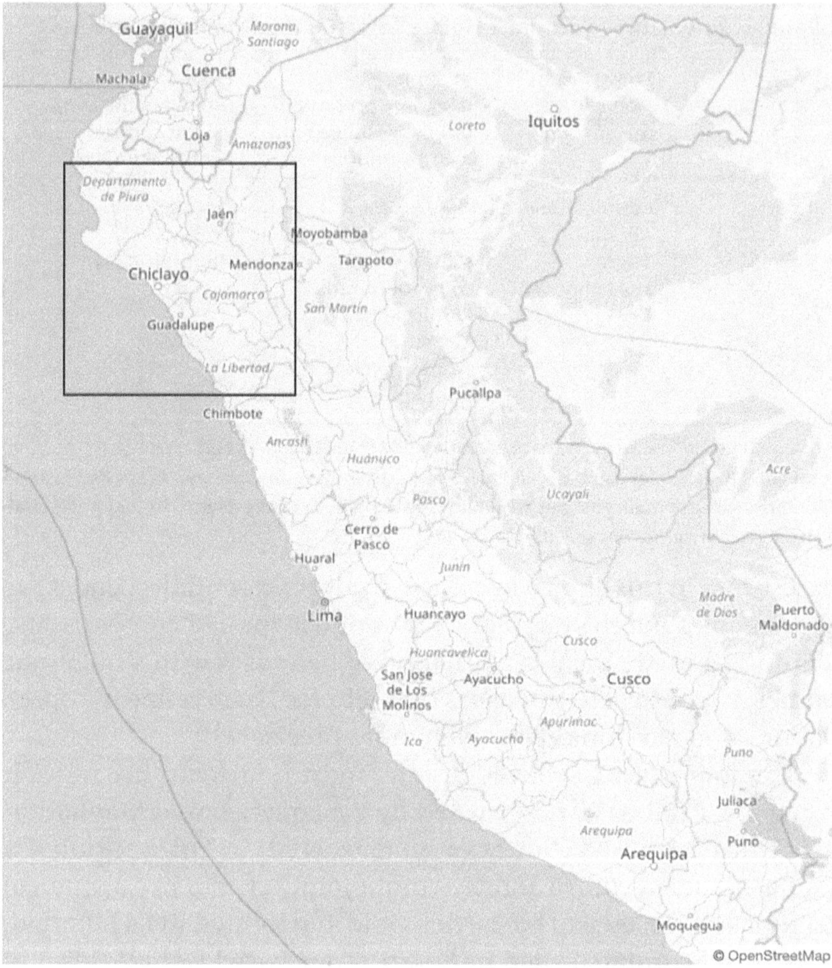

FIGURE 11. Maps of the four mining project sites in northern Peru. Maps of Peru and Northern Peru, © OpenStreetMap contributors (openstreetmap.org and opendatacommons.org).

their processes of learning about these relations; ultimately, I argue, these differences shaped the cases' divergent outcomes. These distinctions help to build and refine the insights drawn from each case. The "most similar systems design" of this comparative analysis helps to shed new light on different theoretical puzzles, such as the effects of different types of corporate social responsibility

programs, and how these work in combination with other corporate strategies, such as intimidation or state repression.

By restricting my focus to one extractive industry (mining), one specific sector (gold), a sub-region (the north) of one country (Peru), and a specific time frame (conflicts active between 2000 and 2015), I could arrive as closely as possible to a controlled comparison of cases. I further narrowed the selection by choosing four cases that, despite their categorical, scalar, and demographic similarities, had different results along the factor to be explained: the levels of violence each conflict reached. This setup allows me to identify, trace, and analyze the dynamics that explain how similar cases can lead to contrasting outcomes—insights that, if they can be abstracted from their local specificities, may be usefully applied in other contexts.[18]

More than just a heuristic device, Northern Peru is a region with a particular history, social fabric, and political and economic traits. The case studies try to bring these insights to light.

Fieldwork and Data Collection Methods

The substance of this study is drawn from field-intensive research methods, namely more than 250 semi-structured interviews, participant-observations at dozens of events, and more than nine hundred archival documents collected during fourteen months of fieldwork (first between August and September of 2014, and then between August 2015 and September 2016). I spent most of my time in the north of Peru, living in districts near the four mining projects, and made frequent visits to Lima.[19]

Interviews cast a broad net and include mining-area residents in various occupations; movement leaders and participants; mining employees, managers, and executives; members of local, national, and international organizations (such as Fedepaz, CONFIEP, FADRE, Cooperacción, EarthWorks, the US Agency for International Development, the US embassy in Lima, UNDP representatives in Peru, the World Bank's International Finance Corporation, Earth Rights International, Amazon Watch, Instituto de Defensa Legal, and many others); municipal, regional, and national government officials across different government agencies and offices in each level (including at the presidential palace, the National Environmental Dialogue Office, officers of the Ministry of Mining and Defensoría del Pueblo at the national and regional levels, and political candidates of different parties); journalists (e.g., from the newspaper *Gestión*); and academics based near the cases as well as in Lima.[20] The study treats participants as complex individuals rather than as representative of any given category, and as research partners whose concerns are central to the analysis.

Archive documents include stakeholder publications, signed agreements, reports, statements and proclamations, more than nine hundred news media clippings, and other records kept by activists, companies, and the state. For secondary sources, I relied heavily on "critical discourse analysis" of news media, especially from the most reputable national journals such as *El comercio* and *La república*, but also including publications from state actors, Defensoría del Pueblo's monthly reports on social conflicts, activist publications, and online blogs.[21]

To make sense of all these sources and forms of data collected in advance, during, and since my fieldwork, I systematically organized most of these sources, except for my interviews and of my field notes, using a free note-keeping software application (wherein I added initial highlights, jottings, and tags or codes). I then used qualitative analysis software ATLAS.ti to code all my sources and archives, including my interviews and field notes alongside scholarly literature and other relevant files.[22]

Positionality, Fieldwork, and Ethics

My aim to make the research reciprocal required forming relationships with participants as partners in a collective inquiry. My main priority was to listen and learn, rather than to impose my assumptions or needs. For example, in interviews, I asked participants to share their own questions and concerns, which I then sought to answer as the central concerns of my overall effort. Ultimately, participants co-created the research throughout: from conceptualization, through the refining of its questions and methods, to the interpretation of its findings. Furthermore, I offered and carried out translation services, paid for interviewee's lunches, helped or accompanied people during events, sought opportunities to collaborate on projects, and formed friendships with many of them—as opposed to merely extracting information from them.

In addition to valorizing the voices traditionally discounted and marginalized in studies such as this, field immersion also meant reading local knowledge producers and historians, prioritizing the contributions of Peruvian thinkers and leaders like Victoria Santa Cruz, María Alvarado, José Mariátegui, Flora Tristán, Dora Mayer de Zulén, Magda Portal, and Hugo Blanco (although I only learned of Hugo Blanco's life of fighting for Indigenous emancipation after

I first met him). Understanding the country's politics required diving deep into history texts.[23] It also meant learning about pre-Columbian cultures and the European arrival in search of wealth to plunder, all while resisting the temptation to reduce my own narrative to a superficial critique of neocolonialism.

Data Analysis Methods

Critical discourse analysis of these sources, assisted by several layers of qualitative coding, provides a thick description of the cases.[24] The primary method I used to systematically analyze the data consists of developing a codebook through several layers of qualitative coding. At first, my coding was inductive, guided by the materials themselves, and keeping my a priori assumptions and theoretical thinking at bay as much as possible. The second layer was more deductive, guided by available theoretical frameworks, my scholarly training, and my prior research. The third and subsequent layers of coding were focused on challenging as well as refining my emergent theory and the early findings I was beginning to formulate.

Together, discourse analysis and thick, within-case process tracing help to weave complex stories about how people perceive events, make choices, frame their perspectives, and shape the outcomes of cases—such as movement demobilization, company concessions, and a more ambiguous normalization of conflict. Then controlled comparison of cases helps to build theory about conflict mechanisms and the prospects of resolution efforts.

Adopting a carefully reflexive, immersive, participatory, and systematic research design, this in-depth comparison of four gold mines in northern Peru contributes original insights about the processes through which conflicts become violent, as well as those that lead actors to eschew violent means of waging conflict.[25]

TABLE 5. Peru's Political Units Visited for this Field Research, 2014–2016

Regions	Provinces	Districts
Autonomous Province of Lima	Metropolitan Municipality	Barranco, Chorrillos, Jesús María, La Molina, LaVictoria, Lima, Magdalena del Mar, Miraflores, Pueblo Libre, Rimac, San Borja, San Isidro, San Miguel, Surquillo, and others
Amazonas	Bagua	Bagua
	Chachapoyas	Chachapoyas
Arequipa	Arequipa	Arequipa
Cajamarca	Cajamarca	Cajamarca and Namora
	Santa Cruz	Santa Cruz de Succhabamba and Pulán
	San Miguel	San Miguel de Pallaques
	Hualgayoc	Bambamarca and Hualgayoc
	Celendín	Celendín
	Chota	Chota
La Libertad	Trujillo	Trujillo and Huanchaco
	Santiago de Chuco	Santiago de Chuco, Cachicadán, and Quiruvilca
	Otuzco	Otuzco
	Sánchez Carrión	Huamachuco
	Julcán	Barro Negro
Lambayeque	Chiclayo	Chiclayo
Piura	Piura	Piura, Tambogrande, and Locuto
	Sullana	Sullana
San Martín	San Martín	Tarapoto

Notes

INTRODUCTION

1. Martín (pseudonym), anonymous former Manhattan Minerals geologist, personal interview, September 16, 2015. Unless otherwise noted, all translations are mine. Translation accuracy and loyalty to original intent were maximized by cross-checking Peruvian slang and cultural references.
2. Maritza Paredes, "El caso de Tambogrande," in *Defendiendo derechos y promoviendo cambios*, ed. Martin Scurrah (Lima: Instituto de Estudios Peruanos, 2008), 283.
3. Liliana Alzamora (teacher and local movement leader), personal interview, September 19, 2015.
4. Brad Evans and Henry A. Giroux, *Disposable Futures: The Seduction of Violence in the Age of Spectacle* (San Francisco: City Lights, 2015); Wendy S. Hesford, *Spectacular Rhetorics: Human Rights Visions, Recognitions, Feminisms* (Durham, NC: Duke University Press, 2011).
5. Global Witness, *Deadly Environments: The Dramatic Rise in Killings of Environmental and Land Defenders 1/1/2002–31/12/2013* (London: Global Witness Limited, 2014); Global Witness, *On Dangerous Ground* (London: Global Witness Limited, 2016).
6. Defensoría del Pueblo, *Violencia en los conflictos sociales* (Lima: Defensoría del Pueblo, 2012); Magali Zevallos, "Perú: Represión y muertes en conflictos mineros," *Gran angular*, May 11, 2015; Observatorio de Conflictos Mineros en el Perú, *20º Informe del OCM* (Lima: Cooperacción, 2017).
7. Defensoría del Pueblo, *Violencia en los conflictos sociales*; Defensoría del Pueblo, *Reporte mensual de conflictos sociales Nº 155—Enero 2017* (Lima: Defensoría del Pueblo, 2017).

8. "De Soto: 'Hay US$70 mil mlls de inversión minera paralizada,'" *El comercio*, May 7, 2015.
9. See, e.g., Stephanie Rose Montesanti and Wilfreda E. Thurston, "Mapping the Role of Structural and Interpersonal Violence in the Lives of Women: Implications for Public Health Interventions and Policy," *BMC Women's Health* 15, no. 100 (2015): 1–13.
10. Anonymous radio journalist in Piura, personal interview, September 21, 2015.
11. Anonymous journalist in Cajamarca, personal interview, July 8, 2016.
12. Wilfredo Saavedra (attorney and leading activist in Cajamarca), personal interview, July 9, 2016.
13. See Timothy Pachirat, *Every Twelve Seconds: Industrialized Slaughter and the Politics of Sight* (New Haven, CT: Yale University Press, 2012). In this book, I borrow the concept of "the everyday" as operationalized by feminist and postcolonial scholars, where it is an explicit attempt to denote the personal immediacy of political conditions; see, e.g., Nancy Scheper-Hughes, *Death without Weeping: The Violence of Everyday Life in Brazil* (Berkeley: University of California Press, 1992).
14. One well-documented example of these gendered and unequally distributed dynamics is how mining activities tend to greatly exacerbate the income gap between men and women. See Katy Jenkins, "Women Anti-Mining Activists' Narratives of Everyday Resistance in the Andes: Staying Put and Carrying on in Peru and Ecuador," *Gender, Place & Culture* 24, no. 10 (2017): 1441–59.
15. Femicide refers to the murder of women because of their gender. The Peruvian state estimated 168 women were killed and 5,140 underage girls were violated in the country in 2019. See "En apenas un mes se violaron sexualmente a 464 menores en el País," *El comercio*, March 4, 2020.
16. "Funcionarios ocultaron contaminación de población de Hualgayoc, en Cajamarca," *Servicio de comunicación intercultural*, May 14, 2015; Wilfredo Cholán, "Hualgayoc: Existen niveles de plomo en la sangre por encima de los límites permisibles," *Noticias SER*, May 13, 2015.
17. David Harvey, *The New Imperialism* (New York: Oxford University Press, 2003).
18. Henri Lefebvre, *The Production of Space* (Cambridge, MA: Blackwell, 1991).
19. See *The Devil Operation*, directed by Stephanie Boyd (Lima, Peru: Guarango Films, 2010), DVD.

20. Alan García, "El síndrome del perro del hortelano," *El comercio*, October 27, 2007; "Presidente Alan García Calificó como un 'Genocidio de Policías,'" *La república*, June 13, 2009.
21. Nancy Lee Peluso and Michael Watts, *Violent Environments* (Ithaca, NY: Cornell University Press, 2001).
22. See, e.g., Keisha-Khan Y. Perry, *Black Women against the Land Grab: The Fight for Racial Justice in Brazil* (Ithaca, NY: Cornell University Press, 2013), xiii. Power and politics are reflected along every step of the research process: who the researcher is, where and when her training and field sites are located, what themes and concepts she selects, the traditions and literatures upon which she situates her work, how she collects and analyzes evidence, whose voices are prominent and whose are left out, and so on—regardless of how apolitical the subject matter may appear to be.
23. See, e.g., Edward Said, *Orientalism* (New York: Vintage Books, 1979).
24. Charles Tilly, "Violent and Nonviolent Trajectories in Contentious Politics" (presentation, Symposium on States in Transition and the Challenge of Ethnic Conflict, Columbia University, New York, December 29, 2010).
25. For an example of problematic perspectives such as this, see Paul Collier and Anke Hoeffler, "Greed and Grievance in Civil War," *Oxford Economic Papers* 56 (2004): 563–95; Robert Hackett, "Objectivity in Reporting," in *The International Encyclopedia of Communication I* (New York: Wiley, 2008); Mick Hume, *Whose War Is It Anyway? The Dangers of the Journalism of Attachment* (London: Living Marxism Special, InformInc., 1997); Wilhelm Kempf, "Conflict Coverage and Conflict Escalation," in *Journalism and the New World Order, Vol. 2: Studying War and the Media*, eds. Wilhelm Kempf and Heikki Luostarien (Göteburg: Nordicom, 2002); Philip Knightly, *The First Casualty* (Baltimore, MD: John Hopkins University Press, 2002); David Loyn, "Good Journalism or Peace Journalism?" *Conflict and Communication Online* 6, no. 2.
26. Roma Chatterji and Deepak Mehta, *Living with Violence: An Anthropology of Events and Everyday Life* (London: Routledge, 2007).
27. For a critique of the insider-outsider binary and an exploration into this embodied ambivalence, see Deianira Ganga and Sam Scott, "Cultural 'Insiders' and the Issue of Positionality in Qualitative Migration Research: Moving 'Across' and Moving 'Along' Researcher-Participant Divides," *Forum: Qualitative Social Research* 7, no. 3 (2006). For a critique of the objective/subjective split, see Deborah E. Reed-Danahay,

"Introduction," in *Auto/Ethnography: Rewriting the Self and the Social*, ed. Deborah E. Reed-Danahay (New York: Berg Publishers, 1997).

28. James Clifford, "On Ethnographic Authority," *Representations* 2 (Spring, 1983): 118–46.

29. For some scholars, especially those aligned with positivist attitudes, being an outsider removed from the contexts I was studying ensured I would be less partial or biased, and more objective in my understandings. On the contrary, for others such as Donna Haraway, it is preferable to emphasize "the partial" perspective and the voices of those whose subjectivity is directly shaped by the events under study. Donna Haraway, "Situated Knowledges: The Science Question in Feminism and the Privilege of Partial Perspective," *Feminist Studies* 14, no. 3 (1998): 583–84. The difficult task is to do so with humility and self-criticism, without appropriating or romanticizing the views of these insiders, without reducing the category of "insiders" itself, and without using categories such as "Peruvian" uncritically. Despite these challenges, I align this study closer to the second of these perspectives, given its potential to better understand and confront violence.

30. For example, one of the narratives which I heard repeatedly was about "state incapacity" to attend to people's grievances to resolve them nonviolently. However, instead of explaining the country's high level of conflicts, this rhetoric turns out to be a trope and an excuse, if one considers how much state capacity there actually is whenever it comes to policing and repression.

31. Carlos Basombrío Iglesias, "Peace in Peru, but Unresolved Tasks," in *In the Wake of War: Democratization and Internal Armed Conflict in Latin America*, ed. Cynthia J. Arnson (Washington, DC: Woodrow Wilson Center Press and Stanford University Press, 2012).

32. Raymundo Casas Navarro, "La prensa chicha: Un análisis cognitivo," *Letras* 80, no. 115 (2009): 63–68; Jacqueline Fowks, *Chichapolitik: La prensa con Fujimori* (Lima: Fundación Friedrich Ebert, 2015).

33. According to the *New York Times*, "Newmont gained undisputed control of Yanacocha in 2000 after years of back-room legal wrangling. Behind the scenes, Newmont and its adversaries . . . reached into the upper levels of the American, French and Peruvian governments, employing a cast of former and active intelligence officials, including Peru's ruthless secret police chief, Vladimiro Montesinos." Jane Perez and Lowell Bergman, "Tangled Strands in Fight over Peru Gold Mine," *New York Times*, June 14, 2010.

34. Although inconclusive in the eyes of many observers, Peru's internal armed conflict spanned roughly between 1980 and 2000. An estimated

69,280 people were killed as a result, and countless others were injured and affected by it. Throughout the conflict, Peruvians endured violence, corruption, and authoritarianism from different sides, including the state, insurgent groups, and terrorists. For a thorough review, see the Truth and Reconciliation Commission's final report: Comisión de la Verdad y Reconciliación, *Informe Final*, 2003, http://cverdad.org.pe/ifinal.

35. "Fujimori ordenó la estirilización forzosa de 200,000 mujeres indígenas en Perú," *El país*, July 25, 2002.
36. Gaile S. Canella and Michelle S. Perez, "Power-Shifting at the Speed of Light: Critical Qualitative Research Post-Disaster," in *Qualitative Inquiry and Social Justice*, eds. Norman K. Denzin and Michael D. Giardina (Walnut Creek, CA: Leftcoast Press, 2009); Gaile S. Canella and Yvonna S. Lincoln, "Deploying Qualitative Methods for Critical Social Purposes," in *Qualitative Inquiry and Social Justice*, eds. Norman K. Denzin and Michael D. Giardina (Walnut Creek, CA: Leftcoast Press, 2009); Chela Sandoval, *Methodology of the Oppressed* (Minneapolis: University of Minnesota Press, 2000); Linda Tuhiwai Smith, *Decolonizing Methodologies: Research and Indigenous Peoples* (London: Zed Books, 2009).
37. Keisha-Khan Y. Perry, personal communication, Nov. 20, 2017.
38. See Mariana Mora, *Kuxlejal Politics: Indigenous Autonomy, Race, and Decolonizing Research in Zapatista Communities* (Austin: University of Texas Press, 2017), 68.
39. Amílcar Cabral, *Revolution in Guinea*, trans. Richard Handyside (London: Stage 1, 1974), 70–72.
40. Arundathi Roy, "We Call This Progress," *Guernica Magazine*, December 17, 2012.
41. For a similar critique, see Marco Avilés, "No soy tu cholo," *Ojo público*, April 9, 2017.

CHAPTER 1

1. Global Witness, *On Dangerous Ground*.
2. Observatory of Economic Complexity, "Peru," Massachusetts Institute of Technology, 2017, https://atlas.media.mit.edu/en.
3. Defensoría del Pueblo, *Violencia en los Conflictos Sociales*; Magali Zevallos, "Perú: represión y muertes en conflictos mineros"; Obser-

vatorio de Conflictos Mineros en el Perú, *20º Informe del OCM*. As a side note, it should be clarified that these statistics have an "immediate bias" in that they discount the numbers of deaths and injuries caused indirectly by pollution, alcoholism, underdevelopment, and gendered or sexual violence that accompany the installation of mining projects.

4. Defensoría del Pueblo, *Reporte Mensual de Conflictos Sociales Nº 155—Enero 2017*.
5. See Laura Soria and Gerardo Castillo, *Gender Justice in Consultation Processes for Extractives Industries in Bolivia, Ecuador and Peru* (Peru: Oxfam and Societas, 2011); Lewis Taylor, "Environmentalism and Social Protest: The Contemporary Anti-Mining Mobilization in the Province of San Marcos and the Condebamba Valley, Peru," *Agrarian Change* 11, no. 3 (2011): 420–39; Bruno Revesz and Julio Oliden, "Piura: Transformación del Territorio Regional," in *Ecuador debate: Acerca del buen vivir*, no. 84 (December 2011): 151–76; Carmen Diana Deere, "Changing Social Relations of Production and Peruvian Peasant Women's Work," *Latin American Perspectives* 14 (Winter/Spring 1977): 48–69; Daniel Franks and Rachel Davis, *The Costs of Conflict* (International Finance Corporation, World Bank Group, 2015); Daniel Franks et al., "Conflict Translates Environmental and Social Risk Into Business Costs," *Proceedings of the National Academy of Sciences* 111, no. 21 (2014): 7576–81.
6. José Carlos Díaz Zanelli, "La contradicción de Alan García con los pueblos indígenas," *Servicios de comunicación intercultural*, January 18, 2016; Patricia Martínez i Álvarez, "Personas de primera," *El país* (Opinión), June 11, 2009.
7. Anthony Bebbington, *Social Conflict, Economic Development and Extractive Industry* (New York: Routledge, 2012), 3–4.
8. Gavin Bridge, "Global Production Networks and the Extractive Sector: Governing Resource Based Development," *Journal of Economic Geography* 8, no. 3 (2008): 389–419.
9. I heard this repeatedly from Lima-based radio and newspapers; e.g., see Verónica Ruíz, and Arturo Pérez, "Advierten nuevos conflictos mineros," *La república*, March 19, 2007.
10. In Peru particularly, the ombuds office, Defensoría del Pueblo, finds that conflicts are more likely against large companies and when the project is surrounded by economically poor or disadvantaged communities. Defensoría del Pueblo, *Violencia en los conflictos sociales* and *Reporte mensual de conflictos sociales Nº 155—Enero 2017*. Besides

the environmental and social grievances people in extractive sites may have about the uneven distribution of benefits and harms of mining activity, studies specifically analyzing mining conflicts in Peru center around three types of explanations: (1) organizations and individuals stir up trouble for economic self-interest and manipulate local ignorance for political gain (a position adopted by many mining supporters); (2) low institutional capacity and poor institutional design lead to a lack of coordination among conflict-response entities, and a business-influenced or "captured" state is unwilling to respect the right of local populations to consultation and consent before development projects that will impact them are constructed; and (3) there is generally poor communication between actors. Beyond Peruvian mining, Marta Conde, Jonathan Gamu, and Philippe Le Billon have reviewed the literature on resource wars and provided the most exhaustive summary of the causes of such conflicts, summarizing these causes into the categories of structural (economic, cultural, and historical), contextual (institutional and political), and proximate (perceptions, livelihood, lack of participation, benefit distribution, distrust, and poor communication). Marta Conde, Jonathan Gamu, and Philippe Le Billon, *The Rise in Conflicts Associated with Extractive Sector Projects—What Lies Beneath?* Vancouver: Canadian International Resources and Development Institute, 2017. For a thicker review of the literature, see this book's Appendix 2.

11. Whereas my own focus is on the question of what causes violent escalation and not company agency itself, see Gustafsson's work for excellent and helpful inroads into these topics. Maria-Therese Gustafsson, "The Struggles Surrounding Ecological and Economic Zoning in Peru," *Third World Quarterly* 38, no. 5 (2017): 9.
12. Adapted from James Ferguson, "Seeing Like an Oil Company: Space, Security, and Global Capital in Neoliberal Africa," *American Anthropologist* 107, no. 3 (2005): 377–82.
13. One study considered company-community conflicts, but not specifically within conflicts over natural resources. See Erica Chenoweth and Tricia Olsen, *Civil Resistance and Corporate Behavior: Mapping Trends and Assessing Impact* (Washington, DC: US Agency for International Development, 2016).
14. See Ian Bannon and Paul Collier, *Natural Resources and Violent Conflict* (Washington: World Bank, 2003).
15. Robert Bates, *Markets and States in Tropical Africa* (Berkeley: University of California Press, 1981); Hazem Beblawi and Giacomo Luciani,

The Rentier State (London: Croom Helm, 1987); Collier and Hoeffler, "Greed and Grievance in Civil War."

16. See Georgina Alonso, "Barrick Gold and CSR: Dynamics of Canadian Extractivism in Peru" (master's thesis, St. Mary's University, 2014) for a thorough review of the CSR literature.
17. See Erica Chenoweth and Maria J. Stephan, *Why Civil Resistance Works: The Strategic Logic of Nonviolent Conflict* (New York: Columbia University Press, 2011).
18. However, see Vanessa Joan Gray, "Nonviolence and Sustainable Resource Use with External Support," *Latin American Perspectives* 39, no. 1 (2012): 43–60; and Maritza Paredes, "El caso de Tambogrande."
19. Clifford Bob, *The Marketing of Rebellion: Insurgents, Media, and International Activism* (Cambridge: Cambridge University Press, 2005). See also Jonathan Fox, "Unpacking Transnational Citizenship," *Annual Review of Political Science* 8 (May 2005); Margaret Keck and Kathryn Sikkink, *Activists beyond Borders: Advocacy Networks in International Politics* (Ithaca, NY: Cornell University Press, 1998).
20. In contrast to my two previous criticisms here, much more has been written about tensions between NGOs and communities. See Amanda Murdie and Tavishi Bhasin, "Aiding and Abetting: Human Rights INGOs and Domestic Protest," *Journal of Conflict Resolution* 55, no. 2 (2011): 163–91; Patricia Widener, "Benefits and Burdens of Transnational Campaigns: A Comparison of Four Oil Struggles in Ecuador," *Mobilization* 12, no. 1 (2007): 21–36.
21. Not all observers have ignored the role of discourse in environmental conflicts. Some interviewees and advisors for this study have analyzed the role of communication and discourse in Peruvian mining conflicts, and this research builds upon their work. See Gerardo Damonte, "El modelo extractivo peruano: Discursos, políticas, y la reproducción de desigualdades sociales," in *Extractivismo minero en Colombia y América Latina*, eds. Barbara Göbel and Astrid Ulloa (Bogotá: Universidad Nacional de Colombia, 2014); Sandro Macassi and Jorge Acevedo, *Confrontación y diálogo: Medios y conflictos en países andinos* (Lima: Pontifícia Universidad Católica del Perú, 2015).
22. For an illustration of this, see Mariella Balbi's interview, on her Canal N television show, with Alberto Pizango, elected leader and spokesperson for the Native communities protesting in Amazonas region in 2009. Televised in the period leading up to the June 5 massacre in Bagua that year, the interview features the pundit aggressively questioning and constantly interrupting Pizango. In one moment, Balbi charges, "Realize that you are putting this whole country at risk!" Pizango remains

astonishingly calm, even as his answer is interrupted by Balbi, who abruptly closes the discussion by arguing that "the country cannot be halted for you [*ustedes*] . . . I am not going to lose electricity because you people do not want to dialogue." For a recording of this televised interview, see *When Two Worlds Collide*, a documentary film directed by Heidi Brandenburg Sierralta and Matthew Orzel (Lima, Peru: Yachaywasi Films, 2016), DVD.

23. While significant opposition to extraction has indeed emerged, there is also widespread support for a lot of these projects. Even where opposition is strong, communities are often divided (in fact, several mining company managers interviewed in this study took credit for such divisions), and even members *within* movements are often divided about their goals. It appears that most people do not oppose extraction per se, but rather seek recognition and a voice in the process. And in some cases, people *in favor* of extractive projects are the ones who organize protests (see Bebbington et al., "Contention and Ambiguity: Mining and the Possibilities of Development." *Development and Change* 39, no. 6: 893). In short, the idea that protesters are "violent anti-miners" minimizes the complex relations between diverse actors in state institutions, companies, local groups, and outside organizations.
24. Daron Acemoglu and James Robinson, *Why Nations Fail* (New York: Crown Press, 2012).
25. While the "visibility" and "invisibilization" metaphor is useful, in this study I refer to these dynamics of concealment and normalization as "the politics of attention," as I detail in this book. This rephrasing can substitute the useful language of "invisibility" while refusing this metaphor's inherent ableism. See Michael Wilson Becerril, "'Invisibilize' This: Ocular Bias and Ableist Metaphors in Anti-Oppressive Discourses," *Feminist Review* 120 (2018): 130–34.
26. See, e.g., Henrik Urdal, "Population, Resources, and Political Violence: A Subnational Study of India," *Journal of Conflict Resolution* 52, no. 4 (2008): 590–617.
27. Violent protest and repression are known to be mutually caused. For a review of interactions between repression and resistance in Peruvian mining conflicts, see Michael Wilson Becerril, "Mining Conflicts in Peru: Civil Resistance and Corporate Counterinsurgency," *Journal of Resistance Studies* 4, no. 1 (2018): 99–132.
28. Systemic exclusion and denial of citizenship based on social categories, such as race, ethnicity, class, sex, and gender, are well documented aspects of Peru's colonial legacies. See Rosemary Thorp and

Maritza Paredes, *Ethnicity and the Persistence of Inequality: The Case of Peru* (Basingstoke: Palgrave Macmillan, 2010); Armando Mendoza Nava, *Inequality in Peru: Reality and Risks*, Oxfam, October 2015, https://peru.oxfam.org/para-no-retroceder-realidad-y-riesgo-de-la-desigualdad-en-el-perú-o.

29. Cecilia Perla, "Extracting from the Extractors: The Politics of Private Welfare in the Peruvian Mining Industry" (PhD diss., Brown University, 2012).
30. "Aurelio Miró Quesada de la Guerra: El ingeniero periodista que dirigió *El comercio*," *El comercio* (Huellas Digitales), May 14, 2015; Media Ownership Monitor, "Peru: Grupo El Comercio" (Reporters without Borders, 2018).
31. Judith Butler, *Frames of War: When Is Life Grievable?* (London: Verso Books, 2009).
32. Richard Matthew, Oli Brown, and David Jensen, *From Conflict to Peacebuilding: The Role of Natural Resources and the Environment* (Geneva: United Nations Environment Programme, 2009), 5.
33. Donatella della Porta, *Clandestine Political Violence* (Cambridge: Cambridge University Press, 2013); Michel Wieviorka, *Violence: A New Approach* (London: Sage Publications, 2009).
34. Andrew Bennett and Colin Elman, "Qualitative Research: Recent Developments in Case Study Materials," *Annual Review of Political Science* 9 (2006): 455–76; David Collier, "Understanding Process Tracing," *PS: Political Science* 44, no. 4 (2011): 823–30.
35. See Arend Lijphart, "Comparative Politics and the Comparative Method," *American Political Science Review* 65, no. 3 (1971): 682–93; Todd Landman, *Issues and Methods in Comparative Politics: An Introduction* (New York: Routledge, 2008).
36. Clifford Geertz, *The Interpretation of Culture* (New York: Basic Books, 1973).

CHAPTER 2

1. The majority of interviewees are anonymized in this study, except as requested by the interviewees themselves.
2. Eduardo Galeano, *Las venas abiertas de America Latina* (Mexico, DF: Siglo XXI Editores, 1971).

3. The mass die-offs of trout have been reported numerous times in Cajamarca. In fact, this has happened on the same river at least three times, in 2002, 2006, and 2012. On the most recent case, see "Acusan a Minera Yanacocha por muerte de truchas en Río Llaucano," *Servicios de comunicación intercultural*, October 26, 2012, https://www.servindi.org/actualidad/75647. In another case, according to its own website, Yanacocha "never denied its responsibility" and promised safety guards would be installed after thirty-six thousand trout died in Porcón in 2002. See "Flora y fauna," Yanacocha, n.d., accessed January 18, 2018. http://www.yanacocha.com/flora-y-fauna.
4. The price of gold per troy ounce in the global market rose from $272.65 at the close of 2000 to $1,420.25 in 2010. "200 Years of Gold Prices," Only Gold, n.d., accessed January 18, 2018. http://onlygold.com/m/Prices/Prices200Years.asp.
5. "Gold Prices," World Gold Council, accessed January 18, 2018. https://www.gold.org/goldhub/data/gold-prices. An estimated 12 percent of all gold is contained in electronic devices such as tablets and computers and is therefore unrecoverable unless those devices are carefully recycled. Hass McCook, "Under the Microscope: The True Costs of Gold Production," *Coin Desk*, June 28, 2014, https://www.coindesk.com/microscope-true-costs-gold-production.
6. Codi Yeager-Kozacek, "Global Gold Rush: The Price of Mining Pursuits on the Water Supply," Circle of Blue, June 15, 2012. http://www.circleofblue.org/2012/world/global-gold-rush-the-price-of-mining-pursuits-on-water-supply.
7. Observatory of Economic Complexity, "Peru."
8. Payal Sampat, "Fact Sheet: The True Cost of Valentine's Day Jewelry" (Washington, DC: Earthworks, 2015).
9. Baker et al., *Vital Waste Graphics*, Geneva: United Nations Environment Programme, October 2004, 44–45. https://www.unenvironment.org/resources/report/vital-waste-graphics.
10. Earthworks and Mining Watch Canada, *Troubled Waters: How Mine Waste Dumping Is Poisoning Our Oceans, Rivers, and Lakes* (Washington, DC: Earthworks, 2012).
11. Ben Hallman and Roxana Olivera, "How the World Bank Is Financing Environmental Destruction," *Huffington Post*, April 15, 2015.
12. Gavin Mudd, "Resource Consumption Intensity and the Sustainability of Gold Mining" (presentation, 2nd International Conference on Sustainability Engineering & Science, Auckland, NZ, February 20–23, 2007); Terry Norgate and Nawshad Haque, "Using Life Cycle Assess-

ment to Evaluate Some Environmental Impacts of Gold Production," *Journal of Cleaner Production* 29, vol. 30 (2012): 53–63. See also Benedicte Bull and Mariel Aguilar-Støen, *Environmental Politics in Latin America: Elite Dynamics, the Left Tide, and Sustainable Development* (New York: Routledge, 2015). Again, this represents the largest and most efficient operations, owned by companies that utilize the most common techniques for gold exploitation available. Less efficient sites, ore sources, and processes require substantially more resources and produce even more waste, and some formal, corporate-owned mines consume much more water. For example, Rio Tinto's Argyle Diamond mine in Australia consumed 3,500 mega-liters of water in 2005; see Perrine Toledano and Clara Roorda, "Leveraging Mining Investments in Water Infrastructure for Broad Economic Development: Models, Opportunities and Challenges," Policy Paper, *Columbia Center on Sustainable Investment*, March 2014.

13. Leah Temper, "Mapping the Global Battle to Protect Our Planet," *Guardian*, March 3, 2015.
14. Bebbington et al., "Contention and Ambiguity."
15. Matthew, Brown, and Jensen, *From Conflict to Peacebuilding*.
16. Heidelberg Institute for International Conflict Research, "Conflict Barometer 2014" (Heidelberg: HIIIK, 2014).
17. Piers M. Blaikie, *The Political Economy of Soil Erosion in Developing Countries* (New York: Longman, 1985); Piers Blaikie and Harold Brookfield, *Land Degradation and Society* (London: Routledge, 1987).
18. Javier Auyero and Debora Alejandra Swistun, *Flammable: Environmental Suffering in an Argentine Shantytown* (Oxford: Oxford University Press, 2009); Victoria Sweet, "Extracting More than Natural Resources: Human Security and Arctic Indigenous Women," *Seattle University Law Review* 37, no. 4 (2014): 1157–78; Heather Turcotte, "Petro-Sexual Politics: Petroleum, Gender Violence, and Transnational Justice" (presentation, Annual Meeting of the American Political Science Association, Seattle, Washington, September 1–4, 2011); Shelly Whitman, "Sexual Violence, Coltan, and the Democratic Republic of Congo," in *Natural Resources and Social Conflict: Towards Critical Environmental Security*, eds. Matthew A. Schnurr and Larry A. Swatuk (New York: Palgrave McMillan, 2012).
19. David Harvey, *The New Imperialism*. It should be noted that the economic valuation of nature might also lend itself toward the conservation of resources rather than their extraction and processing, as in the case of the ecotourism industry. However, even in these cases, the

impetus is still the potential profits that these resources may generate. Like resource extraction, ecotourism involves land- and resource-intensive practices, such as the illegal destruction of mangroves to make room for transnational hotel companies. Moreover, ecotourism tends to reinforce different social inequalities—for instance, via the exploitation of underpaid local workers, especially women—and often leads to conflicts: over land ownership, locals' economic dislocation (and sometimes their incorporation into the service economy), and violent policing to enforce their displacement. See Angele Berland, "Uncovering Spring Break's Hidden Underbelly," Wild Angle Productions, January 19, 2015, https://www.journeyman.tv/film/6342.

20. See Corinna Dengler and Lisa Marie Seebacher, "What about the Global South? Towards a Feminist Decolonial Degrowth Approach," *Ecological Economics* 157 (2019): 246–52; Castriela Hernández Reyes, "Black Women's Struggles against Extractivism, Land Dispossession, and Marginalization in Colombia," *Latin American Perspectives* vol. 46, no. 2 (2019): 217–34; Rocío Silva Saniesteban, "Asesinadas, golpeadas, encarceladas: El impacto de los conflictos sociales ecoterritoriales en los Cuerpos de las Mujeres Peruanas," *Revista pueblos*, January 27, 2015; Women's Earth Alliance and Native Youth Sexual Health Network, "Violence on the Land, Violence on our Bodies," report to the International Indian Treaty Council, Toronto, Canada (2016).

21. Stephen D. Krasner, "State Power and the Structure of International Trade," *World Politics* 28, no. 3 (1976): 317–47; see also Moisés Arce, *La extracción de recursos naturales y la protesta social en el Perú* (Lima, Peru: Fondo Editorial PUCP, 2015). Neoliberalism is furthermore known to concentrate wealth, which exacerbates social inequalities and tensions. Particularly in the developing world, this type of dislocation is becoming more frequent; see William Ascher and Natalia S. Mirovitskaya, *Economic Development Strategies and the Evolution of Violence in Latin America* (New York: Palgrave Macmillan, 2012): 240–41. See also Neil Adger, "Social Capital, Collective Action, and Adaptation to Climate Change," *Economic Geography* 79, no. 4 (2003): 387–404; Raymond L. Bryant, "Power, Knowledge and Political Ecology in the Third World: A Review," *Progress in Physical Geography* 22, no. 1 (1998): 79–94; Raymond Bryant and Sinead Bailey, *Third World Political Ecology* (London: Routledge, 1997); Ronald La Due Lake and Robert Huckfeldt, "Social Capital, Social Networks, and Political Participation," *Political Psychology* 19, no. 3 (1998): 567–84; Silvia Walby, "Globalization and Multiple Inequalities," *Advances in Gender Research* 15 (2011): 17–33.

22. Poverty, inequality, and economic disruption are considered by the Intercontinental Panel on Climate Change (IPCC) as primary "factors known to instigate conflict," and all of these factors are aggravated by resource extraction—ironically, given how these results are the very opposite of what is promised by extractive development. Intercontinental Panel on Climate Change, *Fifth Assessment Report* (New York: United Nations, 2014).
23. Jeffry A. Frieden, "Invested Interests: The Politics of National Economic Policies in a World of International Finance," *International Organization* 45, no. 4 (1991): 434.
24. These distortions are accompanied by economic exposure to vulnerabilities when they become dependent on a smaller range of commodities, the prices of which tend to fluctuate. Exposure to boom and bust cycles, itself the result of neoliberal institutional frameworks that have favored the concentration of investment in extractive sectors, enhances the negative effects of the resource curse. See Scott Pegg, "Mining and Poverty Reduction, Transforming Rhetoric into Reality," *Journal of Cleaner Production* 14, no. 3 (2006): 376–87. See also Javier Arellano-Yanguas, "A Thoroughly Modern Resource Curse? The New Natural Resource Policy Agenda and the Mining Revival in Peru." *Institute of Development Studies* 300 (2008): 5–51; Bannon and Collier, *Natural Resources and Violent Conflict*; Philippe Le Billon, "The Geopolitical Economy or 'Resource Wars,'" *Geopolitics* 9, no. 1 (2004): 1–28; Michael Ross, "Review: The Political Economy of the Resource Curse," *World Politics* 51, no. 2 (1999): 297–332; Jeffrey D., Sachs and Andrew M. Warner, *Natural Resource Abundance and Economic Growth* (Cambridge, MA: National Bureau of Economic Research, 1997); Terry L. Karl, *The Paradox of Plenty: Oil Booms and Petro States* (Berkeley: University of California Press, 1997); Fiorella Triscritti, "Mining, Development, and Corporate-Community Relations in Peru," *Community Development Journal* 48, no. 3 (2013): 437–50.
25. Javier Arellano-Yanguas, *Minería sin fronteras? Conflicto y desarrollo en regiones mineras del Perú* (Lima: Instituto de Estudios Peruanos, 2011), 196.
26. Local and structural cleavages may underlie conflict and cause its escalation. This is especially noticeable, for example, when the environmental and social damages that result from resource extraction are portrayed as acceptable because they mainly affect poor people, people of color, Indigenous or tribal peoples, or rural communities, whereas the benefits are concentrated among the urban, light-skinned,

and globally Northern upper class. Helle Munk Ravnborg and Maria del Pilar Guerrero, "Collective Action and Watershed Management—Experiences from the Andean Hillsides," *Agriculture and Human Values* 16, no. 3 (1999): 257–66. A clear case of this is the La Oroya mineral processing plant in Peru; while its owner lives in a mansion in the Hamptons, children living near La Oroya are evacuated from their hometown daily, due to the air quality during the plant's operating hours; see Bebbington et al., "Contention and Ambiguity."

27. Conflicts may erupt due to disparities in bargaining power, or because actors perceive institutions to be discredited, slanted, or ineffective. Sometimes, miners themselves participate in conflicts, for economic reasons; for example, they may reject the closing of mines, if they feel threatened by environmentalist challenges, or want to prevent their displacement if they are small-scale or artisanal miners whose activities are deemed illegal and subsequently overtaken by corporations. Petra Tschakert, "Digging Deep for Justice: A Radical Re-imagination of the Artisanal Mining Sector in Ghana," *Antipode* 41, no. 4 (2009): 706–40; Petra Tschakert and Kamini Singha, "Contaminated Identities: Mercury and Marginalization in the Artisanal Mining Sector of Ghana," *Geoforum* 38, no. 6 (2007): 1304–21. Conflicts may also be triggered by the low prices paid for locals' relocation, undue pressure on them to sell their land, concerns about workers and miners' rights, companies' minimal employment offer to locals, inadequate compensation for their labor, and unmet expectations or broken promises about the economic growth that would accrue to the community as a result of outside investment (e.g., when instead of feeding the local economies, extractive projects create "enclave economies" by contracting all their necessary services from non-local firms), or the inflationary effects of projects on local markets, including rising prices of services, land, and food. (Labor-oriented complaints were much more common before the 1970s. Since then, the discourses of people who contest resource extraction have become increasingly sensitized to global currents in environmentalism, human rights, social justice, and self-determination.) See Anthony Bebbington et al., "Mining and Social Movements: Struggles over Livelihood and Rural Territorial Development in the Andes," *World Development* 36, no. 12 (2008): 2895. Furthermore, localized resource conflicts may also be instigated by competition between political factions at different levels and branches of the state. Sometimes regional courts suspend projects approved by the central government. In other cases, mayors

take advantage of conflicts to build their reputation, or they demand higher tax revenues from mining companies to satisfy personal goals and campaign promises. See Arellano-Yanguas, *Minería sin fronteras?*

28. In 2015, minerals represented roughly 65 percent of Peru's export income. Gold alone represented 16 percent, making it the second largest mineral source of Peru's income, after copper (23.5 percent). Peru, which has been the region's largest gold producer for more than a decade, had the fastest growing economy in South America between 2013 and 2017 (27.4 percent, which dwarfed the region's usual top performers, Chile and Brazil, which grew by 24.2 percent and 22.3 percent respectively). See Observatory of Economic Complexity, "Peru."
29. José Miguel Morales and Africa Morante, "Aciertos y debilidades de la legislación minera actual," *Círculos de derecho administrativo, PUCP* 8 (2009): 137–47.
30. A common word for these regulations nowadays is *trabas*, which literally means obstructions.
31. Jeffrey Bury "Neoliberalismo, minería, y cambios sociales en Cajamarca," in *Minería, movimientos sociales, y respuestas campesinas*, ed. Anthony Bebbington (Lima: Instituto de Estudios Peruanos, 2007); Kent Eaton, *Territory and Ideology in Latin America: Policy Conflicts between National and Subnational Governments* (Oxford: Oxford University Press, 2017); Mary Thorp and Graciela Zevallos, "Las políticas económicas del régimen de Fujimori: ¿Un retorno al pasado?" *Economía: Revista del Departamento de Economía de la PUCP* 24, no. 47 (2001): 9–42. Production boomed and the value of Peru's mineral exports grew by 6,000 percent during the nineties; see Gerardo Damonte, "Dinámicas rentistas: Transformaciones institucionales en contextos de proyectos de Gran Minería," in *Desarrollo rural y recursos naturales*, ed. Gerardo Damonte (Lima: GRADE, 2012). From 1990 to 2011, over three hundred foreign mining firms established a base in Peru; see Alfredo Gurmendi, "The Mineral Industry of Peru," *Minerals Yearbook* (Washington, DC: United States Geological Survey, 2011).
32. Javier Arellano-Yanguas, "Mining Policies in Humala's Peru: A Patchwork of Improvised Nationalism and Corporate Interests," in *The Political Economy of Natural Resources and Development: From Neoliberalism to Resource Nationalism*, eds. Paul Haslam and Pablo Heidrich (London: Routledge, 2016).
33. Defensoría del Pueblo, *Defensoría del Pueblo dio a conocer relación de acciones humanitarias realizadas ante los lamentables sucesos ocurridos en Bagua* (Lima, Defensoría del Pueblo, 2009).

34. Critics refer pejoratively to these cluster reforms as *paquetazos ambientales*, which could be blandly translated as "environmental packages," but the *-azos* suffix connotes both magnitude and the action of striking or hitting (e.g., as in *latigazos*, which means "lashes from a whip").
35. Francisco Durand, *Cuando el poder extractivo captura el estado: Lobbies, puertas giratorias, y paquetazo ambiental en Perú*" (Lima: Oxfam International, 2016). The 2014 reforms were not the last: new environmental deregulation was approved in early 2018.
36. At least 69,280 people died as a result of this conflict, and countless people were injured and otherwise affected by it. For a thorough review, see Comisión de la Verdad y Reconciliación's final report: *Informe Final*.
37. Cynthia J. Arnson, "Introduction: Conflict, Democratization, and the State," in *In the Wake of War: Democratization and Internal Armed Conflict in Latin America*, ed. Cynthia J. Arnson (Washington, DC: Woodrow Wilson Center Press and Stanford University Press, 2012).
38. Maiah Jaskoski, "Private Financing of the Military: A Local Political Economy Approach," *Studies in Comparative International Development* 48, no. 2 (Summer 2013): 172–95.
39. Damonte, "Dinámicas rentistas," 110.
40. "CIDH Expresa su Preocupación por Criminalización de la Protesta Social," Coordinadora Nacional de Derechos Humanos, November 10, 2014, https://derechoshumanos.pe/2014/11/cidh-expresa-su-preocupacion-por-criminalizacion-de-la-protesta-social.
41. Key cases of these allegations of police-inflicted torture on detained protesters include those of Marco Arana, congressperson since 2016 and, prior to that, a key leader of the protests against Yanacocha in Cajamarca, and of Antonio Coasaca, a farmer detained during a protest against the Tía María mine. Coasaca was beaten while in police custody, and subjected to an attempt by national police to plant weapons on him, incriminate him, and frame him as a violent protestor—all with the full complicity of the nationwide daily newspaper *Correo*; see "Video: Habla Antonio Coasaca, agricultor que fue 'sembrado' por la policía." *El búho*, April 28, 2015; "Grave denuncia sobre la actuación de la DINOES en el Valle del Campo," Coordinadora Nacional de Derechos Humanos, April 24, 2015, http://derechoshumanos.pe/2015/04/grave-denuncia-sobre-la-actuacion-de-la-dinoes-en-el-valle-del-tambo.
42. Fiorella Triscritti, "The Criminalization of Anti-Mining Social Protest in Peru," *State of the Planet: Blogs from the Earth Institute*, Columbia University, September 10, 2012, http://blogs.ei.columbia.

edu/2012/09/10/peru-mining. According to officials from the National Dialogue and Sustainability Office, García's approach toward mining protests borrowed heavily from the state's approach in dealing with the Sendero Luminoso terrorist group. The state's militarized response to internal insurgent groups, infamous for its scant regard for human rights, directly shaped the response to mining conflicts. I would like to thank Kent Eaton for this insight.

43. Mirtha Vásquez, "Criminalización de la protesta en su máxima expresión," *Revista voces*, September 2012.
44. Mirtha Vásquez (human rights and environmental rights attorney), personal interview, March 12, 2016. That these charges are often trumped up to dissuade other protestors is apparent in cases where members of the Rondas Campesinas—rural vigilante groups whose authority and jurisdiction are recognized by the Peruvian constitution—are being tried for "kidnapping" when they arguably have a legitimate right to detain suspects and turn them over to police. Examples include sixteen *ronderos* from Celendín and Sorochuco provinces who had organized a meeting to be heard by their government representatives, but because those officials claim that they were at the meeting against their will, the ronderos are being charged with kidnapping. Another couple of ronderos from the area once detained two suspects who were attempting to purchase lands from neighbors; for questioning these men, despite not using force, they too are charged with kidnapping. Similar charges are trumped up in the case of Dina Mendoza, a well-known social organizer and community leader who participated in a water march and, as of 2018, was condemned to four years in jail (although she was given a suspended sentence) and a fine of 3,000 soles (about US$1,000) for obstructing public roads.
45. Jacqueline Fowks, "Preocupación en Perú por el nivel de concentración de prensa," *El país,* September 10, 2013.
46. See José de Echave, "Hernando de Soto Habla de un 'Sendero Verde' Sin Ningún Sustento," *La república*, May 12, 2016; "*El comercio* censura a . . . ¿Martha Meier Miró Quesada?" *La mula*, February 7, 2015.
47. In my experience and my reading, the vast majority of protesters are not anti-miners. During my fourteen months of fieldwork between 2014 and 2016, I heard repeatedly that people do not oppose extraction, but rather seek fair treatment. And in some cases, people *in favor* of extractive projects are the ones who organize protests; see Bebbington et al., "Mining and Social Movements." To summarize, the idea that protesters are "violent anti-miners," working knowingly or ignorantly for some "NGO conspiracy" against the country's heroic impre-

sarios, might be easy to digest and to sell. However, it reduces and harms the complex relations between diverse actors in state institutions, companies, local groups, and outside organizations. In contrast to this, many interviewees, some from the mining sector, recognized the problem of adopting conspiratorial, demeaning, and polarizing discourses, and some outlined their work to actively debunk these.

48. Butler, *Frames of War*.
49. For a detailed discussion of this, see Michael Wilson Becerril, "Frames in Conflict: Discursive Contestation and the Transformation of Resistance," in *Civil Resistance and Violent Conflict in Latin America*, eds. Cécile Mouly and Esperanza Hernández (New York: Palgrave Macmillan, 2019).
50. Personal communication, March 25, 2016.
51. Wieviorka, *Violence*, 3.

CHAPTER 3

1. José de Echave, "Tantas veces Tambogrande," Cooperacción (blog), February 25, 2014, http://www.cooperaccion.org.pe/opina/43-cooperaccion-opina/1645-tantas-veces-tambogrande.
2. It is key to distinguish at the outset the terms used here. *Tambo Grande*, two words, is the official name of the mining project, whereas the district itself is named *Tambogrande*.
3. Nelson Peñaherrera Castillo (activist and journalist), personal communication, April 19, 2018.
4. Sidney Tarrow, *The New Transnational Activism* (Cambridge, UK: Cambridge University Press, 2005).
5. Karyn Keenan, José De Echave, and Ken Traynor, "Mining Rights and Community Rights: Poverty amidst Wealth," in *Reclaiming Nature: Environmental Justice and Ecological Restoration*, eds. James K. Boyce, Sunita Narain, and Elizabeth A. Stanton (London: Anthem Press, 2007), 195.
6. Håvard Haarstad, "Globalización, narrativas y redes: Conflictos sobre la actividad minera en Tambogrande, Piura," *Espacio y desarrollo* (December 2008): 87–107.
7. See Robert Moran, *An Alternative Look at a Proposed Mine in Tambogrande, Peru* (Washington, DC: Oxfam America, Mineral Policy Center, and Environmental Mining Council of British Columbia, August 15, 2001).

8. Anthony Bebbington, "Social Conflict and Emergent Institutions: Hypotheses from Piura, Peru," in *Social Conflict, Economic Development and the Extractive Industry: Evidence from South America,* ed. Anthony Bebbington (New York, NY: Routledge, 2012), pp. 72.
9. Luis Riofrío (organic mango farmer and movement leader), personal interview, September 17, 2015.
10. "Manhattan to Resume Exploration at Montosa," *Northern Miner*, August 7, 1995; "Manhattan Wins Approvals," *Northern Miner*, May 24, 1999.
11. Fabiana Li, *Unearthing Conflict: Corporate Mining, Activism, and Expertise in Peru* (Durham, NC: Duke University Press, 2015), 8.
12. Luis Riofrío, personal interview, September 17, 2015.
13. Haarstad, "Globalización, narrativas, y redes," 95–96.
14. Alfredo Rengifo Navarrete, personal interview, September 18, 2015.
15. Roldan Muradian, Joan Martinez-Alier, and Humberto Correa, "International Capital versus Local Population: The Environmental Conflict of the Tambogrande Mining Project, Peru," *Society and Natural Resources* 16, no. 9 (2003): 775–92.
16. Gina Alvarado Merino, "Políticas neoliberales en el manejo de los recursos naturales en Perú: El caso del conflicto agrominero de Tambogrande," in *Gestión ambiental y conflicto social en América Latina*, eds. Gina Alvarado Merino et al. (Buenos Aires, Argentina: CLACSO, 2008): 67–103; Moran, "An Alternative Look," 5–18.
17. Francisco Ojeda, "Tambogrande: A Community in Defence of Its Rights," in *Community Rights and Corporate Responsibility: Canadian Mining and Oil Companies in Latin America*, eds. Liisa North, Timothy David Clark, and Viviana Patroni (Toronto, Canada: Between the Lines, 2006), 60–61.
18. Anonymous activist, personal interview, September 17, 2015.
19. Cited in *Tambogrande: Mangoes, Murder, Mining*, documentary film directed by Stephanie Boyd and Ernesto Cabellos (Lima: Guarango Films 2006).
20. Moran, "An Alternative Look," 9.
21. Martín (former Manhattan geologist and explorer), personal interview, September 16, 2015.
22. Liliana Alzamora, personal interview, September 19, 2015.
23. Anonymous journalist, personal interview, September 21, 2015.
24. Anonymous member of ADIMTA, personal interview, September 15, 2015.
25. Anonymous former mayor of a nearby district, personal interview, September 12, 2015.

26. Mariano Fiestas, personal interview, September 17, 2015.
27. Mariano Fiestas, personal interview, September 17, 2015.
28. Boyd and Cabellos, *Tambogrande.*
29. "Tambogrande, una década de impunidad," *Diario correo* (Lima), October 11, 2010.
30. Francisco Ojeda, "Tambogrande," 62.
31. Nelson Peñaherrera Castillo, personal communication, April 19, 2018. See also Hannah Hennessy, "Gold Mine Fails to Glitter in Peru," *BBC News*, December 3, 2003.
32. Allan Robinson, "Manhattan Gold Mine in Peru Faces Vote," *Globe and Mail*, May 10, 2002.
33. Boyd and Cabellos, *Tambogrande.*
34. Almut Schilling-Vacaflor and Riccarda Flemmer, "Conflict Transformation through Prior Consultation? Lessons from Peru," *Journal of Latin American Studies* 47, no. 4 (2015): 818.
35. Keenan, De Echave, and Traynor, "Mining Rights and Community Rights," 196.
36. Moran, "An Alternative Look," v.
37. Maiah Jaskoski makes a similar point about the opportunity created by these EIA audiences in other contexts. See Maiah Jaskoski, "Environmental Licensing and Conflict in Peru's Mining Sector: A Path-Dependent Analysis," *World Development* 64 (December): 873–83.
38. For a movement that had already scaled up, preventing these formalities was easy through mass protest, physical blockades, and legal obstruction. After Tambogrande, lawmakers rescinded the law requiring companies to present their EIA in the local, regional, and national capitals. Peru's mining law now requires, rather nebulously, "formal instances of diffusion and community participation" and "informal instances that applicants must encourage, to incorporate during the environmental impact assessment the perceptions and opinion of the population to be potentially affected or benefitted." See Ministerio del Ambiente, "Ley del sistema nacional de impacto ambiental y su reglamento" (Lima, Peru: Ministerio del Ambiente, Gobierno del Peru, 2011).
39. "Centromin Peru Ruling on Tambogrande Option Agreement," Manhattan Minerals Corp. press release, BusinessWire, December 10, 2003, https://businesswire.com/news/home/20031210005946/en/Manhattan-Minerals-Corp-Centromin-Peru-Ruling-Tambogrande.
40. Aiden Corkery, "Manhattan Pulls Out after US$60mn Tambogrande Loss," *BN Americas*, February 7, 2005; see also "Minera Manhattan

desiste de explotar Tambogrande y anuncia retiro del Perú," *La república*, February 8, 2015.

41. Hernándo de Soto wrote these words in *Mining Press*, one of the industry's leading publications. See Zaraí Toledo Orozco, "Tambogrande ayer y hoy," *Útero*, August 7, 2015.
42. Scholars such as Moisés Arce (2015) have taken the presence of robust and lucrative nonmining activities in the area as the factor that explains the movement's success. This factor certainly sets the case apart from the other three in this book. While I agree that it is important, this thesis is not particularly about movement "success"; rather, my effort here is to illustrate ethnographically the ground-level factors, proximate dynamics, and local agency that often go missing from simplistic accounts that emphasize these structural and economic factors alone.
43. Nelson Peñaherrera Castillo, personal communication, April 19, 2018.
44. See, e.g., Cynthia Enloe, *Globalization and Militarism: Feminists Make the Link* (Landham, MD: Rowman & Littlefield, 2007); Amina Mama, "Challenging Militarized Masculinities," *OpenDemocracy*, May 29, 2013; Laura Sjoberg, *Gendering Global Conflict* (New York: Columbia University Press, 2013).

CHAPTER 4

1. Raúl Benavides (Buenaventura executive), personal interview, February 10, 2016; Jimmy Guarnizo (Buenaventura), personal interview, February 11, 2016; anonymous Buenaventura regional manager, personal interview, March 31, 2016; anonymous Buenaventura local manager, personal interview, March 3, 2016.
2. Yanacocha grew exponentially in its first decade of production; in 1993 it produced eighty-one thousand ounces of gold, but in 2004 it produced three million ounces. See "Big Mining and Its Increasingly Radical Opponents," *Economist*, February 3, 2005. In the 1990s, early protests decried the low prices the company paid for land; for example, as early as 1993, local farmers denounced the intimidation attempts that Yanacocha's employees made to pressure them to sell their lands.
3. Newmont owns 51.35 percent of Yanacocha, Buenaventura has 43.65 percent, and the World Bank's International Finance Corporation owned 5 percent (until 2018). Before Yanacocha, the Peruvian mining

giant Buenaventura had already owned and operated another mine in Cajamarca, the low-profile Colquirrumi mine in the Hualgayoc district, since 1972. It also had worked together with the World Bank well before Yanacocha; the IFC invested in Buenaventura's Uchucchacua mine in the Lima region in 1979. In contrast, La Zanja is a dual-partnership, in which Buenaventura is the majority holder and operator (with 53 percent of stocks), and Newmont is the minority shareholder (47 percent). One side note worth making here is that Buenaventura, as a Peruvian company, has a long history of establishing itself as a key player in Peruvian economy and politics (since its founding by Alberto Benavides in 1953). This may help to explain its success in mobilizing state and media power and overcoming its opposition, although I would rather be careful not to over-rely on this argument alone, and to instead elaborate the mechanisms that may explain how and why.

4. Roger Cabos, "Potencial Minero en la Región Huancavelica," Compañía de Minas Buenaventura, 2005.
5. Freddy Regalado (Buenaventura, Minera La Zanja, Grupo Norte), personal interview, March 9, 2016.
6. Anonymous Pulán shop owner, personal interview, March 27, 2016.
7. See "Tangled Strands in Fight over Peru Gold Mine," *New York Times*, June 14, 2010.
8. Rondas Campesinas are rural, autonomous vigilantes, whose jurisdiction is enshrined in Peruvian law.
9. GRUFIDES, "Para Entender el Conflicto Minero Campesino en La Zanja, Cajamarca," *La Minería y sus impactos*, SERVINDI, no. 57 (2004), https://issuu.com/juancamilo02/docs/serv_57_mineria.
10. Observatorio de Conflictos Mineros en el Perú, *10º Informe del OCM*, 11; Triscritti, "Mining, Development, and Corporate-Community Relations in Peru," 439; Jonathan Kishen Gamu, "Corporate Security Governance: Multinational Mining Companies and the Local Political Economy of Violence in Peru" (PhD diss., University of British Columbia, 2016), 114. See also Wilfredo Ardito Vega, "Sobre el Premio Nacional de Derechos Humanos para Marco Arana," *Adital*, 2004.
11. Rosario Mayorga and Maritza Roncal, "Ronderos de Santa Cruz Exigen Retiro de Minera Buenaventura," *La república*, November 18, 2004.
12. Robert Santillán (Cajamarca journalist), personal interview, March 11, 2016.
13. Adolfo Orejuela Chirinos (mining consultant), personal interview, March 8, 2016.
14. Anonymous Buenaventura officer, personal interview, February 11, 2016.

15. Jimmy Guarnizo (Buenaventura environmental officer), personal interview, February 11, 2016.
16. "Halting the Rush against Gold," *Economist*, February 3, 2005.
17. Maritza Roncal, "Cajamarca: Hoy Se Inicia Paro de 48 Horas en Santa Cruz," *La república*, November 22, 2004.
18. "La Zanja: ¿Solo una protesta ambiental?" *Noticias SER*, November 24, 2004.
19. "Big Mining and Its Increasingly Radical Opponents," *Economist*, February 3, 2005.
20. Rodolfo Orejuela Chirinos, personal interview, March 8, 2016.
21. Anonymous Buenaventura officer, personal interview, August 8, 2016.
22. "Dan ultimatum a Buenaventura-Newmont para abandonar La Zanja-Pulán Cajamarca," *Diario el sol* (Cajamarca), April 29, 2007, https://www.ocmal.org/3759.
23. "Romero Salatiel Alcalde de Pulán," YouTube video, 5:13, posted by Trolatiel, August 17, 2007, https://www.youtube.com/watch?v=Unok2mIwTro.
24. "Coronel Pérez: Comuneros quisieron incendiar campamento La Zanja," *Diario panorama*, May 15, 2007.
25. CNDDHH, "Caso Majaz: Indemnizan a 33 campesinos que fueron torturados en campamento minero," Coordinadora Nacional de Derechos Humanos, July 20, 2011, http://derechoshumanos.pe/2011/07/caso-majaz-indemnizan-a-33-campesinos-que-fueron-torturados-en-campamento-minero; Charis Kamphuis, "Foreign Investment and the Privatization of Coercion: A Case Study of the Forza Security Company in Peru," *Brooklyn Journal of International Law* 37, no. 2 (January 2011): 529–78; Brant McGee, "The Community Referendum: Participatory Democracy and the Right to Free, Prior and Informed Consent to Development," *Berkeley Journal of International Law* 27, no. 2 (2009): 570–635.
26. "Crónica de un reglaje al 'Diablo'," *La república*, December 4. 2006; "Nuevas pruebas acusan a Forza," *La república*, February 3, 2007; "Fiscal archiva caso de espionaje al Padre Arana sin haber citado a nadie de 'Forza,'" *La república*, February 2, 2007.
27. Anonymous social leader (Frente de Defensa) in Pulán, personal interview, March 28, 2016; anonymous woman in Santa Cruz, personal interview, March 26, 2016; Gregorio Santos Guerrero, "Muerte de Alcalde de Pulán: Accidente o atentado?" *El maletero verde*, July 31, 2007; "Alcalde de Pulán Muere en accidente," *Diario panorama*, June 16, 2007.
28. "Falla humana habría generado accidente del Alcalde de Pulán," *El clarín*, June 28, 2007.

29. Anonymous regional La Zanja operator, personal interview, March 31, 2016.
30. "Homenaje a Salatiel Romero, ex alcalde de Pulán, Aventureros," YouTube video, 6:08, posted by 11250416, December 22, 2007, https://www.youtube.com/watch?v=e9HN2Dki2_Y.
31. "Nacionalistas reafirman la estatización de la minería," *Diario panorama* (Cajamarca), June 26, 2007.
32. "Presentan proyecto minero La Zanja ante el gobierno regional Cajamarca," *El clarín*, August 7, 2007.
33. "Minería: Contaminación mata a 5 mil truchas," *La república*, September 5, 2007; Antonio Eneque Soraluz, "Informe de visita a minera La Zanja," *EcoVida* (blog), August 16, 2011, http://eccovidahotmail.blogspot.com/2011/08/informe-de-visita-minera-la-zanja.html.
34. Anonymous member of Cajamarca's regional government, personal interview, March 8, 2016.
35. Andrés Caballero, "Pronunciamiento Municipalidad Distrital de Pulán," *CaballeroVerde*, July 5, 2008.
36. "Proyecto minero La Zanja fue aprobado por distrito cajamarquino de Pulán," *El comercio*, July 4, 2008.
37. "Comuneros cajamarquinos apoyan inicio de operaciones del proyecto minero La Zanja," *Agencia andina*, July 4, 2008.
38. Elizabeth Prado, "Objetan aprobación de estudio técnico de La Zanja," *La república*, July 5, 2008.
39. GRUFIDES, "Caso La Zanja," last modified 2015, http://www.grufides.org/casos/caso-la-zanja.
40. "Agricultores toman las calles de Chiclayo," *La república*, December 12, 2008.
41. "Marcha de Ronderos en Sta Cruz Cajamarca [Parts 1–4]," YouTube videos, posted by Videoreportero William Soberón, January 22, 2009, http://prensadigitaldelperu.blogspot.com/2009/02/ronderos-de-cajamarca-exigen-libertad.html.
42. Coordinadora Nacional de Derechos Humanos, *Informe Anual 2011–2012* (Lima: Coordinadora Nacional de Derechos Humanos, 2012), 23; Wilfredo Ardito Vega, *La promoción del acceso a la justicia en las zonas rurales* (Lima: Poder Judicial del Perú, Oficina Nacional de Justicia y Paz Indígena, 2014), 134.
43. Ronald Ordoñez, "Rondas Campesinas de Santa Cruz exijen nulidad de concesiones Mineras," *Central Única Nacional de Rondas Campesinas del Perú* (blog), November 19, 2009, http://cunarcperu.org/index.php?limitstart=891. On November 16, the Frente held a massive march

in Chiclayo; see "Exigen anular concesión minera a La Zanja," *La república*, November 17, 2009.

44. Tribunal Constitucional del Perú, "Sentencia Expediente No. 01848–2011-PA/TC" (Resolution, Lima, October 19, 2011) http://www.tc.gob.pe/jurisprudencia/2011/01848–2011-AA.html.
45. On the arrest and the cadmium study, see Elizabeth Prado, "Detienen a dirigente que denunció a una minera," *La república*, February 3, 2010. On the blood test results, see Defensoría del Pueblo, "Reporte mensual de conflictos sociales N° 142 – Diciembre 2015" (Lima: Defensoría del Pueblo, 2015); and Gobierno Regional de Cajamarca, "Resolución de Órgano Instructor No. 0004–2016-GR.CAJ-GGR" (report, Cajamarca, March 11, 2016).
46. "Advierten protestas por proyecto minero La Zanja en Santa Cruz," *Coordinadora nacional de radio* (Lima), February 2, 2010.
47. Patricia Zevallos, "Cajamarca: Trabajadores de minera La Zanja continuan paro indefinido," *El comercio*, July 20, 2011; Ronald Ordoñez, "Cajamarca: Reclaman mejora de carretera a minera La Zanja," *Noticias SER*, October 11, 2017. See also Observatorio de Conflictos Mineros en el Perú, *21° Informe del OCM, Segundo Semestre 2017*, (Lima: Cooperacción, November 2017).
48. For example, see Edgar Jara, "DINOES desaloja y recupera el control de vía a Hualgayoc," *La república*, August 30, 2013.
49. Anonymous environmental activist, personal interview, March 28, 2016.
50. Front Line Defenders, *Dispatches: Reports from the Front Line, January–December 2011* (Dublin: Front Line Defenders, 2011), https://www.frontlinedefenders.org/en/file/1428; "Libertad inmediata para Estinaldo Quispe," *Coordinadora nacional de derechos humanos*, August 9, 2011.
51. "Asesinan a dirigente de Rondas Campesinas de Santa Cruz de Cajamarca," *La república*, June 26, 2013.
52. Anonymous member of the mothers' club, personal interview, March 27, 2016.
53. Anonymous, personal interview, March 27, 2016.
54. Specifically, resolutions 89 and 90 by the National Water Authority allowed MLZ to introduce 1,734,480 cubic meters of treated industrial residue liquids from its tailings and refuse deposit. One Chiclayo attorney denounced that this was a flagrant overturning of a 2009 decision by the Health Ministry's Environmental Health Office, in Resolución 22–06–2009, that Minera La Zanja would not be allowed to redirect its residual waste, even if treated, into public waterways due to the risk of pollution through the cyanide-containing waste. See "Explican Autorización para Verter Aguas Residuales de Minera,"

Gobierno Regional de Lambayeque (blog), November 20, 2012, https://www.regionlambayeque.gob.pe/web/noticia/detalle/10897.

55. An investigation into who was responsible for the delay, conducted by the regional government in Cajamarca, reviewed all correspondence and found that the central state in Lima decided to withhold the study results from publication. See Gobierno Regional Cajamarca, "Resolución de Órgano."
56. Anonymous health official in the area near the mine, personal interview, March 28, 2016. See also Defensoría del Pueblo, *Reporte mensual de conflictos sociales N°142*; Defensoría del Pueblo, *Decimonoveno informe anual de la Defensoría del Pueblo, Enero-Diciembre 2015* (Lima: Defensoría del Pueblo, 2016): 108–9; Ronald Ordoñez, "Cajamarca reduce presupuesto para víctimas de contaminación," *Noticias SER*, October 11, 2017; Elizabeth Prado, "Contaminación del Agua y Plomo en Sangre Mobiliza a Pobladores de Hualgayoc," *La república*, June 4, 2015; "Funcionarios ocultaron contaminación"; Magali Zevallos, "Minería y petróleo en Perú son los principales contaminantes de las poblaciones indígenas y andinas," *Gran angular*, December 12, 2017.
57. Anonymous social leader and Frente de Defensa member in Pulán, personal interview, March 28, 2016; anonymous elected official in Pulán's municipality, personal interview, March 28, 2016; anonymous health official in the area near the mine, personal interview, March 28, 2016; anonymous shop owner in Pulán, personal interview, March 27, 2016.
58. Anonymous group of elderly women, personal interviews, March 4, 2016.
59. Freddy Regalado (Buenaventura), personal interview, March 9, 2016; Violeta Vigo, Fondo Los Andes de Cajamarca (Yanacocha's CSR initiative in Cajamarca), personal interview, March 9, 2016.
60. Anonymous academic and social movement leader in Cajamarca, personal interview, February 29, 2016.
61. "La Zanja: Un ejemplo de éxito," in *Conflictos sociales en el Perú (2008–2015)*, eds. Carlos Basombrío, Fernando Rospigliosi, and Ricardo Valdés (Lima: Capital Humano y Social, 2016), 189.

CHAPTER 5

1. Waldemar Espinoza Soriano, "San José de Quiruvilca: Origen y vicisitudes de un asiento minero," *Investigaciones sociales* 15, no. 27 (2001): 133–79.

2. See Jaime de Althaus, "La triste contribución de los antimineros," *Lampadia* (blog), April 1, 2013, http://www.lampadia.com/opiniones/jaime-de-althaus/la-triste-contribucion-de-los-antimineros.
3. Two anonymous Ronderos, personal interview, November 12, 2015.
4. For an example, see Barrick Gold, "Alto Chicama Feasibility Update" (presentation, Denver Gold Forum, Denver, CO, September 24, 2003).
5. Moreover, one former Barrick executive told me that part of the company's success in installing its Lagunas Norte mine so quickly was owed to how Barrick had originally tied the construction of its mine to a project to build a road connecting the Andean interior of the La Libertad region to the coastal, urban, cosmopolitan Trujillo (the regional capital and the third largest city in the country). In the former executive's words, "Barrick was very intelligent," since it needed the road but knew it could exploit its construction as a way to fulfill a social need to integrate the region. Anonymous former Barrick officer, personal interview, November 4, 2015.
6. Companies are beholden to different layers of legal responsibilities. First, there is the 2004 law of tax redistribution, by which they pay 30 percent in taxes—15 percent to the national government and the other 15 percent to be split by their host areas: 3 percent to the regional government, .8 percent to the public university, 1.5 percent to the district municipality, 3.8 percent to the provincial seat, and 6 percent to other municipalities in the region. Second, they were committed to a "good-faith" voluntary contribution program during Alan García's presidency. Third, they have the option of investing in social welfare programs "for the state" instead of paying some income taxes.
7. Arturo, Rondero activist and seasonal mine worker, personal communication, June 14, 2016. See also, "Así fue el enfrentamiento en Barro Negro, Usquil," YouTube video, 13:01, posted by Ozono Television, June 19, 2016, www.youtube.com/watch?v=8Ay4fFS3lt4.
8. Wilson Arenda and Karen Solís, "Campesinos baleados en gresca con policías en Quiruvilca viven un drama," *La república*, June 12, 2016.
9. "Otuzco: Dos policías desaparecidos tras enfrentamientos con Ronderos," *RPP*, June 9, 2016.
10. "Buzos buscan cuerpos de policías desaparecidos en laguna de Quiruvilca," *La república*, June 10, 2016.
11. "Biólogo trujillano advierte el riesgo de construir una carretera en zonas naturales," *Chami radio*, August 12, 2016; "Fuerte enfrentamiento en Quiruvilca," *Lucha indígena* 19, June 12, 2016; "Ronderos defienden lagunas en Otuzco, policía les dispara y hiere a diecinueve – La Libertad – norte de Perú," *Tomate colectivo* (blog), June

12, 2016, https://tomatecolectivo.wordpress.com/2016/06/12/ronderos-defienden-lagunas-en-otuzco-policia-les-dispara-y-hiere-a-diecinueve-la-libertad-norte-de-peru.

12. See for instance Colectivo Alto Chicama's Facebook page: https://www.facebook.com/altochicama.

13. I borrow from Cecilia Perla's reflections on the literature here. See Perla, "Extracting from the Extractors." See also Marina Welker, "Global Capitalism and the 'Caring Corporation': Mining and the Corporate Social Responsibility Movement in Indonesia and Denver (Colorado)" (PhD diss., University of Michigan, 2006).

14. Espinoza Soriano, "San José de Quiruvilca," 136. Needless to say, even though they worked in relatively large scales and with an impressive level of organization, neither the Huamachucos nor the Inca used open-pit excavation, nor cyanide heap-leaching processes, to extract the mineral.

15. See Barrick Peru, "Alto Chicama project, Las Lagunas Norte" (presentation, Trujillo, Peru, November 10, 2004).

16. Mario Rojas Delgado, "Perspectivas de procesamiento y uso del carbón mineral peruano," *Ingeniería industrial* no. 26 (2008): 231–50.

17. See Gregory C. Wilkins, "Building Mines, Building Value" (Barrick Gold Corporation presentation on Investor Day, New York, NY, February 24, 2004). In this presentation, Barrick's regional vice president for the South America region, Igor Gonzales, also detailed Barrick's plans to explore at Veladero, in Argentina, and at Pascua Lama, in Argentina and Chile—projects that both would face fierce opposition over the coming years, especially in contrast to Lagunas Norte.

18. Reports from Defensoría del Pueblo from mid-2004 follow the story of how the mayor of Quiruvilca was almost beaten, then had to operate remotely for security reasons, after he announced that Barrick's contracts office had moved to Huamachuco in June. See Defensoría del Pueblo, *Reporte mensual de conflictos sociales N° 7* (Lima: Defensoría del Pueblo, 2004).

19. See Gregory C. Wilkins, "Building Mines, Building Value"; see also Barrick Peru, "Alto Chicama project, Las Lagunas Norte."

20. Anonymous former Barrick officer, personal interview, November 4, 2015.

21. See "La producción de oro en el Perú caería hasta 9%," *La prensa* (Peru), February 26, 2013; Jean F. Ramos Beltrán, "Situación y perspectiva de desarrollo de la minería en el Perú: 2000–2010" (PhD diss., Universidad Nacional de Trujillo, August 2010).

22. These 2011 statistics from the Peruvian State's National Statistics and Information Institute (INEI in Spanish) are cited in Giulliana Tamblyn,

"Quiruvilca: The Silver Tooth of the Peruvian Andes" (master's thesis, National University of British Columbia, January 2014), 62.

23. To be sure, this looms as a significant difference between this case and the La Zanja case, for example.
24. *Los conflictos mineros se agudizan y el gobierno incumple creación de comisión de alto nivel*, proclamation, Confederación Nacional de Comunidades Afectadas por la Minería (CONACAMI), 25 July 2005. The same statement listed Minera La Zanja as "violating the right to territory" in Santa Cruz, in the adjacent region of Cajamarca.
25. Anonymous biologist, personal interview, November 18, 2015.
26. César Medina Tafur et al., "El índice 'Biological Monitoring Working Party' (BMWP), modificado y adaptado a tres microcuencas del Alto Chicama. La Libertad. Perú. 2008," *Sciéndo: Ciencia para el desarrollo* (UNT, Peru), 13, no. 2 (2010): 5–20.
27. See also César Medina Tafur, Walter Pereda, Manuel Hora, Ivonne Asencio, Ronal Gabriel, and José Polo, "Calidad del agua en las cuencas del Alto Chicama utilizando macroinvertebrados bentónicos como indicadores biológicos, La Libertad, Peru (2008–2009)" (presentation, Universidad Nacional de Trujillo, 2010).
28. César Medina Tafur (UNT biologist), personal interview, November 18, 2015.
29. Ivonne Asencio Guzmán (Universidad César Vallejo biologist), personal interview, November 6, 2015.
30. César Medina Tafur (UNT biologist), personal interview, November 18, 2015.
31. Anonymous public defendant, personal interview, November 6, 2015.
32. Anonymous Rondero, personal interview, November 12, 2015; anonymous regional Ministry of Energy and Mining official, personal interview, November 23, 2015; anonymous officer from the Nacional Office on Dialogue and Sustainability, personal interview, November 20, 2015.
33. Anonymous municipal clerk, personal interview, November 8, 2015.
34. See Asociación Interétnica de Desarrollo de la Selva Peruana and Coordinadora Nacional de Derechos Humanos, *Pueblos indígenas del Perú: Balance 2014 sobre el cumplimiento del convenio 169 de la OIT* (Lima: CNDH and AIDESEP, 2009), 61.
35. Once again, this accords with Maiah Jaskoski's argument about the disruptive opportunity afforded by these meetings. See Jaskoski, "Environmental Licensing and Conflict in Peru's Mining Sector."
36. "El Otro Lado de la Barrick," YouTube video, 5:15, posted by "Maria Fe Celi," October 16, 2010, https://www.youtube.com/watch?v=5m56DkYpb-Y.

37. Anonymous official in the municipal development office, personal interview, November 11, 2015.
38. Anonymous local attorney, personal interview, November 9, 2015.
39. Anonymous Rondero and miner, personal interview, November 12, 2015.
40. See Policía Nacional del Perú, "RD No. 2373-2006-DIRGEN/EM" (agreement, Lima, November 7, 2006). Via this agreement, the company representative Manuel Fumagalli Drago and PNP representative PNP General Pedro Edgardo Moreno Ruidías, director of the Special Operations Division, signed the private security agreement. See also Asociación Pro Derechos Humanos, "La transformación ausente: Industrias extractivas y situación de las DESCA," (Lima: APRODEH, 2012), 175. Note: DIROES is not to be mistaken with DINOES, the PNP Division of Special Operations counterterrorism and antisubversion unit housed under DIROES. For more on these two police entities, see Renata Bregaglio et al., *Diagnóstico nacional sobre la situación de la seguridad y el respeto a los derechos humanos referencia particular al sector extractivo en el Perú* (Lima: Instituto de Democracia y Derechos Humanos de la Pontificia Universidad Católica del Perú, November 2003).
41. However, an area mayor lamented how the company provided very little of the work opportunities and social development investment it had promised to quell conflict. He also argued that the social movement had not been violent, unlike police. Anonymous area mayor, personal interview, November 9, 2015.
42. See Kent Eaton, "Disciplining Regions: Subnational Contention in Neoliberal Peru," *Territory, Politics, Governance* 3, no. 2 (2015): 124–46.
43. Barrick Peru, "Alto Chicama Project, Las Lagunas Norte."
44. The PMSP was a reversal of García's promises during the 2006 presidential campaign, when he vowed to tax mining companies on the additional profits they were reaping during the boom in global mineral prices. García had adopted these promises after feeling their widespread popularity, which had, up to that point, contributed to public support behind his main opponent in the election, Ollanta Humala Tasso. But after narrowly winning the second round of the presidential election, with 52.6 percent of the vote compared to Humala's 47.4 percent, García was perceived as capitulating to the mining lobbies when he instead proposed this voluntary scheme. See Javier Arellano-Yanguas, *Minería sin fronteras?*, 46.
45. See Igor Ybañez Gamboa, "Día decisivo en el diálogo entre comuneros de Quiruvilca y Barrick," *La república*, February 24, 2013; "Barrick amenaza 5 lagunas en Santiago de Chuco," *Lucha indígena* 79, March

2013; "Bloqueo en Otuzco," *Lucha indígena* 82, June 2013; "Minera Barrick daña lagunas en Quiruvilca," *Lucha indígena* 67, March 2012; "Quiruvilca: Pobladores exigen que compañía minera se retire," *La industria* (Trujillo), August 29, 2017.

46. Anonymous municipal environmental officer, personal interview, November 11, 2015.
47. Wilson Castro, "Quince heridos deja enfrentamiento entre policías y trabajadores de Quiruvilca," *La república*, June 13, 2015; "Informe de contacto: Infernal enfrentamiento en Quiruvilca," *UCV satelital*, June 15, 2015.
48. Anonymous official in the municipal development office, personal interview, November 11, 2015.
49. Anonymous Ministry of Energy and Mining official, personal interview, November 23, 2016; anonymous Rondero and activist, personal interview, November 13, 2016.
50. Véronique Dudouet, *Civil Resistance and Conflict Transformation: Transitions from Armed to Nonviolent Struggle* (New York: Routledge, 2015).
51. Actors who benefit from repression engage in different strategies to prevent it from backfiring. If they can portray themselves as benefactors who must sometimes make use of force, rather than as oppressors, social movement opponents—in this case, mining companies—can avoid the backfire effect. Brian Martin, *Justice Ignited: The Dynamics of Backfire* (New York: Rowman & Littlefield Publishers, 2006). Companies and movements use framing and other tactics to inhibit and promote outrage strategically.

CHAPTER 6

1. Juan Luis Kruger Sayán and Germán Roberto Polack Belaúnde, *Memoria anual y reporte de sostenibilidad 2011* (Lima: Gold Fields, 2012), 12.
2. Anonymous Gold Fields field manager, personal interview, July 13, 2016.
3. Kruger Sayán and Polack Belaúnde, *Memoria anual y reporte de sostenibilidad 2011*, 13.
4. Teresa Santillán, "Hualgayoc, la remediación ambiental sigue pendiente," *Noticias SER*, April 6, 2014.
5. "Gold Fields suspende sus operaciones en Cajamarca por protestas," *Perú21*, October 24, 2006.
6. "Minera Gold Fields se apodera de terrenos de humildes campesinas," *El clarín,* September 27, 2007, www.ocmal.org/3953.

7. Wilmer Delgado Fernández, "Conflicto y negociación," *Observatorio de conflictos mineros de América Latina* (blog), August 27, 2009, https://www.ocmal.org/4940.
8. "Continúa paro indefinido contra Minera Gold Fields en Hualgayoc," *La República*, August 20, 2009.
9. Delgado Fernández, "Conflicto y negociación."
10. See "Hualgayoc exige pronta solución a conflicto minero," *La república*, July 6, 2010.
11. Ministerio de Energía y Minas, *Informe trimestral Julio-Septiembre 2010*. Lima: Gobierno del Perú. http://www.minem.gob.pe/minem/archivos/Informe%20Trimestral%20Julio%20Setiembre%202010%20_ultimo%20WEB__opt.pdf.
12. Ministerio de Salud, *Evaluación de la calidad sanitaria de las aguas del Río Llaucano y tributarios principales, 2011* (Lima: Gobierno del Perú, Dirección General de Salud Ambiental, 2011). http://www.digesa.minsa.gob.pe/DEPA/rios/2011/RIO_LLAUCANO_2011.pdf.
13. Santillán, "Hualgayoc, la remediación ambiental sigue pendiente."
14. "Hualgayoc: Denuncian a Minera Gold Fields por rajaduras de viviendas," *Noticias SER*, April 4, 2012.
15. "Gold Fields aclara que no contamina agua del Río Tingo Maygasbamba," *Panorama cajamarquino*, November 8, 2012.
16. "Protesta Rondera contra Minera Gold Field y Coimolache en Hualgayoc," *Red verde* (blog), March 10, 2013, http://caballeroredverde.blogspot.com/2013/03/protesta-rondera-contra-minera-gold.html.
17. "Mineros protestan contra Gold Fields por pago de utilidades," *La república*, March 23, 2013.
18. "Alcalde de Bambamarca se opone a Conga pero trabaja con Gold Fields," *La república*, April 1, 2013.
19. Jara, "DINOES desaloja y recupera el control de vía a Hualgayoc." Caruajulca is one of several movement leaders who have, as a result of their community leadership, entered institutional, professional, and electoral politics—where she has faced tremendous sexism.
20. Wilfredo Huanachín, "Gold Fields La Cima ampliará operaciones en Cerro Corona," *Gestión*, October 9, 2014.
21. "Hay 43 empresas mineras vinculadas a conflictos," *Gestión*, September 6, 2015.
22. "Hualgayoc acata paro contra contaminación de ríos por mineras," *La república*, May 15, 2016.
23. "From Conflict to Cooperation," *Economist*, February 6, 2016.
24. I obtained a copy of this document, which I can provide to readers upon written request.

25. Anonymous Gold Fields official, personal interview, July 7, 2016.
26. "Gold Fields Halts Peru Exploration Project on Protest," *Bloomberg*, September 18, 2009.
27. Anonymous movement leader, personal interview, July 17, 2016.
28. GRUFIDES, "Conflicto Minero Gold Fields," last modified 2015, http://www.grufides.org/sites/default/files//Documentos/fichas_casos/CONFLICTO%20MINERO%20GOLD%20FIELDS.pdf.
29. Several anonymous Hualgayoc residents, personal interviews, July 2016.
30. Roland Ordoñez, "Comuneros de Cajamarca protestan por más de 950 pasivos ambientales," *La mula*, May 19, 2016.
31. Here I borrow Rob Nixon's term. Nixon uses "slow violence" in other contexts to describe "incremental and accretive" forms of structural violence related to socio-environmental damages. Rob Nixon, *Slow Violence and the Environmentalism of the Poor* (Cambridge: Harvard University Press, 2011), 2.
32. Anonymous environmental activist, personal interview, July 15, 2016.
33. Mónica Belling, "Juan Luis Kruger (Gold Fields La Cima): Conflictos sociales no deben afectar competitividad," *Mining Press*, January 31, 2012.
34. Anonymous Gold Fields field manager, personal interview, July 13, 2016.
35. Anonymous Gold Fields regional manager, personal interview, July 7, 2016.
36. "Gold Fields Fires 8,500 Strikers at South Africa Mine," *Reuters*, October 23, 2012. "Sindicato de trabajadores de Abosso Gold Fields rechaza despido de 340 mineros en Ghana," *IndustriAll*, April 3, 2018.

CONCLUSION

1. Paulo Freire, *Pedagogy of the Oppressed* (New York: Continuum, 1970), 55.
2. I would like to thank Kim Reimann and Philippe Le Billon for influencing these reflections.
3. For seminal works on backfire, see, Brian Martin, "From Political Jiu-Jitsu to the Backfire Dynamic: How Repression Can Promote Mobilization," in *Civil Resistance: Comparative Perspectives on Nonviolent Struggle*, ed. Kurt Schock (Minneapolis: University of Minnesota Press, 2015).
4. Lefebvre, *The Production of Space*.

5. See e.g., Patricia Hill Collins, "The Tie That Binds: Race, Gender, and US Violence," *Ethnic and Racial Studies* 21, no. 5 (1998): 917–38; Yasmin Jiwani, *Discourses of Denial: Mediation, Race, Gender, and Violence* (Vancouver: University of British Columbia Press, 2006); Samantha Sabo et al., "Everyday Violence, Structural Racism, and Mistreatment at the US-Mexico Border," *Social Science and Medicine* 109 (May 2014): 66–74; and Ximena S. Warnaars, "Territorial Transformations in El Pangui, Ecuador: Understanding How Mining Conflict Affects Territorial Dynamics, Social Mobilization, and Daily Life," in *Subterranean Struggles: New Dynamics of Mining, Oil, and Gas in Latin America*, eds. Anthony Bebbington and Jeffrey Bury, 149–72 (Austin: University of Texas Press, 2013). As a Lima-based human rights advocate, Warnaars was also interviewed for this research.
6. Ranajit Guha, *Elementary Aspects of Peasant Insurgency in Colonial India* (Delhi: Oxford University Press, 1983); Krupa Shandilya, "Writing/Reading the Subaltern Woman: Narrative Voice and Subaltern Agency in Upamanyu Chatterjee's *English, August*," *Postcolonial Text* 9, no. 3 (2014).
7. For example, in 2018, the congressperson Carlos Tubino tweeted about Indigenous Shipibo and Conibo leaders, concerned with the killing of one of their leaders, as Ayahuasca-driven "savages." See Dan Collins, "Peru's Brutal Murders Renew Focus on Tourist Boom for Hallucinogenic Brew," *Guardian*, April 29, 2018.; Another intersectional illustration of this is the classist, racist, and sexist Paisana Jacinta TV character, which human rights organizations have denounced before the United Nations and Organization of American States' offices in charge of monitoring racism.
8. Charis Kamphuis, "Foreign Investment and the Privatization of Coercion"; "Caso Majaz: Indemnizan a 33 campesinos que fueron torturados en campamento minero," Coordinadora Nacional de Derechos Humanos, July 20, 2011, http://derechoshumanos.pe/2011/07/caso-majaz-indemnizan-a-33-campesinos-que-fueron-torturados-en-campamento-minero; "Crónica de un reglaje al 'diablo'," *La república*, December 4, 2006; "Fiscal archiva caso de espionaje al Padre Arana sin haber citado a nadie de 'Forza'," *La república*, February 2, 2007; Public Citizen, "On Fifth Anniversary of Peru FTA Bagua Massacre of Indigenous Protestors, State Department Cables Published on Wikileaks Reveal US Role," Intercontinental Cry, June 9, 2014, https://intercontinentalcry.org/fifth-anniversary-peru-fta-bagua-massacre-indigenous-protestors-state-department-cables-published-

wikileaks-reveal-u-s-role; McGee, "The Community Referendum"; "Nuevas pruebas acusan a Forza," *La república*, February 3, 2007; US Embassy in Peru, "Ollanta Humala claims he can save Peru from extremists," Wikileaks Cable: 08LIMA1107_a, dated June 26, 2008, http://wikileaks.org/cable/2008/06/08LIMA1107.html.

9. For more concrete policy proposals that can be gleaned from this study, please see Michael Wilson Becerril, "Entendiendo y previniendo la violencia en conflictos mineros," *Noticias SER*, August 2019.
10. Another such myth this research casts doubt upon is the idea that a district's history with mining can be a factor that explains the outcomes of conflicts. With the exception of the Tambo Grande project proposal, the three other cases in this study all had a history of mining, yet they each experienced different outcomes.

APPENDIX 1

1. Javier Arellano-Yanguas, "A Thoroughly Modern Resource Curse?"; Karl, *The Paradox of Plenty*; Michael Ross, "Review."
2. Carlos Meléndez, "Mediaciones y conflictos: Las transformaciones de la intermediación política y los estallidos de violencia en el Perú actual," in *El estado está de vuelta: Desigualdad, diversidad, y democracia*, ed. Víctor Vich (Lima: Instituto de Estudios Peruanos, 2005); Alfredo F. Ponce and Cynthia McClintock, "The Explosive Combination of Inefficient Local Bureaucracies and Mining Production: Evidence from Localized Societal Protests in Peru," *Latin American Politics and Society* 56, no. 3 (2014): 118–40.
3. Liz Puma and César Bedoya *Transformación de Conflictos* (Lima: ProDialogo, Prevención y Resolución, 2015); Leire Urkidi and Mariana Walter, "Dimensions of Environmental Justice in Anti-Gold Mining Movements in Latin America" *Geoforum* 42 (2011): 683–95.
4. Moisés Arce, *Resource Extraction and Protest in Peru* (Pittsburg: University of Pittsburg Press, 2014); Anthony Bebbington and Jeffrey Bury, *Subterranean Struggles: New Dynamics of Mining, Oil, and Gas in Latin America* (Austin: University of Texas Press, 2014); Bebbington et al., "Contention and Ambiguity."
5. Jeffrey Bury, "Livelihoods in Transition: Transnational Gold Mining Operations and Local Change in Cajamarca, Peru," *Geographic Journal* 170, no. 1 (2004): 78–91; Guillermo Salas, *Dinámica social y minería: Familias pastorales de Puna y la presencia del proyecto antamina (1997–2002)* (Lima: Instituto de Estudios Peruanos, 2008); Kurt Weyland, *The*

Politics of Market Reform in Fragile Democracies: Argentina, Brazil, Peru, and Venezuela (Princeton: Princeton University Press, 2002).

6. Javier Arellano-Yanguas, "Aggravating the Resource Curse: Decentralisation, Mining, and Conflict in Peru," *Journal of Development Studies* 47, no. 4 (2011): 617–38.
7. Anthony Bebbington and Denise Humphreys Bebbington, "Actores y ambientalismos: Continuidades y cambios en los conflictos socioambientales en el Perú," in *Minería y territorio en el Perú: Conflictos, resistencias, y propuestas en tiempos de globalización*, eds. José de Echave, Raphael Hoetmer, and Mario Palacios Panéz. Lima: Programa Democracia y Transformación Global, 2009; Taylor, "Environmentalism and Social Protest."
8. Shane Greene, "Getting Over the Andes: The Geo-Eco-Politics of Indigenous Movements in Peru's Twenty-First Century Inca Empire," *Journal of Latin American Studies* 38, no. 2 (2006): 327–54; Kay Treakle, "Ecuador: Structural Adjustment and Indigenous Environmentalist Resistance," in *The Struggle for Accountability: The World Bank, NGOs, and Grassroots Movements*, eds. Jonathan Fox and David Brown (Boston: MIT Press, 1998); Patricia I. Vásquez, *Oil Sparks in the Amazon: Local Conflicts, Indigenous Populations, and Natural Resources* (Athens: University of Georgia Press, 2014).
9. Alain Joxe, "A Critical Examination of Qualitative Studies Applied to Research in the Causes of Violence," in *Violence and its Causes*, ed. Alan Joxe (Paris: UNESCO, 1981).
10. Wilber Chafee, *The Economics of Violence in Latin America* (London: Praeger, 1992).
11. David Meyer and Nancy Whittier, *Social Movements: Identity, Culture, and the State* (Oxford: Oxford University Press, 2002).
12. Daniel M. Goldstein, "'In Our Own Hands': Lynching, Justice, and the Law in Bolivia," *American Ethnologist* 30, no. 1 (2003): 22–43; Hank Johnston, "Ritual, Strategy, and Deep Culture in the Chechen National Movement," *Critical Studies on Terrorism* 1, no. 3 (2008): 321–42.
13. Valpy Fitzgerald, Frances Stewart, and Rajesh Venugopal, *Globalization, Violent Conflict, and Self-Determination* (New York: Palgrave Macmillan, 2006).
14. Robert Pape, *Dying to Win: The Strategic Logic of Suicide Terrorism* (New York: Random House, 2001).
15. Henrik Urdal, "Population, Resources, and Political Violence."
16. Paivi Lujala, Nils Peter Gleditsch, and Elisabeth Gilmore, "A Diamond Curse? Civil War and a Lootable Resource," *Journal of Conflict Resolution* 49, no. 4 (2005): 538–62.

17. Peter Ackerman and Berel Rodal, "The Strategic Dimensions of Civil Resistance," *Survival: Global Politics and Strategy* 50, no. 3 (2008): 111–26; Brian Martin, *Social Defence, Social Change* (London, UK: Freedom Press, 1993); Sharon Erickson Nepstead, *Nonviolent Revolutions* (Oxford: Oxford University Press, 2011); Adam Roberts, ed., *The Strategy of Civilian Defence: Non-violent Resistance to Aggression* (London: Faber and Faber, 1967); Kurt Schock, *Unarmed Insurrections: People Power Movements in Nondemocracies* (Minneapolis: University of Minnesota Press, 2004).
18. Véronique Dudouet, "Dynamics and Factors of Transition from Violence to Nonviolent Resistance," webinar at the International Center on Nonviolent Conflict (2014); Véronique Dudouet, *Civil Resistance and Conflict Transformation*; Jason MacLeod, "From the Mountains and Jungles to the Villages and Streets: Transitions from Violent to Nonviolent Resistance in West Papua," in *Civil Resistance and Conflict Transformation: Transitions from Armed to Nonviolent Struggle*, ed. Véronique Dudouet (New York: Routledge, 2015).
19. Wendy Pearlman, "Precluding Nonviolence, Propelling Violence: The Effect of Internal Fragmentation on Movement Protest," *Studies in Comparative International Development* 47, no. 1 (2012): 23–46. The factors that attract people to civil resistance are clearly embedded in systems of symbolic meaning, encompassing identities, ideologies, commitments, and justifications.

APPENDIX 2

1. Victoria Fontan, *Decolonizing Peace* (Lake Oswego, OR: Dignity Press, 2012); Stuart Hall, "Racist Ideologies and the Media," in *Media Studies: A Reader*, eds. Paul Marris and Sue Thornham (New York: New York University Press, 2000); David Harvey, "Militant Particularism and Global Ambition: The Conceptual Politics of Place, Space, and Environment in the Work of Raymond Williams," *Social Text* 42 (Spring 1995): 69–98; Reinhart Koselleck, "The Modern Concept of Revolution as a Historical Category," *Studium Generale* 22, no. 8 (1969): 825–38; Raymond Williams, *Keywords: A Vocabulary of Culture and Society* (Oxford: Oxford University Press, 1985).
2. Charles Tilly, "Violent and Nonviolent Trajectories in Contentious Politics." I do not believe that there is a single, unitary definition of violence or even political violence. In my view, all violence is politi-

cal, from macro-level "structural violence" such as racism or poverty to direct physical damage to living things, and this applies even in micro-level aggressions. In peace studies literature, many scholars see almost any affront to dignity as a form of violence, since it creates the conditions that prevent human development or happiness. Raymond Williams, who warns that "the emotional power of the word can be very confusing," identifies at least seven senses: (a) physical assault, (b) use of physical force, and (c) the sense of portrayal, as in violence on television, which "can include the reporting of physical events but indicates mainly the dramatic portrayal of such events" (Williams, *Keywords*, 329). It becomes more difficult when we speak of (d) violence as threat, (e) violence as unruly behavior, (f) violence as a way to denote intensity (as in "violently in love"), and (g) something that wrenches meaning or significance from another thing (330).

3. Gabriela Torres, "Imagining Social Justice amidst Guatemala's Post-Conflict Violence," *Studies in Social Justice* 2, no. 1 (2008): 1–11.
4. See della Porta, *Clandestine Political Violence*; Wieviorka, *Violence: A New Approach.*
5. In contrast to this overly deterministic perspective, scholars such as della Porta have provided path-breaking, contextualized insights into the role of friendship and kinship groups in violent activism, noting that young militants are radicalized by group pressures, social status, and personal significance. Donatella della Porta, *It Was Like a Fever: Storytelling and Protest in Politics* (University of Chicago Press, 2006). See Andrew Dey et al., *Handbook for Nonviolent Campaigns* (New York: War Resisters League, 2014).
6. It is unfortunately common to confuse conflict with violence, perhaps because their causes are often attributed to the same phenomena: unequal patterns of access to wealth, resources, and power; polarization; ideology; religion; and others. For example, see Andrés Solimano, *Political Violence and Economic Development in Latin America: Issues and Evidence* (Santiago, Chile: United Nations Economic Commission for Latin America and the Caribbean, 2004).
7. For example, see Bannon and Collier, *Natural Resources and Violent Conflict*; James Fearon, "Primary Commodity Exports and Civil War," *Journal of Conflict Resolution* 49, no. 4 (2005): 483–507; Ross, "Review: The Political Economy of the Resource Curse"; Jeffrey Sachs and Andrew M. Warner, *Natural Resource Abundance and Economic Growth.*
8. della Porta, *Clandestine Political Violence*; Wieviorka, *Violence: A New Approach.*

9. Bennett and Elman, "Qualitative Research."
10. See the Observatory of Economic Complexity, "Peru." In the 1990s, Alberto Fujimori's administration cemented the importance of mining in Peru by declaring it a "national interest" activity and enacting a number of liberal mining reforms, which have been expanded by subsequent regimes. Experts on Latin America argue that Peru has modified its regulatory framework to adopt one of the most neoliberal, no-holds-barred approaches to extraction in the region. Since 1990, more than three hundred foreign mining companies have established a base in Peru. Gurmendi, "The Mineral Industry of Peru."
11. Richard Snyder, "Scaling Down: The Subnational Comparative Method," *Studies in Comparative International Development* 36, no. 1 (2001): 93–110.
12. See Lijphart, "Comparative Politics and the Comparative Method"; Landman, *Issues and Methods in Comparative Politics*; Giovanni Sartori, "Comparing and Miscomparing," *Journal of Theoretical Politics* 3, no. 3 (1991): 243–57.
13. See, e.g., John Andrew McNeish, "Resource Extraction and Conflict in Latin America," *Colombia internacional* 93 (2018): 3–16. The problems described here apply to comparisons across sectors and localities; however, interesting comparisons of various forms of extractivism in one particular site are fruitful, as they include similar controls. See, e.g., Flora Lu, Gabriela Valdivia, and Néstor L. Silva, "Neoextractivism and Its Contestation in Ecuador," in *Oil, Revolution, and Indigenous Citizenship in Ecuadorian Amazonia*, eds. Flora Lu, Gabriela Valdivia, and Néstor L Silva (New York: Palgrave Macmillan, 2017).
14. On these forms of contestation, see "How Peru Excludes Indigenous Voices in its Quest to Develop the Amazon," *The Conversation*, February 8, 2018.
15. Triscritti, "Mining, Development, and Corporate-Community Relations in Peru."
16. An alternative typology is José de Echave's distinction between "coexistence" conflicts, where contention surrounds the redistribution of mining benefits through investment, work contracts, and philanthropy, and conflicts based on "rejection," where opponents refuse mining in their districts entirely. See José de Echave et al., *Minería y conflicto social* (Lima: Instituto de Estudios Peruanos, 2009). While this distinction is useful, my findings suggest that in most cases, groups and individuals make both rejection and redistribution claims, even within the same case and period of the conflict. Sometimes, the

majority of protesters may reject a project initially, then adopt redistributive positions once the mine begins construction and production, and then again reject plans to expand the project later. Therefore, I have opted for a simpler typology, if only to analyze the representativeness of cases and select a few for this comparative study.

17. On paired comparisons, see Rachel M. Gisselquist, "Paired Comparison and Theory Development: Considerations for Case Selection," *PS: Political Science and Politics* 47, no. 2 (April 2014): 477–84.
18. See David Collier, "Understanding Process Tracing."
19. Peru's subnational political units are broken down as follows: at the local level, thousands of neighborhoods (or *caseríos*) are organized into 1854 districts (or municipalities), which are spread unevenly into 196 provinces, which in turn belong to 24 regions (or departments).
20. Barrick Gold representatives in both La Libertad and Lima refused multiple requests for interviews sent via phone and email between 2015 and 2016.
21. Critical discourse analysis is a well-established qualitative method in the social sciences and humanities. See Teun A. van Dijk, "Principles of Critical Discourse Analysis," *Discourse and Society* 4, no. 2: 249–83. For an example of how to apply this method, see Said, *Orientalism*.
22. I have previously used ATLAS.ti in a research project sponsored by the US Minerva Research Initiative, a comparative analysis of 150 interviews focused on the reasons why radicals in several countries chose or eschewed violent tactics to spur social change or pursue their political goals. To review our qualitative and quantitative findings, please see Maiah Jaskoski, Michael Wilson Becerril, and Berny Lazareno, "Approving of but Not Choosing Violence: Paths of Nonviolent Radicals," *Terrorism and Political Violence* (September 2017). In addition to this multi-layered coding experience, I was also trained in ATLAS at the Institute of Qualitative and Mixed-Methods Research (a two-week program hosted at Syracuse University) in the summer of 2015.
23. E.g., see María Rostworowski, *La mujer en el Perú prehispánico* (Lima: Instituto de Estudios Peruanos, 1995); Santiago Roncagliolo, *Abril Rojo* (Lima: Alfaguara, 2006).
24. Edward Said argued that discourse is supported by "institutions, vocabulary, scholarship, doctrines, and even colonial bureaucracies and colonial style." It is a constant exchange of ideas between the scholarly and popular imagination's construction of the other. But in the case of the discourses around mining in Peru, these are mainly supported, intentionally, by corporate institutions including media

that make statements, authorize views, describe, teach, settle things, rule over them, and encourage others to take these imaginaries and then even exaggerate them. To understand the sources, effects, and power of violence, one must study how meaning travels, generates and alters relations, and conditions material relations; in other words, one must analyze discourse, compare how people in different positions think and what they say, what they write, and the way this travels, their access to media of dissemination, etc. See Said, *Orientalism*.

25. For more on methods, see the notes on methodology in the second annex of this book.

Bibliography

"200 Years of Gold Prices." Only Gold, n.d., accessed January 18, 2018. http://onlygold.com/m/Prices/Prices200Years.asp.

Acemoglu, Daron, and James Robinson. *Why Nations Fail.* New York: Crown Press, 2012.

Ackerman, Peter, and Berel Rodal. "The Strategic Dimensions of Civil Resistance." *Survival: Global Politics and Strategy* 50, no. 3 (2008): 111–26.

"Acusan a Minera Yanacocha por muerte de truchas en Río Llaucano." Servicios de comunicación intercultural [SERVINDI], October 26, 2012. https://www.servindi.org/actualidad/75647.

Adger, Neil. "Social Capital, Collective Action, and Adaptation to Climate Change." *Economic Geography* 79, no. 4 (2003): 387–404.

"Advierten protestas por proyecto minero La Zanja en Santa Cruz." *Coordinadora nacional de radio* (Lima), February 2, 2010.

"Agricultores toman las calles de Chiclayo." *La república*, December 12, 2008.

"Alcalde de Bambamarca se opone a Conga pero trabaja con Gold Fields." *La república*, April 1, 2013.

"Alcalde de Pulán Muere en accidente." *Diario panorama*, June 16, 2007.

Alonso, Georgina. "Barrick Gold and CSR: Dynamics of Canadian Extractive Capitalism in Peru." Master's thesis, St. Mary's University, April 2014.

Alvarado Merino, Gina. "Politicas neoliberales en el manejo de los recursos naturales en Perú: El caso del conflicto agrominero de Tambogrande." In *Gestión ambiental y conflicto social en América Latina*, edited by Gina Alvarado Merino, Gian Carlo Delgado Ramos, Diego

Domínguez, Cecília Campello do Amaral Mello, Iliana Monterroso, and Guillermo Wilde. Buenos Aires: CLACSO, 2008.

Arce, Moisés. *La extracción de recursos naturales y la protesta social en el Perú*. Lima: Fondo Editorial PUCP, 2015.

Arce, Moisés. *Resource Extraction and Protest in Peru*. Pittsburg, PA: University of Pittsburg Press, 2014.

Arellano-Yanguas, Javier. "Aggravating the Resource Curse: Decentralisation, Mining, and Conflict in Peru." *Journal of Development Studies* 47, no. 4 (2011): 617–38.

______. "A Thoroughly Modern Resource Curse? The New Natural Resource Policy Agenda and the Mining Revival in Peru." *Institute of Development Studies* 300 (2008): 5–51.

______. *Minería sin fronteras? Conflicto y desarrollo en regiones mineras del Perú*. Lima: Instituto de Estudios Peruanos, 2011.

______. "Mining Policies in Humala's Peru: A Patchwork of Improvised Nationalism and Corporate Interests." In *The Political Economy of Natural Resources and Development: From Neoliberalism to Resource Nationalism*, edited by Paul Haslam and Pablo Heidrich. London: Routledge, 2016.

Arenda, Wilson, and Karen Solís. "Campesinos baleados en gresca con policías en Quiruvilca viven un drama." *La república*, June 12, 2016.

Ardito Vega, Wilfredo. *La promoción del acceso a la justicia en las zonas rurales*. Lima: Poder Judicial del Perú, Oficina Nacional de Justicia y Paz Indígena, 2014.

Ardito Vega, Wilfredo. "Sobre el Premio Nacional de Derechos Humanos para Marco Arana." Peruvian Reflections, AgenciaPeru, December 12, 2004. http://web.archive.org/web/20060709091608/http://www.agenciaperu.com/columnas/2004/dic/reflexiones3.htm.

Arnson, Cynthia J. "Introduction: Conflict, Democratization, and the State." In *In the Wake of War: Democratization and Internal Armed Conflict in Latin America*, edited by Cynthia J. Arnson. Washington, DC: Woodrow Wilson Center Press and Stanford University Press, 2012.

Ascher, William, and Natalia S. Mirovitskaya. *Economic Development Strategies and the Evolution of Violence in Latin America*. New York: Palgrave Macmillan, 2012.

"Asesinan a dirigente de Rondas Campesinas de Santa Cruz de Cajamarca." *La república*, June 26, 2013.

"Así fue el enfrentamiento en Barro Negro, Usquil." YouTube video, 13:01. Posted by Ozono Television on June 19, 2016. www.youtube.com/watch?v=8Ay4fFS3lt4.

Asociación Interétnica de Desarrollo de la Selva Peruana and Coordinadora Nacional de Derechos Humanos. *Pueblos indígenas del Perú: Balance 2014 sobre el cumplimiento del convenio 169 de la OIT*. Lima: CNDH and AIDESEP, 2009.

Asociación Pro Derechos Humanos. "La transformación ausente: Industrias extractivas y situación de las DESCA." Lima: APRODEH, 2012.

"Aurelio Miró Quesada de la Guerra: El ingeniero periodista que dirigió *El comercio*." *El comercio* (Huellas Digitales), May 14, 2015. https://elcomercio.pe/blog/huellasdigitales/2015/05/aurelio-miro-quesada-de-la-guerra-el-ingeniero-periodista-que-dirigio-el-comercio.

Auyero, Javier, and Debora Alejandra Swistun. *Flammable: Environmental Suffering in an Argentine Shantytown*. New York: Oxford University Press, 2009.

Avilés, Marco. "No soy tu cholo." *Ojo público*, April 9, 2017.

Baker, Elaine, Emmanuelle Bournay, Akiko Harayama, and Philippe Rekacewicz. *Vital Waste Graphics*. Geneva: United Nations Environment Programme. October 2004. https://www.unenvironment.org/resources/report/vital-waste-graphics.

Bannon, Ian, and Paul Collier. *Natural Resources and Violent Conflict*. Washington: World Bank, 2003.

"Barrick amenaza 5 lagunas en Santiago de Chuco." *Lucha indígena* 79, March 2013.

Barrick Gold. "Alto Chicama Feasibility Update." Presentation, Denver Gold Forum, Denver, CO, September 24, 2003.

Barrick Peru. "Alto Chicama Project, Las Lagunas Norte." Presentation, Trujillo, Peru, November 10, 2004.

Basombrío Iglesias, Carlos. "Peace in Peru, but Unresolved Tasks." In *In the Wake of War: Democratization and Internal Armed Conflict in Latin America*, edited by Cynthia J. Arnson. Washington, DC: Woodrow Wilson Center Press and Stanford University Press, 2012.

Bates, Robert. *Markets and States in Tropical Africa*. Berkeley: University of California Press, 1981.

Bebbington, Anthony. "Social Conflict and Emergent Institutions: Hypotheses from Piura, Peru." In *Social Conflict, Economic Development and the Extractive Industry: Evidence from South America*, edited by Anthony Bebbington. New York: Routledge, 2012.

______. *Social Conflict, Economic Development and Extractive Industry*. New York: Routledge, 2012.

Bebbington, Anthony, and Denise Humphreys Bebbington. "Actores y ambientalismos: Continuidades y cambios en los conflictos socioambientales en el Perú." In *Minería y territorio en el Perú: Conflictos, resistencias, y propuestas en tiempos de globalización*, edited by José de Echave, Raphael Hoetmer, and Mario Palacios Panéz. Lima: Programa Democracia y Transformación Global, 2009.

Bebbington, Anthony, and Jeffrey Bury. *Subterranean Struggles: New Dynamics of Mining, Oil, and Gas in Latin America*. Austin: University of Texas Press, 2014.

Bebbington, Anthony, Jeffrey Bury, Denise Humphreys-Bebbington, Jeannet Lingan, Juan Pablo Muñoz, and Martin Scurrah. "Mining and Social Movements: Struggles over Livelihood and Rural Territorial Development in the Andes." *World Development* 36, no. 12 (2008): 2888–905.

Bebbington, Anthony, Leonith Hinojosa, Denise Humphreys Bebbington, Maria Luisa Burneo, and Ximena Warnaars. "Contention and Ambiguity: Mining and the Possibilities of Development." *Development and Change* 39, no. 6: 887–914.

Beblawi, Hazem, and Giacomo Luciani. *The Rentier State*. London: Croom Helm, 1987.

Belling, Mónica. "Juan Luis Kruger (Gold Fields La Cima): Conflictos sociales no deben afectar competitividad." *Mining Press*, January 31, 2012.

Bennett, Andrew, and Colin Elman. "Qualitative Research: Recent Developments in Case Study Materials." *Annual Review of Political Science* 9 (2006): 455–76.

Berland, Angèle. "Uncovering Spring Break's Hidden Underbelly." Wild Angle Productions, January 19, 2015, https://www.journeyman.tv/film/6342.

"Big Mining and Its Increasingly Radical Opponents." *Economist*, February 3, 2005.

"Biólogo trujillano advierte el riesgo de construir una carretera en zonas naturales." *Chami radio*, August 12, 2016.

Blaikie, Piers M. *The Political Economy of Soil Erosion in Developing Countries*. New York: Longman, 1985.

Blaikie, Piers M., and Harold Brookfield. *Land Degradation and Society*. London: Routledge, 1987.

"Bloqueo en Otuzco." *Lucha indígena* 82, June 2013.

Bob, Clifford. *The Marketing of Rebellion: Insurgents, Media, and International Activism*. Cambridge: Cambridge University Press, 2005.

Boyd, Stephanie, dir. *The Devil Operation*. Lima: Guarango Films, 2010. DVD.

Boyd, Stephanie, and Ernesto Cabellos, dirs. *Tambogrande: Mangoes, Murder, Mining*. 2006; Lima: Guarango Films. DVD.

Brandenburg Sierralta, Heidi, and Matthew Orzel, dirs. *When Two Worlds Collide*. Lima: Yachaywasi Films, 2016. DVD.

Bregaglio, Renata, Jean Franco Olivera, Rosa Arévalo, Rubén Vargas, and José A. Godoy. *Diagnóstico nacional sobre la situación de la seguridad y el respeto a los derechos humanos referencia particular al sector extractivo en el Perú*. Lima: Instituto de Democracia y Derechos Humanos de la Pontificia Universidad Católica del Perú, 2003.

Bridge, Gavin. "Global Production Networks and the Extractive Sector: Governing Resource Based Development." *Journal of Economic Geography* 8, no. 3 (2008): 389–419.

Bryant, Raymond L. "Power, Knowledge and Political Ecology in the Third World: A Review." *Progress in Physical Geography* 22, no. 1 (1998): 79–94.

Bryant, Raymond L., and Sinead Bailey. *Third World Political Ecology*. London: Routledge, 1997.

Bull, Benedicte, and Mariel Aguilar-Støen. *Environmental Politics in Latin America: Elite Dynamics, the Left Tide, and Sustainable Development*. New York: Routledge, 2015.

Bury, Jeffrey. "Livelihoods in Transition: Transnational Gold Mining Operations and Local Change in Cajamarca, Peru." *Geographic Journal* 170, no. 1 (2004): 78–91.

Bury, Jeffrey. "Neoliberalismo, minería, y cambios sociales en Cajamarca." In *Minería, movimientos sociales, y respuestas campesinas*, edited by Anthony Bebbington. Lima: Instituto de Estudios Peruanos, 2007.

Butler, Judith. *Frames of War: When Is Life Grievable?* London: Verso Books, 2009.

"Buzos buscan cuerpos de policías desaparecidos en laguna de Quiruvilca." *La república*, June 10, 2016.

Caballero, Andrés. "Pronunciamiento Municipalidad Distrital de Pulán." *CaballeroVerde*, July 5, 2008.

Cabos, Roger. *Potencial minero en la región Huancavelica*. San Borja: Compañía de Minas Buenaventura, 2005. https://www.academia.edu/35045849/potencial_minero_en_la_región_huancavelica.

Cabral, Amílcar. *Revolution in Guinea*. Translated by Richard Handyside. London: Stage 1, 1974.

Canella, Gaile S., and Yvonna S. Lincoln, "Deploying Qualitative Methods for Critical Social Purposes." In *Qualitative Inquiry and Social Justice: Toward a Politics of Hope*, edited by Norman K. Denzin and Michael D. Giardina, 53–72. Walnut Creek, CA: Leftcoast Press, 2009.

Canella, Gaile S., and Michelle S. Perez. "Power-Shifting at the Speed of Light: Critical Qualitative Research Post-Disaster." In *Qualitative Inquiry and Social Justice: Toward a Politics of Hope*, edited by Norman K. Denzin and Michael D. Giardina, 165–85. Walnut Creek, CA: Leftcoast Press, 2009.

Casas Navarro, Raymundo. "La prensa chicha: Un análisis cognitivo." *Letras* 80, no. 115 (2009): 63–68.

"Caso Majaz: Indemnizan a 33 campesinos que fueron torturados en campamento minero." Coordinadora Nacional de Derechos Humanos. July 20, 2011. http://derechoshumanos.pe/2011/07/caso-majaz-indemnizan-a-33-campesinos-que-fueron-torturados-en-campamento-minero.

Castro, Wilson. "Quince heridos deja enfrentamiento entre policías y trabajadores de Quiruvilca." *La república*, June 13, 2015.

"Centromin Peru Ruling on Tambogrande Option Agreement." Press release. Manhattan Minerals Corp., BusinessWire, December 10, 2003. https://businesswire.com/news/home/20031210005946/en/Manhattan-Minerals-Corp-Centromin-Peru-Ruling-Tambogrande.

Chafee, Wilber. *The Economics of Violence in Latin America*. London: Praeger, 1992.

Chatterji, Roma, and Deepak Mehta. *Living with Violence: An Anthropology of Events and Everyday Life*. London: Routledge, 2007.

Chenoweth, Erica, and Maria J. Stephan. *Why Civil Resistance Works: The Strategic Logic of Nonviolent Conflict*. New York: Columbia University Press, 2011.

Chenoweth, Erica, and Tricia Olsen. *Civil Resistance and Corporate Behavior: Mapping Trends and Assessing Impact*. Washington, DC: US Agency for International Development, 2016.

Cholán, Wilfredo. "Hualgayoc: Existen niveles de plomo en la sangre por encima de los límites permisibles." *Noticias SER*, May 13, 2015.

"CIDH expresa su preocupación por criminalización de la protesta social." Coordinadora Nacional de Derechos Humanos, November 10, 2014. https://derechoshumanos.pe/2014/11/cidh-expresa-su-preocupacion-por-criminalizacion-de-la-protesta-social.

Clifford, James. "On Ethnographic Authority." *Representations* 2 (Spring 1983): 118–46.

CNDDHH. "Caso Majaz: Indemnizan a 33 campesinos que fueron torturados en campamento minero." Coordinadora Nacional de Derechos Humanos, July 20, 2011. http://derechoshumanos.pe/2011/07/caso-majaz-indemnizan-a-33-campesinos-que-fueron-torturados-en-campamento-minero.

Colectivo Alto Chicama. Facebook page. Accessed July 2016. https://www.facebook.com/altochicama.

Collier, David. "Understanding Process Tracing." *PS: Political Science* 44, no. 4 (2011): 823–30.

Collier, Paul, and Anke Hoeffler. "Greed and Grievance in Civil War." *Oxford Economic Papers* 56 (2004): 563–95.

Collins, Dan. "Peru's Brutal Murders Renew Focus on Tourist Boom for Hallucinogenic Brew." *Guardian*, April 29, 2018.

Collins, Patricia Hill. "The Tie that Binds: Race, Gender, and US Violence." *Ethnic and Racial Studies* 21, no. 5 (1998): 917–38.

Comisión de la Verdad y Reconciliación. *Informe Final.* 2003. http://cverdad.org.pe/ifinal.

"Comuneros cajamarquinos apoyan inicio de operaciones del proyecto minero La Zanja." *Agencia andina*, July 4, 2008.

Conde, Marta, Jonathan Gamu, and Philippe Le Billon. *The Rise in Conflicts Associated with Extractive Sector Projects—What Lies Beneath?* Vancouver: Canadian International Resources and Development Institute, 2017.

"Continúa paro indefinido contra Minera Gold Fields en Hualgayoc." *La república*, August 20, 2009.

Coordinadora Nacional de Derechos Humanos. *Informe Anual 2011–2012.* Lima: Coordinadora Nacional de Derechos Humanos, 2012.

Corkery, Aiden. "Manhattan Pulls Out after US$60mn Tambogrande Loss." *BN Americas*, February 7, 2005.

"Coronel Pérez: Comuneros quisieron incendiar campamento La Zanja." *Diario panorama*, May 15, 2007.

"Crónica de un reglaje al 'Diablo.'" *La república*, December 4, 2006.

Damonte, Gerardo. "Dinámicas rentistas: Transformaciones institucionales en contextos de proyectos de Gran Minería." In *Desarrollo rural y recursos naturales*, edited by Gerardo Damonte. Lima: GRADE, 2012.

Damonte, Gerardo. "El modelo extractivo peruano: Discursos, políticas, y la reproducción de desigualdades sociales." In *Extractivismo minero en Colombia y América Latina*, edited by Barbara Göbel and Astrid Ulloa. Bogotá: Universidad Nacional de Colombia, 2014.

"Dan ultimatum a Buenaventura-Newmont para abandonar La Zanja-Pulán Cajamarca." *Diario el sol* (Cajamarca), April 29, 2007. https://www.ocmal.org/3759.

de Althaus, Jaime. "La triste contribución de los antimineros." *Lampadia* (blog), April 1, 2013. http://www.lampadia.com/opiniones/jaime-de-althaus/la-triste-contribucion-de-los-antimineros.

de Echave, José. "Hernando de Soto habla de un 'sendero verde' sin ningún sustento." *La república*, May 12, 2016.

______. "Tantas veces Tambogrande." *Cooperacción* (blog), February 25, 2014. http://www.cooperaccion.org.pe/opina/43-cooperaccion-opina/1645-tantas-veces-tambogrande.

de Echave, José, Alejandro Diez, Ludwig Huber, Bruno Revesz, Xavier Ricard Lanata, and Martín Tanaka. *Minería y conflicto social*. Lima: Instituto de Estudios Peruanos, 2009.

Deere, Carmen Diana. "Changing Social Relations of Production and Peruvian Peasant Women's Work." *Latin American Perspectives* 14 (Winter/Spring 1977): 48–69.

Defensoría del Pueblo. *Decimonoveno informe anual de la Defensoría del Pueblo, Enero-Diciembre 2015*. Lima: Defensoría del Pueblo, 2016.

______. *Defensoría del Pueblo dio a conocer relación de acciones humanitarias realizadas ante los lamentables sucesos ocurridos en Bagua*. Lima: Defensoría del Pueblo, 2009.

______. *Reporte mensual de conflictos sociales N° 7—Septiembre 2004*. Lima: Defensoría del Pueblo, 2004.

______. *Reporte mensual de conflictos sociales N° 142—Diciembre 2015*. Lima: Defensoría del Pueblo, 2015.

______. *Reporte Mensual de Conflictos Sociales N° 155—Enero 2017* Lima: Defensoría del Pueblo, 2017.

______. *Violencia en los Conflictos Sociales*. Lima: Defensoría del Pueblo, 2012.

Delgado Fernández, Wilmer. "Conflicto y negociación." *Observatorio de conflictos mineros de América Latina* (blog), August 27, 2009. https://www.ocmal.org/4940.

della Porta, Donatella. *Clandestine Political Violence*. Cambridge: Cambridge University Press, 2013.

______. *It Was Like a Fever: Storytelling and Protest in Politics*. Chicago: University of Chicago Press, 2006.

Dengler, Corinna, and Lisa Marie Seebacher. "What about the Global South? Towards a Feminist Decolonial Degrowth Approach." *Ecological Economics* 157 (2019): 246–52.

"De Soto: 'Hay US$70 mil mlls de inversión minera paralizada.'" *El comercio*, May 7, 2015.

Dey, Andrew, Javier Garate, Subhash Kattel, Christine Schweitzer, and Joanne Sheehan. *Handbook for Nonviolent Campaigns*. New York: War Resisters League, 2014.

Díaz Zanelli, José Carlos. "La contradicción de Alan García con los pueblos indígenas." *Servicios de comunicación intercultural*, January 18, 2016. https://www.servindi.org/actualidad/18/01/2016/la-contradiccion-de-alan-garcia-con-los-pueblos-indigenas.

Dudouet, Véronique. "Dynamics and Factors of Transition from Violence to Nonviolent Resistance." Webinar at the International Center on Nonviolent Conflict (2014).

______. *Civil Resistance and Conflict Transformation: Transitions from Armed to Nonviolent Struggle*. New York: Routledge, 2015.

Durand, Francisco. *Cuando el poder extractivo captura el estado: Lobbies, puertas giratorias, y paquetazo ambiental en Perú*. Lima: Oxfam International, 2016.

Earthworks and Mining Watch Canada. *Troubled Waters: How Mine Waste Dumping Is Poisoning Our Oceans, Rivers, and Lakes*. Washington, DC: Earthworks, 2012.

Eaton, Kent. "Disciplining Regions: Subnational Contention in Neoliberal Peru." *Territory, Politics, Governance* 3, no. 2 (2015): 124–46.

______. *Territory and Ideology in Latin America: Policy Conflicts between National and Subnational Governments*. Oxford: Oxford University Press, 2017.

"*El comercio* censura a . . . ¿Martha Meier Miró Quesada?" *La mula*, February 7, 2015.

"El otro lado de la Barrick." YouTube video, 5:15. Posted by Maria Fe Celi, on October 16, 2010. https://www.youtube.com/watch?v=5m56DkYpb-Y.

"En apenas un mes se violaron sexualmente a 464 menores en el País." *El comercio*, March 4, 2020.

Encque Soraluz, Antonio. "Informe de visita a minera La Zanja," *EcoVida* (blog), August 16, 2011. http://eccovidahotmail.blogspot.com/2011/08/informe-de-visita-minera-la-zanja.html.

Enloe, Cynthia. *Globalization and Militarism: Feminists Make the Link*. Landham, MD: Rowman & Littlefield, 2007.

Espinoza Soriano, Waldemar. "San José de Quiruvilca: Origen y vicisitudes de un asiento minero." *Investigaciones sociales* 15, no. 27 (2001): 133–79.

Evans, Brad, and Henry A. Giroux. *Disposable Futures: The Seduction of Violence in the Age of Spectacle*. San Francisco: City Lights, 2015.

"Exigen anular concesión minera a La Zanja." *La república*, November 17, 2009.

"Explican autorización para verter aguas residuales de minera." *Gobierno Regional de Lambayeque* (blog), November 20, 2012. https://www.regionlambayeque.gob.pe/web/noticia/detalle/10897.

"Falla humana habría generado accidente del Alcalde de Pulán." *El clarín*, June 28, 2007.

Fearon, James D. "Primary Commodity Exports and Civil War." *Journal of Conflict Resolution* 49, issue 4 (2005): 483–507.

Ferguson, James. "Seeing Like an Oil Company: Space, Security, and Global Capital in Neoliberal Africa." *American Anthropologist* 107, no. 3 (2005): 377–82.

"Fiscal archiva caso de espionaje al Padre Arana sin haber citado a nadie de 'Forza.'" *La república*, February 2, 2007.

Fitzgerald, Valpy, Frances Stewart, and Rajesh Venugopal. *Globalization, Violent Conflict, and Self-Determination*. New York: Palgrave Macmillan, 2006.

"Flora y fauna." Yanacocha, n.d., accessed January 18, 2018. http://www.yanacocha.com/flora-y-fauna.

Fontan, Victoria. *Decolonizing Peace*. Lake Oswego, OR: Dignity Press, 2012.

Fox, Jonathan. "Unpacking Transnational Citizenship." *Annual Review of Political Science* 8 (May 2005).

Fowks, Jacqueline. *Chichapolitik: La prensa con Fujimori*. Lima: Fundación Friedrich Ebert, 2015.

______. "Preocupación en Perú por el nivel de concentración de prensa." *El país*, September 10, 2013.

Franks, Daniel, and Rachel Davis. *The Costs of Conflict*. International Finance Corporation, World Bank Group, 2015.

Franks, Daniel, Rachel Davis, Anthony J. Bebbington, Saleem H. Ali, Deanna Kemp, and Martin Scurrah. "Conflict Translates Environmental and Social Risk into Business Costs." *Proceedings of the National Academy of Sciences* 111, no. 21 (2014): 7576–81.

Freire, Paulo. *Pedagogy of the Oppressed*. New York: Continuum, 1970.

Frieden, Jeffry A. "Invested Interests: The Politics of National Economic Policies in a World of International Finance." *International Organization* 45, no. 4 (1991): 425–51.

"From Conflict to Cooperation." *Economist*, February 6, 2016.

Front Line Defenders. *Dispatches: Reports from the Front Line, January–December 2011*. Dublin: Front Line Defenders, 2011. https://www.frontlinedefenders.org/en/file/1428.

"Fuerte enfrentamiento en Quiruvilca." *Lucha indígena* 19, June 12, 2016.

"Fujimori ordenó la estirilización forzosa de 200,000 mujeres indígenas en Perú." *El país*, July 25, 2002.

"Funcionarios ocultaron contaminación de población de Hualgayoc, en Cajamarca." *Servicio de comunicación intercultural*, May 14, 2015.

Galeano, Eduardo. *Las venas abiertas de America Latina*. Mexico, DF: Siglo XXI Editores, 1971.

Gamu, Jonathan Kishen. "Corporate Security Governance: Multinational Mining Companies and the Local Political Economy of Violence in Peru." PhD diss., University of British Columbia, 2016.

Ganga, Deianira, and Sam Scott. "Cultural 'Insiders' and the Issue of Positionality in Qualitative Migration Research: Moving 'Across' and Moving 'Along' Researcher-Participant Divides." *Forum: Qualitative Social Research* 7, no. 3 (2006). DOI: http://dx.doi.org/10.17169/fqs-7.3.134.

García, Alan. "El síndrome del perro del hortelano." *El comercio*, October 27, 2007.

Geertz, Clifford. *The Interpretation of Culture*. New York: Basic Books, 1973.

Gisselquist, Rachel M. "Paired Comparison and Theory Development: Considerations for Case Selection." *PS: Political Science and Politics* 47, no. 2 (April 2014): 477–84.

Global Witness. *Deadly Environments: The Dramatic Rise in Killings of Environmental and Land Defenders 1/1/2002–31/12/2013*. London: Global Witness Limited, 2014.

______. *On Dangerous Ground*. London: Global Witness Limited, 2016.

Gobierno Regional de Cajamarca. "Resolución de Órgano Instructor No. 0004–2016-GR.CAJ-GGR." Report, Cajamarca, March 11, 2016.

"Gold Fields aclara que no contamina agua del Río Tingo Maygasbamba." *Panorama cajamarquino*, November 8, 2012.

"Gold Fields Fires 8,500 Strikers at South Africa Mine." *Reuters*, October 23, 2012.

"Gold Fields Halts Peru Exploration Project on Protest." *Bloomberg*, September 18, 2009.

"Gold Fields suspende sus operaciones en Cajamarca por protestas." *Perú21*, October 24, 2006.

Goldstein, Daniel M. "'In Our Own Hands': Lynching, Justice, and the Law in Bolivia." *American Ethnologist* 30, no. 1 (2003): 22–43.

"Grave denuncia sobre la actuación de la DINOES en el Valle del Campo." Coordinadora Nacional de Derechos Humanos, April 24, 2015. http://derechoshumanos.pe/2015/04/grave-denuncia-sobre-la-actuacion-de-la-dinoes-en-el-valle-del-tambo.

Gray, Vanessa Joan. "Nonviolence and Sustainable Resource Use with External Support." *Latin American Perspectives* 39, no. 1 (2012): 43–60.

Greene, Shane. "Getting Over the Andes: The Geo-Eco-Politics of Indigenous Movements in Peru's Twenty-First Century Inca Empire." *Journal of Latin American Studies* 38, no. 2 (2006): 327–54.

GRUFIDES. "Caso La Zanja." Last modified 2015. http://www.grufides.org/casos/caso-la-zanja.

______. "Conflicto Minero Gold Fields." Last modified 2015. http://www.grufides.org/sites/default/files//Documentos/fichas_casos/CONFLICTO%20MINERO%20GOLD%20FIELDS.pdf.

______. "Para Entender el Conflicto Minero Campesino en La Zanja, Cajamarca." *La Minería y sus impactos*, SERVINDI, no. 57 (2004). https://issuu.com/juancamilo02/docs/serv_57_mineria.

Guha, Ranajit. *Elementary Aspects of Peasant Insurgency in Colonial India*. Delhi: Oxford University Press, 1983.

Gurmendi, Alfredo. "The Mineral Industry of Peru." *Minerals Yearbook*. Washington, DC: United States Geological Survey, 2011.

Gustafsson, Maria-Therese. "The Struggles Surrounding Ecological and Economic Zoning in Peru." *Third World Quarterly* 38, no. 5 (2017): 1–19.

Haarstad, Håvard. "Globalización, narrativas y redes: Conflictos sobre la actividad minera en Tambogrande, Piura." *Espacio y desarrollo* (December 2008): 87–107.

Hackett, Robert. "Objectivity in Reporting." In *The International Encyclopedia of Communication I*. New York: Wiley, 2008.

Hall, Stuart. "Racist Ideologies and the Media." In *Media Studies: A Reader*, edited by Paul Marris and Sue Thornham. New York: New York University Press, 2000.

Hallman, Ben, and Roxana Olivera. "How the World Bank Is Financing Environmental Destruction." *Huffington Post*, April 15, 2015.

"Halting the Rush against Gold." *Economist*, February 3, 2005.

Haraway, Donna. "Situated Knowledges: The Science Question in Feminism and the Privilege of Partial Perspective." *Feminist Studies* 14, no. 3 (1998): 575–99.

Harvey, David. "Militant Particularism and Global Ambition: The Conceptual Politics of Place, Space, and Environment in the Work of Raymond Williams." *Social Text* 42 (Spring 1995): 69–98.

Harvey, David. *The New Imperialism*. New York: Oxford University Press, 2003.

"Hay 43 empresas mineras vinculadas a conflictos." *Gestión*, September 6, 2015.

Heidelberg Institute for International Conflict Research. "Conflict Barometer 2014." Heidelberg: HIIIK, 2014.

Hennessy, Hannah. "Gold Mine Fails to Glitter in Peru." *BBC News*, December 3, 2003.

Hernández Reyes, Castriela. "Black Women's Struggles against Extractivism, Land Dispossession, and Marginalization in Colombia." *Latin American Perspectives* 46, no. 2 (2019): 217–34.

Hesford, Wendy S. *Spectacular Rhetorics: Human Rights Visions, Recognitions, Feminisms*. Durham, NC: Duke University Press, 2011.

"Homenaje a Salatiel Romero, ex alcalde de Pulán, Aventureros." YouTube video, 6:08. Posted by 11250416, on December 22, 2007. https://www.youtube.com/watch?v=e9HN2Dki2_Y.

"How Peru Excludes Indigenous Voices in its Quest to Develop the Amazon." *The Conversation*, February 8, 2018.

"Hualgayoc: Denuncian a Minera Gold Fields por rajaduras de viviendas." *Noticias SER*, April 4, 2012.

"Hualgayoc exige pronta solución a conflicto minero." *La república*, July 6, 2010.

"Hualgayoc acata paro contra contaminación de ríos por mineras." *La república*, May 15, 2016.

Huanachín, Wilfredo. "Gold Fields La Cima ampliará operaciones en Cerro Corona." *Gestión*, October 9, 2014.

Hume, Mick. *Whose War Is It Anyway? The Dangers of the Journalism of Attachment*. London: Living Marxism Special, InformInc., 1997.

"Informe de contacto: Infernal enfrentamiento en Quiruvilca." *UCV satelital*, June 15, 2015.

"Interactive Market Chart." World Gold Council, n.d. Accessed January 18, 2018. www.gold.org/data/gold-supply-and-demand/gold-market-chart.

Intercontinental Panel on Climate Change. *Fifth Assessment Report*. New York: United Nations, 2014.

Jara, Edgar. "DINOES desaloja y recupera el control de vía a Hualgayoc." *La república*, August 30, 2013.

Jaskoski, Maiah. "Environmental Licensing and Conflict in Peru's Mining Sector: A Path-Dependent Analysis." *World Development* 64 (December): 873–83.

______. "Private Financing of the Military: A Local Political Economy Approach." *Studies in Comparative International Development* 48, no. 2 (Summer 2013): 172–95.

Jaskoski, Maiah, Michael Wilson Becerril, and Berny Lazareno. "Approving of but Not Choosing Violence: Paths of Nonviolent Radicals." *Terrorism and Political Violence*, September 2017.

Jenkins, Katy. "Women Anti-Mining Activists' Narratives of Everyday Resistance in the Andes: Staying Put and Carrying on in Peru and Ecuador." *Gender, Place & Culture* 24, no. 10 (2017): 1441–59.

Jiwani, Yasmin. *Discourses of Denial: Mediation, Race, Gender, and Violence*. Vancouver: University of British Columbia Press, 2006.

Johnston, Hank. "Ritual, Strategy, and Deep Culture in the Chechen National Movement." *Critical Studies on Terrorism* 1, no. 3 (2008): 321–42.

Joxe, Alain. "A Critical Examination of Qualitative Studies Applied to Research in the Causes of Violence." In *Violence and its Causes*, edited by Alan Joxe. Paris: UNESCO, 1981.

Kamphuis, Charis. "Foreign Investment and the Privatization of Coercion: A Case Study of the Forza Security Company in Peru." *Brooklyn Journal of International Law* 37, no. 2 (January 2011): 529–78.

Karl, Terry L. *The Paradox of Plenty: Oil Booms and Petro States*. Berkeley: University of California Press, 1997.

Keck, Margaret, and Kathryn Sikkink. *Activists beyond Borders: Advocacy Networks in International Politics*. Ithaca, NY: Cornell University Press, 1998.

Keenan, Karyn, José De Echave, and Ken Traynor. "Mining Rights and Community Rights: Poverty amidst Wealth." In *Reclaiming Nature: Environmental Justice and Ecological Restoration*, edited by James K. Boyce, Sunita Narain, and Elizabeth A. Stanton. London: Anthem Press, 2007.

Kempf, Wilhelm. "Conflict Coverage and Conflict Escalation." In *Journalism and the New World Order, Vol. 2: Studying War and the Media*, edited by Wilhelm Kempf and Heikki Luostarien. Göteburg: Nordicom, 2002.

Knightly, Philip. *The First Casualty*. Baltimore, MD: John Hopkins University Press, 2002.

Koselleck, Reinhart. "The Modern Concept of Revolution as a Historical Category." *Studium Generale* 22, no. 8 (1969): 825–38.

Krasner, Stephen D. "State Power and the Structure of International Trade." *World Politics* 28, no. 3 (1976): 317–47.

Kruger Sayán, Juan Luis, and Germán Roberto Polack Belaúnde. *Memoria anual y reporte de sostenibilidad 2011*. Lima: Gold Fields, 2012.

Lake, Ronald La Due, and Robert Huckfeldt. "Social Capital, Social Networks, and Political Participation." *Political Psychology* 19, no. 3 (1998): 567–84.

Landman, Todd. *Issues and Methods in Comparative Politics: An Introduction*. New York: Routledge, 2008.

"La producción de oro en el Perú caería hasta 9%." *La prensa* (Peru), February 26, 2013.

"La Zanja: ¿Solo una protesta ambiental?" *Noticias SER*, November 24, 2004.

"La Zanja: Un ejemplo de éxito." In *Conflictos sociales en el Perú (2008–2015)*, edited by Carlos Basombrío, Fernando Rospigliosi, and Ricardo Valdés. Lima: Capital Humano y Social, 2016.

Le Billon, Philippe. "The Geopolitical Economy or 'Resource Wars.'" *Geopolitics* 9, no. 1 (2004): 1–28.

Lefebvre, Henri. *The Production of Space*. Cambridge, MA: Blackwell, 1991.

Li, Fabiana. *Unearthing Conflict: Corporate Mining, Activism, and Expertise in Peru*. Durham, NC: Duke University Press, 2015.

"Libertad inmediata para Estinaldo Quispe." *Coordinadora nacional de derechos humanos*, August 9, 2011.

Lijphart, Arend. "Comparative Politics and the Comparative Method," *American Political Science Review* 65, no. 3 (1971): 682–93.

Los conflictos mineros se agudizan y el gobierno incumple creación de comisión de alto nivel. Proclamation. Confederación Nacional de Comunidades Afectadas por la Minería (CONACAMI), 25 July 2005.

Loyn, David. "Good Journalism or Peace Journalism?" *Conflict and Communication Online* 6, no. 2.

Lu, Flora, Gabriela Valdivia, and Néstor L. Silva. "Neoextractivism and Its Contestation in Ecuador." In *Oil, Revolution, and Indigenous Citizenship in Ecuadorian Amazonia*, edited by Flora Lu, Gabriela Valdivia, and Néstor L Silva. New York: Palgrave Macmillan, 2017.

Lujala, Paivi, Nils Peter Gleditsch, and Elisabeth Gilmore. "A Diamond Curse? Civil War and a Lootable Resource." *Journal of Conflict Resolution* 49, no. 4 (2005): 538–62.

Macassi, Sandro, and Jorge Acevedo. *Confrontación y diálogo: Medios y conflictos en países andinos*. Lima: Pontifícia Universidad Católica del Perú, 2015.

MacLeod, Jason. "From the Mountains and Jungles to the Villages and Streets: Transitions from Violent to Nonviolent Resistance in West Papua." In *Civil Resistance and Conflict Transformation: Transitions from Armed to Nonviolent Struggle*, edited by Véronique Dudouet. New York: Routledge, 2015.

Mama, Amina. "Challenging Militarized Masculinities." *OpenDemocracy*, May 29, 2013.

"Manhattan to Resume Exploration at Montosa." *Northern Miner*, August 7, 1995.

"Manhattan Wins Approvals." *Northern Miner*, May 24, 1999.

"Marcha de Ronderos en Sta Cruz Cajamarca" [Parts 1–4]. YouTube videos (series in four parts). Posted by Videoreportero William Soberón, on January 22, 2009. http://prensadigitaldelperu.blogspot.com/2009/02/ronderos-de-cajamarca-exigen-libertad.html.

Martin, Brian. "From Political Jiu-Jitsu to the Backfire Dynamic: How Repression Can Promote Mobilization." In *Civil Resistance: Comparative Perspectives on Nonviolent Struggle*, edited by Kurt Schock. Minneapolis: University of Minnesota Press, 2015.

______. *Justice Ignited: The Dynamics of Backfire*. New York: Rowman & Littlefield Publishers, 2006.

______. *Social Defence, Social Change*. London: Freedom Press, 1993.

Martínez i Álvarez, Patricia. "Personas de primera." *El país* (Opinión), June 11, 2009.

Matthew, Richard, Oli Brown, and David Jensen. *From Conflict to Peacebuilding: The Role of Natural Resources and the Environment*. Geneva: United Nations Environment Programme, 2009.

Mayorga, Rosario, and Maritza Roncal. "Ronderos de Santa Cruz exigen retiro de Minera Buenaventura." *La república*, November 18, 2004.

McCook, Hass. "Under the Microscope: The True Costs of Gold Production." Coin Desk, June 28, 2014. https://www.coindesk.com/microscope-true-costs-gold-production.

McGee, Brant. "The Community Referendum: Participatory Democracy and the Right to Free, Prior and Informed Consent to Development." *Berkeley Journal of International Law* 27, no. 2 (2009): 570–635.

McNeish, John Andrew. "Resource Extraction and Conflict in Latin America." *Colombia Internacional* 93 (2018): 3–16.

Media Ownership Monitor. "Peru: Grupo El Comercio." Reporters without Borders, 2018. https://peru.mom-rsf.org/en/owner/companies/detail/company/company/show/grupo-el-comercio-hoy-vigenta-inversiones-sa.

Medina Tafur, César, Manuel Hora-Revilla, Ivonne Asencio-Guzmán, Walter Pereda Ruíz, and Ronal Gabriel Aguilar. "El índice 'Biological Monitoring Working Party' (BMWP), modificado y adaptado a tres microcuencas del Alto Chicama, La Libertad, Perú, 2008." *Sciéndo: Ciencia para el desarrollo* (UNT, Peru) 13, no. 2 (2010): 5–20.

Medina Tafur, César, Walter Pereda, Manuel Hora, Ivonne Asencio, Ronal Gabriel, and José Polo. "Calidad del agua en las cuencas del Alto Chicama utilizando macroinvertebrados bentónicos como indicadores biológicos, La Libertad, Peru (2008–2009)." Presentation, Universidad Nacional de Trujillo, 2010.

Meléndez, Carlos. "Mediaciones y conflictos: Las transformaciones de la intermediación política y los estallidos de violencia en el Perú actual." In *El estado está de vuelta: Desigualdad, diversidad, y democracia*, edited by Víctor Vich. Lima: Instituto de Estudios Peruanos, 2005.

Mendoza Nava, Armando. *Inequality in Peru: Reality and Risks*. Oxfam, October 2015. https://peru.oxfam.org/para-no-retroceder-realidad-y-riesgo-de-la-desigualdad-en-el-perú-o.

Meyer, David, and Nancy Whittier. *Social Movements: Identity, Culture, and the State*. Oxford: Oxford University Press, 2002.

"Minera Barrick daña lagunas en Quiruvilca." *Lucha indígena* 67, March 2012.

"Minera Gold Fields se apodera de terrenos de humildes campesinas." *El clarín*, September 27, 2007. www.ocmal.org/3953.

"Minera Manhattan desiste de explotar Tambogrande y anuncia retiro del Perú." *La república*, February 8, 2015.

"Mineros protestan contra Gold Fields por pago de utilidades." *La república*, March 23, 2013.

"Minería: Contaminación mata a 5 mil truchas." *La república*, September 5, 2007.

Ministerio de Energía y Minas. *Informe trimestral Julio-Septiembre 2010*. Lima: Gobierno del Perú. http://www.minem.gob.pe/minem/archivos/Informe%20Trimestral%20Julio%20Setiembre%202010%20_ultimo%20WEB__opt.pdf.

Ministerio del Ambiente, "Ley del sistema nacional de impacto ambiental y su reglamento." Lima, Peru: Ministerio del Ambiente, Gobierno del Peru, 2011.

Ministerio de Salud, *Evaluación de la calidad sanitaria de las aguas del Río Llaucano y tributarios principales, 2011*. Lima: Gobierno del Perú, Dirección General de Salud Ambiental, 2011. http://www.digesa.minsa.gob.pe/DEPA/rios/2011/RIO_LLAUCANO_2011.pdf.

Montesanti, Stephanie Rose, and Wilfreda E. Thurston. "Mapping the Role of Structural and Interpersonal Violence in the Lives of Women: Implications for Public Health Interventions and Policy." *BMC Women's Health* 15, no. 100 (2015): 1–13.

Mora, Mariana. *Kuxlejal Politics: Indigenous Autonomy, Race, and Decolonizing Research in Zapatista Communities*. Austin: University of Texas Press, 2017.

Morales, José Miguel, and Africa Morante. "Aciertos y debilidades de la legislación minera actual." *Círculos de derecho administrativo, PUCP* 8 (2009): 137–47.

Moran, Robert. *An Alternative Look at a Proposed Mine in Tambogrande, Peru*. Washington, DC: Oxfam America, Mineral Policy Center, and Environmental Mining Council of British Columbia, August 15, 2001.

Mudd, Gavin. "Resource Consumption Intensity and the Sustainability of Gold Mining." Presentation, 2nd International Conference on Sustainability Engineering & Science, Auckland, NZ, February 20–23, 2007.

Muradian, Roldan, Joan Martinez-Alier, and Humberto Correa. "International Capital versus Local Population: The Environmental Conflict of the Tambogrande Mining Project, Peru." *Society and Natural Resources* 16, no. 9 (2003): 775–92.

Murdie, Amanda, and Tavishi Bhasin. "Aiding and Abetting: Human Rights INGOs and Domestic Protest." *Journal of Conflict Resolution* 55, no. 2 (2011): 163–91.

"Nacionalistas reafirman la estatización de la minería." *Diario panorama* (Cajamarca), June 26, 2007.

Nepstead, Sharon Erickson. *Nonviolent Revolutions*. Oxford: Oxford University Press, 2011.

Nhât Hanh, Thích. *The Heart of Understanding*. Berkeley, CA: Parallax Press, 1988.

Nixon, Rob. *Slow Violence and the Environmentalism of the Poor*. Cambridge: Harvard University Press, 2011.

Norgate, Terry, and Nawshad Haque. "Using Life Cycle Assessment to Evaluate Some Environmental Impacts of Gold Production." *Journal of Cleaner Production* 29, vol. 30 (2012): 53–63.

"Nuevas pruebas acusan a Forza." *La república*, February 3, 2007.

Observatorio de Conflictos Mineros en el Perú, *10º Informe del OCM, Primer Semestre de 2012*. Lima: CooperAcción, 2012.

______. *20º Informe del OCM, Primer Trimestre 2017*. Lima: Cooperacción, 2017.

______. *21º Informe del OCM, Segundo Semestre 2017*. Lima: Cooperacción, 2017.

Observatory of Economic Complexity. "Peru." Massachusetts Institute of Technology, 2017. https://atlas.media.mit.edu/en.

Ojeda, Francisco. "Tambogrande: A Community in Defence of Its Rights." In *Community Rights and Corporate Responsibility: Canadian Mining and Oil Companies in Latin America*, edited by Liisa North, Timothy David Clark, and Viviana Patroni. Toronto, Canada: Between the Lines, 2006.

Ordoñez, Ronald. "Cajamarca: Reclaman mejora de carretera a minera La Zanja." *Noticias SER*, October 11, 2017.

______. "Cajamarca reduce presupuesto para víctimas de contaminación." *Noticias SER*, October 11, 2017.

______. "Comuneros de Cajamarca Protestan por más de 950 pasivos ambientales." *La mula*, May 19, 2016.

______. "Rondas Campesinas de Santa Cruz exijen nulidad de concesiones mineras." *Central Única Nacional de Rondas Campesinas del Perú* (blog), November 19, 2009. http://cunarcperu.org/index.php?limitstart=891.

"Otuzco: Dos policías desaparecidos tras enfrentamientos con Ronderos." *RPP*, June 9, 2016.

Pachirat, Timothy. *Every Twelve Seconds: Industrialized Slaughter and the Politics of Sight*. New Haven, CT: Yale University Press, 2012.

Pape, Robert. *Dying to Win: The Strategic Logic of Suicide Terrorism*. New York: Random House, 2001.

Paredes, Maritza. "El caso de Tambogrande." In *Defendiendo derechos y promoviendo cambios*, edited by Martin Scurrah. Lima: Instituto de Estudios Peruanos, 2008.

Pearlman, Wendy. "Precluding Nonviolence, Propelling Violence: The Effect of Internal Fragmentation on Movement Protest." *Studies in Comparative International Development* 47, no. 1 (2012): 23–46.

Pegg, Scott. "Mining and Poverty Reduction, Transforming Rhetoric into Reality." *Journal of Cleaner Production* 14, no. 3 (2006): 376–87.

Peluso, Nancy Lee, and Michael Watts. *Violent Environments*. Ithaca, NY: Cornell University Press, 2001.

Perez, Jane, and Lowell Bergman. "Tangled Strands in Fight over Peru Gold Mine." *New York Times*, June 14, 2010.

Perla, Cecilia. "Extracting from the Extractors: The Politics of Private Welfare in the Peruvian Mining Industry." Phd diss., Brown University, 2012.

Perry, Keisha-Khan Y. *Black Women against the Land Grab: The Fight for Racial Justice in Brazil*. Ithaca, NY: Cornell University Press, 2013.

Policía Nacional del Perú. "RD No. 2373–2006-DIRGEN/EM." Agreement, Lima, November 7, 2006.

Ponce, Alfredo F., and Cynthia McClintock. "The Explosive Combination of Inefficient Local Bureaucracies and Mining Production: Evidence from Localized Societal Protests in Peru." *Latin American Politics and Society* 56, no. 3 (2014): 118–40.

Prado, Elizabeth. "Contaminación del agua y plomo en sangre mobiliza a pobladores de Hualgayoc." *La república*, June 4, 2015.

______. "Detienen a dirigente que denunció a una minera." *La república*, February 3, 2010.

______. "Objetan aprobación de estudio técnico de La Zanja." *La república*, July 5, 2008.

"Presentan proyecto minero La Zanja ante el gobierno regional Cajamarca." *El clarín*, August 7, 2007.

"Presidente Alan García Calificó como un 'Genocidio de Policías.'" *La República*, June 13, 2009.

"Protesta Rondera contra Minera Gold Field y Coimolache en Hualgayoc." *Red verde* (blog), March 10, 2013. http://caballeroredverde.blogspot.com/2013/03/protesta-rondera-contra-minera-gold.html.

"Proyecto minero La Zanja fue aprobado por distrito cajamarquino de Pulán." *El comercio*, July 4, 2008.

Public Citizen. "On Fifth Anniversary of Peru FTA Bagua Massacre of Indigenous Protestors, State Department Cables Published on WikiLeaks Reveal US Role." Intercontinental Cry, June 9, 2014. https://intercontinentalcry.org/fifth-anniversary-peru-fta-bagua-massacre-Indigenous-protestors-state-department-cables-published-wikileaks-reveal-u-s-role.

Puma, Liz, and César Bedoya. *Transformación de Conflictos*. Lima: ProDialogo, Prevención y Resolución, 2015.

"Quiruvilca: Pobladores exigen que compañía minera se retire." *La industria* (Trujillo), August 29, 2017.

Ramos Beltrán, Jean F. "Situación y perspectiva de desarrollo de la minería en el Perú: 2000–2010." PhD diss., Universidad Nacional de Trujillo, August 2010.

Ravnborg, Helle Munk, and Maria del Pilar Guerrero. "Collective Action and Watershed Management—Experiences from the Andean Hillsides." *Agriculture and Human Values* 16, no. 3 (1999): 257–66.

Reed-Danahay, Deborah E. "Introduction." In *Auto/Ethnography: Rewriting the Self and the Social*, edited by Deborah E. Reed-Danahay. New York: Berg Publishers, 1997.

Revesz, Bruno, and Julio Oliden. "Piura: Transformación del Territorio Regional." *Ecuador debate: Acerca del buen vivir*, no. 84 (December 2011): 151–76.

Roberts, Adam. *The Strategy of Civilian Defence: Non-violent Resistance to Aggression*. London: Faber and Faber, 1967.

Robinson, Allan. "Manhattan Gold Mine in Peru Faces Vote." *Globe and Mail*, May 10, 2002.

Rojas Delgado, Mario. "Perspectivas de procesamiento y uso del carbón mineral peruano." *Ingeniería industrial*, no. 26 (2008): 231–50.

"Romero Salatiel Alcalde de Pulán." YouTube video, 5:13. Posted by Trolatiel on August 17, 2007. https://www.youtube.com/watch?v=Unok2mIwTro.

Roncagliolo, Santiago. *Abril Rojo*. Lima: Alfaguara, 2006.

Roncal, Maritza. "Cajamarca: Hoy se inicia paro de 48 horas en Santa Cruz." *La república*, November 22, 2004.

"Ronderos defienden lagunas en Otuzco, policía les dispara y hiere a diecinueve—La Libertad—norte de Perú." *Tomate colectivo* (blog), June 12, 2016. https://tomatecolectivo.wordpress.com/2016/06/12/ronderos-defienden-lagunas-en-otuzco-policia-les-dispara-y-hiere-a-diecinueve-la-libertad-norte-de-peru.

Ross, Michael. "Review: The Political Economy of the Resource Curse." *World Politics* 51, no. 2 (1999): 297–332.

Rostworowski, María. *La mujer en el Perú prehispánico*. Lima: Instituto de Estudios Peruanos, 1995.

Roy, Arundathi. "We Call This Progress." *Guernica Magazine*, December 17, 2012.

Ruíz, Verónica, and Arturo Pérez. "Advierten nuevos conflictos mineros." *La república*, March 19, 2007.

Sabo, Samantha, Susan Shaw, Maia Ingram, Nicolette Teufel-Shone, Scott Carvajal, Jill Guernsey de Zapien, Cecilia Rosales, Flor Redondo, Gina Garcia, and Raquel Rubio-Goldsmith. "Everyday Violence, Structural

Racism, and Mistreatment at the US-Mexico Border." *Social Science and Medicine* 109 (May 2014): 66–74.

Sachs, Jeffrey D., and Andrew M. Warner. *Natural Resource Abundance and Economic Growth*. Cambridge, MA: National Bureau of Economic Research, 1997.

Sandoval, Chela. *Methodology of the Oppressed*. Minneapolis: University of Minnesota Press, 2000.

Salas, Guillermo. *Dinámica social y minería: Familias pastorales de Puna y la presencia del proyecto antamina (1997–2002)*. Lima: Instituto de Estudios Peruanos, 2008.

Said, Edward. *Orientalism*. New York: Vintage Books, 1979.

Sampat, Payal. "Fact Sheet: The True Cost of Valentine's Day Jewelry." Washington, DC: Earthworks, 2015.

Santillán, Teresa. "Hualgayoc, la remediación ambiental sigue pendiente." *Noticias SER*, April 6, 2014.

Santos Guerrero, Gregorio. "Muerte de Alcalde de Pulán: Accidente o atentado?" *El maletero verde*, July 31, 2007.

Sartori, Giovanni. "Comparing and Miscomparing." *Journal of Theoretical Politics* 3, no. 3 (1991): 243–57.

Scheper-Hughes, Nancy. *Death without Weeping: The Violence of Everyday Life in Brazil*. Berkeley: University of California Press, 1992.

Schilling-Vacaflor, Almut, and Riccarda Flemmer. "Conflict Transformation through Prior Consultation? Lessons from Peru." *Journal of Latin American Studies* 47, no. 4 (2015): 811–39.

Schock, Kurt. *Unarmed Insurrections: People Power Movements in Nondemocracies*. Minneapolis: University of Minnesota Press, 2004.

Shandilya, Krupa. "Writing/Reading the Subaltern Woman: Narrative Voice and Subaltern Agency in Upamanyu Chatterjee's *English, August*." *Postcolonial Text* 9, no. 3 (2014). https://www.postcolonial.org/index.php/pct/article/view/1877.

Silva Saniesteban, Rocío. "Asesinadas, golpeadas, encarceladas: El impacto de los conflictos sociales ecoterritoriales en los Cuerpos de las Mujeres Peruanas." *Revista pueblos*, January 27, 2015.

"Sindicato de trabajadores de Abosso Gold Fields rechaza despido de 340 mineros en Ghana." *IndustriAll*, April 3, 2018.

Sjoberg, Laura. *Gendering Global Conflict*. New York: Columbia University Press, 2013.

Smith, Linda Tuhiwai. *Decolonizing Methodologies: Research and Indigenous Peoples*. London: Zed Books, 2009.

Snyder, Richard. "Scaling Down: The Subnational Comparative Method." *Studies in Comparative International Development* 36, no. 1 (2001): 93–110.

Solimano, Andrés. *Political Violence and Economic Development in Latin America: Issues and Evidence*. Santiago, Chile: United Nations Economic Commission for Latin America and the Caribbean, 2004.

Soria, Laura, and Gerardo Castillo. *Gender Justice in Consultation Processes for Extractives Industries in Bolivia, Ecuador and Peru*. Peru: Oxfam and Societas, 2011.

Sweet, Victoria. "Extracting More than Natural Resources: Human Security and Arctic Indigenous Women." *Seattle University Law Review* 37, no. 4 (2014): 1157–78.

Tamblyn, Giulliana. "Quiruvilca: The Silver Tooth of the Peruvian Andes." Master's thesis, National University of British Columbia, January 2014.

"Tambogrande, una decada de impunidad." *Diario correo* (Lima), October 11, 2010.

"Tangled Strands in Fight over Peru Gold Mine." *New York Times*, June 14, 2010.

Tarrow, Sidney. *The New Transnational Activism*. Cambridge, UK: Cambridge University Press, 2005.

Taylor, Lewis. "Environmentalism and Social Protest: The Contemporary Anti-Mining Mobilization in the Province of San Marcos and the Condebamba Valley, Peru." *Agrarian Change* 11, no. 3 (2011): 420–39.

Temper, Leah. "Mapping the Global Battle to Protect Our Planet." *Guardian*, March 3, 2015.

Thorp, Mary, and Graciela Zevallos. "Las políticas económicas del régimen de Fujimori: ¿Un retorno al pasado?" *Economía: Revista del Departamento de Economía de la PUCP* 24, no. 47 (2001): 9–42.

Thorp, Rosemary, and Maritza Paredes. *Ethnicity and the Persistence of Inequality: The Case of Peru*. Basingstoke: Palgrave Macmillan, 2010.

Tilly, Charles. "Violent and Nonviolent Trajectories in Contentious Politics." Presentation, Symposium on States in Transition and the Challenge of Ethnic Conflict, Columbia University, New York, December 29, 2010.

Toledano, Perrine, and Clara Roorda. "Leveraging Mining Investments in Water Infrastructure for Broad Economic Development: Models,

Opportunities and Challenges." Policy Paper, *Columbia Center on Sustainable Investment*, March 2014.

Toledo Orozco, Zaraí. "Tambogrande ayer y hoy." *Útero*, August 7, 2015.

Torres, Gabriela. "Imagining Social Justice amidst Guatemala's Post-Conflict Violence." *Studies in Social Justice* 2, no. 1 (2008): 1–11.

Treakle, Kay. "Ecuador: Structural Adjustment and Indigenous Environmentalist Resistance." In *The Struggle for Accountability: The World Bank, NGOs, and Grassroots Movements*, edited by Jonathan Fox and David Brown. Boston: MIT Press, 1998.

Tribunal Constitucional del Perú. "Sentencia Expediente No. 01848–2011-PA/TC." Resolution, Lima, October 19, 2011. http://www.tc.gob.pe/jurisprudencia/2011/01848–2011-AA.html.

Triscritti, Fiorella. "Mining, Development, and Corporate-Community Relations in Peru," *Community Development Journal* 48, no. 3 (2013): 437–50.

______. "The Criminalization of Anti-Mining Social Protest in Peru." *State of the Planet: Blogs from the Earth Institute*. Columbia University, September 10, 2012. http://blogs.ei.columbia.edu/2012/09/10/peru-mining.

Tschakert, Petra. "Digging Deep for Justice: A Radical Re-imagination of the Artisanal Mining Sector in Ghana." *Antipode* 41, no. 4 (2009): 706–40.

Tschakert, Petra, and Kamini Singha. "Contaminated Identities: Mercury and Marginalization in the Artisanal Mining Sector of Ghana." *Geoforum* 38, no. 6 (2007): 1304–21.

Turcotte, Heather. "Petro-Sexual Politics: Petroleum, Gender Violence, and Transnational Justice." Presentation, Annual Meeting of the American Political Science Association, Seattle, Washington, September 1–4, 2011.

Urdal, Henrik. "Population, Resources, and Political Violence: A Subnational Study of India." *Journal of Conflict Resolution* 52, no. 4 (2008): 590–617.

Urkidi, Leire, and Mariana Walter. "Dimensions of Environmental Justice in Anti-Gold Mining Movements in Latin America." *Geoforum* 42 (2011): 683–95.

US Embassy in Peru. "Ollanta Humala Claims He Can Save Peru from Extremists." Wikileaks Cable: 08LIMA1107_a. Dated June 26, 2008. http://wikileaks.org/cable/2008/06/08LIMA1107.html.

van Dijk, Teun A. "Principles of Critical Discourse Analysis." *Discourse and Society* 4, no. 2: 249–83.

Vásquez, Mirtha. "Criminalización de la protesta en su máxima expresión." *Revista voces*, September 2012.

Vásquez, Patricia I. *Oil Sparks in the Amazon: Local Conflicts, Indigenous Populations, and Natural Resources*. Athens: University of Georgia Press, 2014.

"Video: Habla Antonio Coasaca, agricultor que fue 'sembrado' por la policía." *El búho*, April 28, 2015.

Walby, Silvia. "Globalization and Multiple Inequalities." *Advances in Gender Research* 15 (2011): 17–33.

Warnaars, Ximena S. "Territorial Transformations in El Pangui, Ecuador: Understanding How Mining Conflict Affects Territorial Dynamics, Social Mobilization, and Daily Life." In *Subterranean Struggles: New Dynamics of Mining, Oil, and Gas in Latin America*, edited by Anthony Bebbington and Jeffrey Bury. Austin: University of Texas Press, 2013.

Welker, Marina. "Global Capitalism and the 'Caring Corporation': Mining and the Corporate Social Responsibility Movement in Indonesia and Denver (Colorado)." PhD diss., University of Michigan, 2006.

Weyland, Kurt. *The Politics of Market Reform in Fragile Democracies: Argentina, Brazil, Peru, and Venezuela.* Princeton, NJ: Princeton University Press, 2002.

Whitman, Shelly. "Sexual Violence, Coltan, and the Democratic Republic of Congo." In *Natural Resources and Social Conflict: Towards Critical Environmental Security*, edited by Matthew A. Schnurr and Larry A. Swatuk. New York: Palgrave McMillan, 2012.

Wieviorka, Michel. *Violence: A New Approach.* London: Sage Publications, 2009.

Widener, Patricia. "Benefits and Burdens of Transnational Campaigns: A Comparison of Four Oil Struggles in Ecuador." *Mobilization* 12, no. 1 (2007): 21–36.

Wilkins, Gregory C. "Building Mines, Building Value." Barrick Gold Corporation. Presentation on Investor Day, New York, NY, February 24, 2004.

Williams, Raymond. *Keywords: A Vocabulary of Culture and Society*. Oxford: Oxford University Press, 1985.

Wilson Becerril, Michael. "Entendiendo y previniendo la violencia en conflictos mineros." *Noticias SER*, August 2019.

______. "Mining Conflicts in Peru: Civil Resistance and Corporate Counterinsurgency." *Journal of Resistance Studies* 4, no. 1 (2018): 99–132.

______. "Frames in Conflict: Discursive Contestation and the Transformation of Resistance." In *Civil Resistance and Violent Conflict in Latin America*, edited by Cécile Mouly and Esperanza Hernández. New York: Palgrave Macmillan, 2019.

______. "'Invisibilize' This: Ocular Bias and Ableist Metaphors in Anti-Oppressive Discourses." *Feminist Review* 120 (2018): 130–34.

Women's Earth Alliance and Native Youth Sexual Health Network. "Violence on the Land, Violence on our Bodies: Building an Indigenous Response to Environmental Violence." Report to the International Indian Treaty Council, Toronto, CAN (2016).

Ybañez Gamboa, Igor. "Día decisivo en el diálogo entre comuneros de Quiruvilca y Barrick." *La república*, February 24, 2013.

Yeager-Kozacek, Codi. "Global Gold Rush: The Price of Mining Pursuits on the Water Supply," Circle of Blue, June 15, 2012. http://www.circleofblue.org/2012/world/global-gold-rush-the-price-of-mining-pursuits-on-water-supply.

Zevallos, Magali. "Minería y petróleo en Perú son los principales contaminantes de las poblaciones indígenas y andinas." *Gran angular*, December 12, 2017.

______. "Perú: Represión y muertes en conflictos mineros." *Gran angular*, May 11, 2015.

Zevallos, Patricia. "Cajamarca: Trabajadores de minera La Zanja continuan paro indefinido." *El comercio*, July 20, 2011.

Index

The letter *t* following a page number denotes a table; the letter *f* denotes a figure.

www.ingramcontent.com/pod-product-compliance
Lightning Source LLC
LaVergne TN
LVHW092117300926
849161LV00002B/157
* 9 7 8 0 8 2 6 5 0 1 5 8 5 *